Discover Acadia
National Park

A Guide to Hiking, Biking, and Paddling

Jerry & Marcy Monkman

Also available from Appalachian Mountain Club Books...

Trail Guides

Hiking Guide to Mount Washington and the Presidential Range
Massachusetts and Rhode Island Trail Guide
North Carolina Hiking Trails
West Virginia Hiking Trails
White Mountain Guide

Paddling Guides

Classic Northeastern Whitewater Guide
Quiet Water Canoe Guide: Maine
Quiet Water Canoe Guide: Massachusetts/Connecticut/Rhode Island
Quiet Water Canoe Guide: New Hampshire/Vermont
Quiet Water Canoe Guide: New York
Sea Kayaking along the New England Coast
Sea Kayaking along the Mid-Atlantic Coast
Whitewater Handbook

Outdoor Skill Guides

Guide to Trail Building and Maintenance
Organizing Outdoor Volunteers
River Rescue
Ultimate Guide to Backcountry Travel
Watercolor Painting on the Trail

Discover Acadia National Park

A Guide to Hiking, Biking, and Paddling

Jerry & Marcy Monkman

APPALACHIAN MOUNTAIN CLUB BOOKS
BOSTON, MASSACHUSETTS

Cover Photograph: Jerry and Marcy Monkman
All photographs by the author unless otherwise noted
Cover Design: Ola Frank
Book Design: Carol Bast Tyler

Distributed by The Globe Pequot Press, Inc.

Library of Congress Cataloging-in-Publication Data
Monkman, Jerry.
    Discover Acadia / Jerry & Marcy Monkman.
        p. cm.
    Includes bibliographical references and index.
    ISBN 1-878239-92-9 (alk. paper)
        1. Hiking--Maine--Acadia National Park--Guidebooks. 2. Cycling--Maine--Acadia National Park--Guidebooks. 3. Canoes and canoeing--Maine--Acadia National Park--Guidebooks. 4. Acadia National Park (Me.)--Guidebooks. I. Monkman, Marcy. II. Title.

GV199.42.M22 A326 2000
917.41'450443--dc21
                                                99-087916

The paper used in this publication meets the minimum requirements of the American National Standard for Information Sciences—Permanence of Paper for Printed Library Materials, ANSI Z39.48–1984.∞

Due to changes in conditions,
use of the information in this book
is at the sole risk of the user.

Printed on recycled paper using soy-based inks.
Printed in the United States of America.

10 9 8 7 6 5 4 3 2 1   00 01 02 03 04 05

contents

v

introduction

SWEEPING MOUNTAIN VIEWS, rugged ocean scenery, and abundant wildlife all contribute to the splendor that is Acadia National Park. Acadia's 46,000 acres stretch from Isle au Haut in the southwest to the Schoodic Peninsula in the northeast. However, the heart and soul of Acadia is Mount Desert Island, a place of scenic pink-granite mountains, deep glacial ponds, cobblestone beaches, and ocean-side cliffs. Bald eagles, ospreys, and peregrine falcons patrol the skies while seals, porpoises, and seabirds fish the cold waters of Frenchman Bay and beyond. Mount Desert Island is the third largest island in the continental United States and boasts such natural wonders as Somes Sound, the only fiord on the East Coast, and Cadillac Mountain, the highest point on the East Coast north of Brazil.

While it is the dramatic scenery that lures most visitors, it is the more intimate moments in Acadia that become a part of those who come here: Listening to the steady sound of the surf in Monument Cove on a quiet morning in June, inhaling the delicious smell of pitch pine on a rocky trail on a warm September day, or watching in surprise as a harbor porpoise surfaces next to your kayak on a calm August afternoon. Although your experiences in Acadia most likely will be different from ours, our hope is that this book will help you discover your own special moments in Acadia.

acknowledgments

WE WOULD FIRST and foremost like to extend our gratitude to Mark Russell, our editor, for his guidance, his great sense of humor, his gentle but instructive editing style, and his willingness to meet with us over chocolate croissants at Café Brioche. We'd also like to thank Elisabeth Brady and Jessica Church of AMC Books for all their effort on our behalf. So many of the rangers from Acadia National Park were instrumental in helping us gather tidbits of information about the natural science, trails, and rules of the park: Wanda Moran, Deborah Wade, Shirley Beccue, Paul Super, Don Beals, Charlie Jacobi, and John Cousins. We also had invaluable help from Ken Olson and the staff at Friends of Acadia. For the kayaking section, we are indebted to Glenn Tucker, Natalie Springel, and the guides at Coastal Kayaking for showing us the best kayaking in the area.

We would also like to express our gratitude to Lou and Coleene at Little Luigi's for feeding us many wonderful meals after long days of hiking, biking, and paddling. Karen Gladstone at Maptech was generous enough to donate their very helpful CD-ROM version of Acadia's USGS maps. And, of course, this book wouldn't have been possible without the love and support of our families and friends: Pat Monkman gave us our first AMC *White Mountain Guide* when we moved to New England ten years ago, inspiring us to discover New

England's backcountry. Carol and Jerry Wolin were kind enough to buy prints of every one of our photographs they liked, encouraging us to pursue nature photography and writing as a career. Jeff Monkman looked after our often deserted house. Tom, Jane, and Eddie Ferrini missed us so much they came with us to Acadia. Our friends Eric Reimer and John Muller spent many selfless hours of their own time over the last few years teaching us to write readable prose.

1

Acadia National Park
basic information

IT IS HARD TO SAY exactly what draws so many people to Acadia, although the juxtaposition of granite-clad mountain peaks overlooking the deep blue waters of the Atlantic Ocean probably lures most visitors. With mountains next to the ocean, Acadia gives visitors the chance to participate in almost any outdoor activity they can dream up, all with spectacular scenic rewards. Of course, the mountains of Acadia are modest, even by New England standards, with the tallest peak, Cadillac Mountain, reaching a height of only 1,530 feet. Nonetheless, hiking is probably the most popular park activity, as most of the summits are treeless and provide spectacular views of the surrounding bays and islands. Trails vary from easy ocean-side walks to steep cliff-side climbs up iron ladders. Biking is also a popular activity in the park, particularly on the scenic system of gravel carriage roads built by John Rockefeller Jr. in the 1920s and 1930s. Just a few thousand years ago, glaciers left behind numerous deep lakes and ponds which now give visitors the opportunity to canoe or kayak below the rocky scenery of the mountains. Over the last ten years, sea kayaking has become one of the premier activities of the more adventurous visitors to Acadia National Park. Chapters 4 through 7 give detailed descriptions of hiking, biking, and paddling trips, from one-hour excursions to all-day adventures.

Other activities such as rock climbing, birding, and whale watching give the outdoor enthusiast plenty of alternative ways to experience Acadia. Chapter 9 provides information for participating in these other vacation adventures. The rest of this introductory chapter provides some basic information you can use to get started on your visit to Acadia National Park and Mount Desert Island.

Climate

Acadia has a typical New England coastal climate. Cold, wet conditions are common, but so are sunny and warm days. In general, Acadia's climate is no problem for the outdoor adventurer who comes prepared for unexpected weather. **Spring** is often foggy, with temperatures ranging between thirty and seventy degrees. **Summer** is mild, with daytime temperatures usually in the seventies and eighties. Evenings are cool, especially when there is a sea breeze, and, with ocean temperatures in the fifties, any activity on the ocean requires an extra layer of clothing. **Fall** in Acadia varies from sub-freezing temperatures at night to warm days in the seventies. Rain and fog are common, but so are perfect, clear, leaf-peeping days. **Winter** is cold, with daytime temperatures usually in the thirties and lows ranging to below zero. Acadia averages sixty-one inches of snow per year.

Getting There

Bar Harbor and Acadia National Park are located forty-five miles southeast of Bangor, Maine. From Bangor, drive east on Alternate Route 1 to Route 3 in Ellsworth. Following Route 3 south will take you to Mount Desert Island. The entrance to Acadia National Park is located off Maine Route 3 in Hulls Cove, just north of Bar Harbor. During the summer months, Vermont Transit (207-288-3366) provides bus service between Bangor and Bar Harbor. For getting around the island, see "Take the Bus" below.

Lodging

There are two campgrounds in the national park: Blackwoods and Seawall. Blackwoods is open year-round, while Seawall is open Memorial Day through Columbus Day. Many private campgrounds are also in the area and are listed on page 268–269. Bar Harbor, Northeast Harbor, and Southwest Harbor are full of inns, hotels, and bed-and-breakfasts. A complete listing of these can be attained by calling the local areas' chambers of commerce. These are listed on page 267.

Food

Restaurants are located throughout the island, with the biggest selection in Bar Harbor. The IGA on Cottage Street in Bar Harbor is the island's largest grocery store. The Alternative Market, located across from the Bar Harbor town green, has a good selection of health foods.

National Park Service Information

First-time visitors to Acadia National Park should begin their visit by stopping in at the Hulls Cove Visitor Center on Maine Route 3. Here you can pick up a schedule of ranger-led events, talk to a ranger about your park visit, and pick up fliers and books about Acadia. The Hulls Cove Visitor Center is open from May through October. During the winter months, visitors should check in at park headquarters on Maine Route 233, west of Bar Harbor. The Park Service maintains a website at www.nps.gov.acad/anp.html. You can also request information about the park before your visit by writing to or calling the Park Service at Acadia National Park, P.O. Box 177, Bar Harbor, ME 04609; 207-288-3338.

Fees

There are fees for using the Park Loop Road and the park campgrounds. In 1999, a one-week pass for driving the Park Loop Road was $10. An Acadia annual pass is available for $20. A campsite at

Blackwoods or Seawall costs $18 per night. However, you can reach many of the hiking trails, carriage roads, and ponds from public roads where no fee is required.

Handicapped Access

Most park facilities, including the visitor center and Blackwoods and Seawall Campgrounds, are accessible to handicapped persons. The exceptions are the Nature Center at Sieur de Monts, the Frazer and Pretty Marsh Picnic Areas, Sand Beach, and the Thunder Hole Gift Shop. To see the backcountry, the park's carriage roads are the best option since they tend to have level, firm surfaces. The two easiest sections of the carriage roads can be reached from Eagle Lake and Bubble Pond. Wildwood Stables near Jordan Pond also has carriage rides that are accessible to the handicapped. For more information, contact the Park Service and ask for their excellent eight-page access guide. Call 207-288-3338 and have them send you the guide, or pick one up at the visitor center. The visitor center phone number has TDD access.

Emergencies

All injuries that happen in the park should be reported to a ranger. In the event of an emergency, you should call one of the following numbers:

Bar Harbor Emergency: 911
Bar Harbor Police (nonemergency calls): 207-288-3391
Mount Desert Police (nonemergency calls): 207-276-5111

Southwest Harbor Emergency: 207-244-5552
Southwest Harbor (nonemergency calls): 207-244-7911

Acadia National Park Emergency: 207-288-3369
Acadia National Park (nonemergency calls): 207-288-3338

U.S. Coast Guard Emergency: 207-244-5121
U.S. Coast Guard (nonemergency calls): 207-244-5121

Choosing Your Trip

The forty hiking, biking, and paddling trips in this book provide a variety of outdoor experiences. Before heading out on the trail or on the water, you should decide what the focus of your trip is (beachcombing, mountain views, wildlife watching, etc.). You should also decide how strenuous a trip you and your group are willing and able to complete. The highlight chart following this introduction has an easy-to-follow listing of all the trips, including their difficulty, length, and highlights. Once you have narrowed down your choices, read the detailed trip descriptions in the individual chapters to get a better idea of what the trip entails and what you might encounter. Hikers interested in trails other than those listed in the hiking chapter can read through a complete listing of hiking trails in appendix A.

Protect the Resource!

Acadia National Park consistently ranks as one of the ten most visited national parks in the United States. With 3 million visitors entering the park every year, it sees the same amount of use as much bigger parks, such as Yellowstone and Yosemite. With that many people enjoying Acadia's limited and fragile resources, it is imperative that everyone learn and adhere to Leave No Trace principles. These principles were developed by the National Outdoor Leadership School in order to promote and inspire responsible outdoor recreation. In Acadia, follow these principles:

Plan ahead and prepare

When going into Acadia's backcountry, plan an outing that you know everyone in your group can finish. Be prepared for unexpected events by having extra food, water, and clothing. A well-planned day will prevent the need for an unnecessary night out in the woods, where you may be forced to build fires and trample delicate vegetation. Keep your group size to ten or fewer, splitting into smaller groups if necessary. Try to avoid travel in wet and muddy conditions and use extra care when in Acadia's delicate subalpine zone.

Camp and travel on durable surfaces

Camping in Acadia's backcountry is prohibited. When hiking, try to stay on trails and rocks. When you are on a trail, stay in the center of the trail, even when it is wet and muddy. Use your boots! Trails are hardened sites where use should be concentrated. Avoid contributing to the widening and braiding of trails. Hiking off-trail into pristine areas is allowed, but requires great understanding and diligence. First consider if hiking off-trail is necessary. If you decide to hike off-trail, do it only on durable surfaces such as rock, gravel, or grasses. Spread your group out, take different routes, and avoid places where unofficial "social" trails are just beginning to show.

Dispose of waste properly

Pack out *all* that you bring in. This includes any and all food you may drop while eating. Urinate at least 200 yards from any water source and pack out your used toilet paper. To dispose of solid human waste in the backcountry, dig an individual "cat hole" at least 200 yards from a trail or water source. Organic topsoil is preferable to sandy mineral soil. Dig a hole four to eight inches deep and about six inches in diameter. After use, mix some soil into the cat hole with a stick and cover it with the remainder of the soil. Disguise the hole by covering it with leaves or other brush. Pack out your toilet paper in an odor-proof bag. It is especially important in Acadia not to pollute near any watercourse, as it probably leads to a town water source.

Leave what you find

Leave all natural and historical items as you find them. Of particular concern to naturalists in the park is the moving of rocks, large and small, in order to build rock cairns or sculptures. This detracts from the natural and scenic qualities of the landscape. It wreaks havoc on the environment, causing soil erosion and removing vital habitats for small plants and animals. Building unauthorized cairns is also a safety concern, as an improperly located cairn can cause hikers to get lost.

There is much human history in and around Acadia in the form of Native American shell heaps and arrowheads, as well as stone walls and old cellar holes from early European settlements. It is illegal to disturb any such cultural artifacts in the national park. It is also illegal to move or take home natural features of the park, whether they are wildflowers, rocks, or animal parts such as feathers or antlers. The only exception to this in Acadia is that you are allowed to pick fruit, nuts, and berries for personal consumption. However, the taking of pine or spruce cones, mushrooms, fungi, and fiddlehead ferns is prohibited.

Minimize campfire impacts

Campfires are allowed only in designated fire pits in campgrounds and picnic areas.

Respect wildlife

Remain quiet while in the backcountry, and give animals enough space so that they feel secure. If you notice wildlife changing their behavior, it is most likely because you are too close. In that case, back off and give the animals space. Avoid nesting or calving sites, and *never* attempt to feed any wildlife, even sea gulls and those cute little red squirrels. While kayaking around the island, do not land on any island that has an active seabird colony or nesting bald eagles. To verify the location of any such islands, check with the Park Service before your paddle. Also, remember that residents of the intertidal zone are wildlife too. Do not remove starfish, sea urchins, or other creatures from their natural habitat. For low-impact wildlife-watching tips, visit Watchable Wildlife's website, www.watchablewildlife.org.

Be considerate of other visitors

Stay quiet. Refrain from using cell phones and radios. When hiking, take rests on the side of the trail so that other hikers do not have to walk around you. When on the water, remember that sound carries a long, long way. Also, it is required that you keep your dog on a leash while in the park. Dogs are not allowed on Sand Beach, Echo Lake Beach, or ladder trails.

You can learn more about the Leave No Trace program by visiting their website, www.lnt.org, or by writing them at LNT Inc., P.O. Box 997, Boulder, CO 80306.

Take the Bus

Using Mount Desert Island's new *free* bus system, the *Island Explorer*, is a great way to help "leave no trace." This system of propane-powered buses can help you to avoid spending your vacation driving and finding places to park at crowded trailheads. It also gives hikers and bicyclists the opportunity to complete longer one-way trips without spotting cars. All six routes can be boarded at the village green in Bar Harbor. The six routes go to Blackwoods and Seawall Campgrounds, Sand Beach and Otter Cliffs, Jordan Pond, Eagle Lake, Northeast Harbor, Southwest Harbor, Bass Harbor, Tremont, and many places in between. Once again, the buses are free! For a schedule, contact Downeast Transportation at 207-667-5796.

Trail Maintenance

It takes a huge amount of work to keep hiking trails and carriage roads in good condition. Volunteering to help with trail maintenance is a great way to give back to the park. Friends of Acadia runs a volunteer trail-maintenance program in conjunction with the national park. Currently, maintenance is scheduled for Tuesdays, Thursdays, and Saturdays. For more information, call Friends of Acadia at 207-288-3340 or the Park Service at 207-288-3338. The AMC's Echo Lake Camp (207-244-3747) also leads trail-maintenance trips twice a week.

2
history

EVERY HIKING TRAIL, carriage road, and stretch of shoreline in Acadia National Park contains clues about the history of the area. In some places you can see bedrock that formed at the
bottom of an ancient ocean 500 million years ago. Mountaintops
show the marks of glaciers that retreated 18,000 years ago. Shell
heaps and spear tips are reminders of the first human inhabitants of
Mount Desert Island, while stone foundations mark the locations of
old teahouses from the nineteenth century. Even a seemingly wild
forest can tell you about the past, revealing the places where fire
burned out of control in 1947. While we have included historical
tidbits throughout the trip descriptions in this book, the following
summary of Mount Desert Island's history provides you with an
introduction to the world of Acadia National Park.

Geological History

The story of what is now Acadia National Park began about 500 million years ago at the bottom of an ancient sea called the Iapetus
Ocean. In this prehistoric ocean, silt and volcanic ash accumulated
at the rate of an inch every 100 years until the material was thousands of feet deep. This accumulated matter solidified into shales
and tuffs before the heat and pressure associated with being deep

within the Earth metamorphosed the rock into a dark gray or green schist composed of quartz, feldspar, and chlorite. This rock is now called Ellsworth schist and forms an incomplete ring around Mount Desert Island. It can be seen along the shore near the Thompson Island Picnic Area.

Around 400 million years ago, another round of silt accumulation formed a layer of sedimentary rock composed of sandstone and shale. Known as the Bar Harbor Formation, this rock is black to rusty brown in color and can be seen from the town pier in Bar Harbor, as well as around the Porcupine Islands and in Northeast Harbor. At about the same time, the Cranberry Island Series of sedimentary rock formed around the Cranberry Islands. This rock is lighter in color, with embedded rock fragments, and was formed by the sedimentation of volcanic ash.

These sedimentary and metamorphic bedrocks were an easily eroded covering that now makes up just a small part of the island. Between 380 million and 420 million years ago, the bulk of what is now Mount Desert Island literally bubbled up from deep within the Earth. At this time, North America was colliding with what is known as the Avalonian plate. This collision, called the Acadian Orogeny, created the mountains of Acadia and caused great movements of magma (molten rock) below the Earth's crust. Under Mount Desert Island, molten magma moved upward through the Earth's crust, consuming and altering the existing layers of bedrock. At one point a huge balloon of magma, eight or more miles in diameter, worked its way upward. This magma eventually cooled into what is now known as Cadillac granite. It makes up much of the island and all of the mountains, and has characteristic pink shading which is due to a mineral called feldspar. Other minerals that are easily visible upon inspection of the granite are quartz, hornblende, and biotite.

As North America moved away from Europe and Africa, fissures occasionally formed in the crust. Molten black diabase rose from the Earth's mantle to fill these fissures. These diabase dikes can be seen in many places around Acadia. They are on mountain summits, such as Pemetic Mountain, as well as on the shoreline. The Schoodic Peninsula and Isle au Haut have some excellent examples.

While plate tectonics following millions of years of sedimentation are responsible for building the mountains and bedrock of Acadia National Park, it is the more recent phenomenon of glaciation that has shaped the park into its current form. Over the last 2–3 million years, New England has experienced twenty to thirty glacial cycles, each lasting about 100,000 years. Glacial periods take up about 80,000 years of that time, while interglacial periods last 15,000 to 20,000 years. During these glacial cycles, thick layers of ice up to a mile deep move over the landscape, breaking the weaker rocks and grinding them into sand and gravel. The dominant Cadillac granite in Acadia withstood this glacial grinding better than the weaker sedimentary and metamorphic rocks on Mount Desert Island. While the glaciers did not obliterate the granite, they were powerful enough to wear down Acadia's granite-topped mountains into the rounded shapes you see today.

The last ice age was named after the Wisconsin Glacier, which reached as far south as Long Island about 18,000 years ago. At this time, the ice had to be at least a mile thick, as it covered the entire 5,267 vertical feet of Katahdin in northern Maine. The ice was not stationary; it flowed toward the ocean as all water does, and it wore its way through rock, creating deep U-shaped valleys like the one between Dorr Mountain and Huguenot Head. Between Acadia and Norumbega Mountains, the glacier dug so deep it created the only fiord in the eastern U.S., Somes Sound. Most of the lakes and ponds on Mount Desert Island are also a result of glacial carving.

Acadia has other evidence of glacial activity. As the ice surged through the valleys, it carried small rocks that dug out striations in the remaining granite. These shallow grooves in the rock can be found throughout the park. Two examples are on the coast around Bar Island, and on Flying Mountain. The glaciers also carried large boulders from many miles away and deposited them on Mount Desert Island. The two most obvious examples of these glacial "erratics" are Bubble Rock, which sits high up on the South Bubble, and Balance Rock, which can be seen from the Shore Path in Bar Harbor. Both Balance Rock and Bubble Rock can be identified as erratics because, unlike other rocks on Mount Desert Island, they consist of a light-colored granite called Lucerne granite, which originates in Lucerne, Maine, about forty miles to the northwest.

By 14,000 years ago, most of the ice had retreated from Mount Desert Island, leaving a treeless expanse of tundra surrounded by a constantly changing shoreline. As the glacial period ended, the ice melted, raising sea levels so that by 12,000 years ago, the shoreline of Mount Desert Island was much as it is now. Ice is heavy, however, and it had depressed the island by as much as 0.3 mile. With the ice gone, the land began to rebound. By 11,000 years ago, the land had rebounded faster than the sea was rising and Frenchman Bay and Blue Hill Bay were dry land. Ice continued to melt around the Earth's polar regions, and sea level finally rose to its current level about 8,000 years ago. By then, all the tree species now present in Acadia had colonized the island. Since that time, most of the shaping of Acadia's landscape has been done by pounding surf, wind and rain, and people.

Human History

Available archaeological evidence suggests that Native Americans were living on Mount Desert Island at least 6,000 years ago. It is likely they were on the island even earlier, but Maine's wet coastal climate has caused any older evidence to decay into oblivion. Shell middens, deep heaps of discarded clam and mussel shells which also harbor stone tools and other artifacts, can be found throughout this part of coastal Maine. The Abenaki Indians lived throughout Maine and spent at least part of the year on Mount Desert Island, which they called "Pemetic," which means "Sloping Land." It was originally believed that the Abenaki spent summers on the island and wintered inland. However, archaeological evidence suggests the opposite was true. Avoiding the brutally cold winters of inland Maine, the Abenaki most likely wintered on the coast, living off fish and shellfish. In the summers they moved inland to take advantage of runs of Atlantic salmon. More can be learned about Maine's Native American heritage at the Abbe Museum, located in the park at Sieur de Monts Spring.

It is possible that Leif Ericson and his crew of Viking sailors in search of timber encountered Mount Desert Island around 1000 A.D. However, most of the known history of Mount Desert Island begins with the arrival of Europeans, who came after Columbus. Sailing for France, Italian explorer Giovanni da Verazzano was the first to make note of the island in 1500. However, Samuel de Champlain is generally given credit for "discovering" Mount Desert Island in 1604 when he ran aground near Otter Point. Champlain, who was mapping the area for the French, named the island l'Isle des Monts-Deserts, or "Island of the Desert Mountains." He also called the area La Cadie, from the Abenaki word for "where it is plentiful." Most of what was to become New France, from Down East Maine to Nova Scotia, would be known for many years as L'Acadie, or Acadia.

The first permanent European settlement on Mount Desert Island was short-lived. In 1613 two French Jesuit priests, Father Biard and Father Masse established a mission on Fernald Point, near the entrance to Somes Sound. They called their mission Saint Sauveur, now the name of the mountain just to the northwest of Fernald Point. The local Abenaki, led by their chief, Asticou, welcomed the Jesuits' attempt to build a fort, plant corn, and baptize the natives. However, before they finished building the mission, an English ship, under the leadership of Captain Samuel Argall, destroyed their fledgling settlement. For the next 150 years, this part of Maine became a no man's land as the French and English fought for control of North America. During this period, Mount Desert Island was used primarily as a landmark for passing ships, and some say as a hideout for pirates.

In 1688 Louis XIV granted 100,000 acres on the Maine coast to Antoine de Mothe Cadillac, who briefly settled on Mount Desert Island before moving on to found Detroit. While he bestowed upon himself the important-sounding title of Sieur de la Mothe Cadillac, he had little influence on the history of Mount Desert Island. Shortly after the Revolutionary War, however, his granddaughter, Madame de Gregoire, asked the United States to give her the land from her grandfather's grant. Feeling friendly toward the French after their help in the war, the Massachusetts legislature agreed to uphold part of her claim and granted her rights to the entire eastern half of Mount Desert Island. Mount Desert Island is the only place in the United States outside of Louisiana where land titles can be traced back to the French crown. Madame de Gregoire and her husband settled at Hulls Cove in 1788, but they proved to be rather ill suited to the pioneer lifestyle. They gradually sold off their land holdings in order to support themselves, and their family grant was completely used up by the time of their deaths in 1810 and 1811.

The English began settling Mount Desert Island after their victory in the French and Indian War in 1759. In 1760 John Bernard, governor of Massachusetts, obtained a royal land grant on Mount

Desert Island and attempted to secure his claim by offering free land to settlers. Abraham Somes and John Richardson of Gloucester, Massachusetts, took advantage of Bernard's offer and settled in what is now Somesville. Bernard lost his grant as a result of the Revolutionary War, but the early U.S. government granted his son the western half of the island at about the same time they deeded the eastern half to Madame de Gregoire. However, the grants of Bernard and de Gregoire had little effect on the settlers homesteading on the island, and by the middle of the nineteenth century Mount Desert Island was a thriving place with a diverse economy revolving around farming, lumbering, and fishing.

Things started to change in the 1850s as visiting artists and journalists began to tell the world about the beauty of Mount Desert Island. The most prominent of these early visitors were painters of the Hudson River school, such as Thomas Cole and Frederic Church. Their dramatically lit renditions of landscapes such as Eagle Lake, the Beehive, and the Porcupine Islands lured more visitors from the big cities on the East Coast. These early visitors, known as "rusticators," rented rooms from local farmers and fishermen and ate simple meals with their hosts. Of course, as word got out about Mount Desert Island's simple life, salty spruce-scented air, and mild summer climate, tourism grew substantially. By 1870, steamers began landing in Southwest Harbor, and they soon made their way to Bar Harbor. By 1871, Bar Harbor had eleven hotels and was visited by four steamers a week. Daniel Rodick built the largest of the hotels, the Rodick House, which by 1882 could hold more than 600 guests. Magazines such as *Harpers* began calling Bar Harbor a "fashionable spa," and soon tourists from around the world were spending their summers on Mount Desert Island.

The 1880s saw the beginning of the building of summer "cottages" by America's wealthy elite. These estates of fifty or more rooms, complete with ten to fifteen servants, were the summer residences of families such as the Rockefellers, Astors, Fords, Morgans, and Carnegies. At one point, there were as many as ninety of these estates. These families also bought up huge pieces of the most desirable pieces of real estate on Mount Desert Island. For example, J. P. Morgan owned Great Head and Sand Beach, which he gave to his daughter in 1910. The wealthy summer residents also contributed generously to the towns on the island, greatly improving sanitation

The Tarn Trail, originally called the Kane Path, was designed by George Dorr who was the first superintendent of Acadia National Park.

and building libraries and hospitals. It was this spirit of philanthropy that would lead to the establishment of Acadia National Park.

In 1901 Charles Eliot, president of Harvard and a summer resident of Northeast Harbor, became concerned that the invention of the portable sawmill was going to bring about the demise of the tranquil beauty that existed on Mount Desert Island. He asked Charles Dorr, a wealthy Bostonian and fellow summer visitor to Mount Desert Island, to help him preserve the best of the island. Dorr convinced other summer residents such as John S. Kennedy and George Vanderbilt to help him start a nonprofit organization whose sole purpose was "to acquire by devise, gift, or purchase, and to own, arrange, hold, maintain, or improve for public use lands in Hancock County, Maine, which by reason of scenic beauty, historical interest, sanitary advantage or other like reasons may become available for such purpose." So began the Hancock County Trustees of Public Reservations.

With George Dorr at the helm, the Trustees acquired substantial pieces of Mount Desert Island, including the summit of Cadillac Mountain and Otter Cliffs. Dorr worked tirelessly for years to persuade landowners to donate land to the Trustees. By 1913, 6,000 acres had been acquired, and in 1916 the land was given to the federal government for the creation of Sieur de Monts National Monument. Dorr continued to acquire land for the park, and in 1919 the national monument became Lafayette National Park, the first national park east of the Mississippi River. Dorr was hired as the park's first superintendent and is generally thought of as the father of Acadia National Park, which became the park's official name in 1929. Acadia now protects 46,000 acres on Mount Desert Island, the Schoodic Peninsula, and Isle au Haut, and is the only national park in the U.S. where all of the land was donated to the government.

In 1947, an event occurred that still has an effect on Acadia today. That summer Maine received only 50 percent of its normal rainfall, and by October Mount Desert Island was as dry as it has ever been. On October 17 the fire department received a call that smoke was rising from a cranberry bog near a dump on Crooked Road, west of Hulls Cove. At the time it was a modest blaze, and it burned only 167 acres during the next three days. But on October 21 strong winds took control, and soon another 2,000 acres were burning. The fire continued to intensify as firefighters proved no match for the gale force winds, which blew the fire south and east. At one point, the fire moved six miles in less than three hours and burned sixty-seven summer cottages in the section of Bar Harbor known as Millionaires' Row. Downtown Bar Harbor itself was spared, although the fire came close enough that 400 people fled by sea to Winter Harbor across Frenchman Bay.

After burning more than 17,000 acres, 10,000 of them in Acadia, the fire burned itself out in a massive fireball over the Atlantic Ocean at Ocean Drive. For such an intense fire, casualties were low: one person had died in the fire while trying to rescue a cat from his burning home, and two people died in a car accident while fleeing the island. Park rangers believed that most animals were able to outrun the fire and take refuge in lakes and ponds. However, the nature in the park was altered dramatically. Before the fire, spruce and fir dominated the landscape, but with the spruce-fir canopy gone, sunloving species such as birch and aspen were able to grow. Today, a mosaic forest has reclaimed the burned areas of the park. This mosaic forest is a mix of spruce, fir, white pine, hemlock, beech, maple, birch, and aspen, and it supports a variety of wildlife including beaver, white-tailed deer, and ruffed grouse. On the exposed, rocky ledges of the mountains that burned, fire-resistant pitch pine flourishes. All in all, the park now contains a more diverse mix of flora and fauna than it did before the fire.

The fire of 1947 brought about the end of the era of huge summer cottages, although this lifestyle of conspicuous consumption had already been in decline due to such factors as the introduction of the income tax, the Great Depression, and World War II. However, tourism remains the largest part of the economy for Mount Desert Island, and more than 3 million people a year visit Acadia to walk its wooded paths, breathe in the salty scent of the Atlantic, and watch the wildlife of Maine's wild coast. Acadia National Park has healed its fire scars and is now a vibrant and healthy ecosystem.

trip highlights chart

SPORT	SECTION	TRIP #	TRIP	DIFFICULTY	DISTANCE
Walking	Eastern		Shore Path	Easy	0.7 mi. one-way
Walking	Eastern		Ocean Trail	Easy	2.0 mi. one-way
Walking	Eastern		Jordan Pond Shore Trail	Easy	1.5 mi. one-way
Walking	Eastern		Jessup Path	Easy	1.0 mi. one-way
Walking	Western		Wonderland Trail	Easy	0.5 mi. one-way
Hiking	Western	1	Ship Harbor Nature Trail	Easy	1.3 mi.
Hiking	Western	2	Flying Mountain	Moderate	1.2 mi.
Hiking	Eastern	3	Great Head & Sand Beach	Moderate	1.8 mi.
Hiking	Eastern	4	Bubbles	Strenuous but short	1.6 mi.
Hiking	Eastern	5	Gorham Mountain–Ocean Trail Loop	Moderate, then easy	3.5 mi.

ELEVATION	ESTIMATED HIKING TIME	FEATURES	PAGE
Minimal	30 min.	A flat walk along Frenchman Bay that starts from downtown Bar Harbor. Great for families with small children.	32
100 ft.	1 hr.	A gentle walk along the ocean with awesome views of the rocky coast and Otter Cliffs. A great walk for anyone; lots for small children to explore.	33
Minimal	45 min.	An easy walk along the eastern shore of scenic Jordan Pond. Great for families.	33
Minimal	40 min.	This easy walk is close to Bar Harbor. It passes beaver ponds, winds through forests, and ends at Sieur de Monts Spring.	33
Minimal	30 min.	An excellent place to explore a cobble beach and tide-pool area with beautiful ocean views. Great for families.	33
25 ft.	30 min.	A flat, easy hike to pink-granite outcroppings with views of Blue Hill Bay, several islands, and the Atlantic Ocean. A great family trip.	34
275 ft.	45 min.	A short hike to good views of the waters surrounding the entrance of Somes Sound	36
200 ft.	1 hr.	A beach walk followed by a wooded climb to the cliffs of Great Head, overlooking the Atlantic Ocean. Good for families.	38
550 ft.	1.5 hrs.	A short but irresistible climb to the summits of Jordan Pond's distinctive mountains. Great reward for short hike.	41
500 ft.	2 hrs.	A moderate hike up to wide-open views of the ocean, followed by a walk along the dramatic coastline between Sand Beach and Otter Cliffs. Great family hike.	45

SPORT	SECTION	TRIP #	TRIP	DIFFICULTY	DISTANCE
Hiking	Eastern	6	Beehive & Bowl	Ladder	1.3 mi.
Hiking	Western	7	Beech Mountain	Moderate	2.0 mi.
Hiking	Eastern	8	Huguenot Head & Champlain Mountain	Moderate, with one short, strenuous section	3.3 mi.
Hiking	Eastern	9	Pemetic Mountain & Bubble Pond	Strenuous, then moderate, then easy	4.1 mi.
Hiking	Western	10	Acadia & Saint Sauveur Mountains	Strenuous	3.7 mi.
Hiking	Eastern	11	Penobscot & Sargent Mountains	Strenuous	5.2 mi.
Hiking	Western	12	Mansell & Bernard Mountains	Strenuous	4.2 mi.
Hiking	Eastern	13	Peak-Baggers' Delight: Bald, Parkman, Gilmore & Sargent Mountains	Strenuous	4.0 mi.
Hiking	Eastern	14	Dorr Mountain, the Gorge, & Sieur de Monts Spring	Strenuous	4.0 mi.

ELEVATION	ESTIMATED HIKING TIME	FEATURES	PAGE
450 ft.	1 hrs.	A challenging climb up iron rungs to spectacular views, and a visit to a quiet and beautiful mountain pond.	50
700 ft.	1.5 hrs.	An enjoyable hike over rocky ledges to the summit of Beech Mountain with excellent views.	53
1,100 ft.	2.5 hrs.	A classic Acadia hike up steep pink granite through a pitch pine forest to extraordinary mountain and ocean views. Good wildlife-watching opportunities.	55
950 ft.	2.5 hrs.	A strenuous hike to some of Mount Desert Island's most spectacular views combined with a gentle walk along the scenic Bubble Pond.	60
1,050 ft.	3 hrs.	A strenuous hike through a beautiful pitch pine forest to the best views of Somes Sound, the only fiord on the East Coast of the U.S.	65
1,300 ft.	3.5 hrs.	A strenuous hike to two of Acadia's highest peaks, with long periods of hiking on open ledges with magnificent views. Great hawk-watching in the fall.	69
1,350 ft.	3.5 hrs.	A peaceful yet strenuous hike to the highest peaks on the western side of Mount Desert Island.	74
1,500 ft.	3.5 hrs.	A challenging hike over four peaks, including Sargent Mountain, Acadia's second highest peak. Great views and lots of endorphins.	78
1,200 ft.	4 hrs.	A challenging hike to spectacular views, a narrow gorge, and quiet forests.	82

SPORT	SECTION	TRIP #	TRIP	DIFFICULTY	DISTANCE
Hiking	Eastern	15	Cadillac Mountain	Moderate	7.0 mi.
Biking	Eastern, Carriage Roads	16	Maple Spring–Hadlock Brook Loop	Easy	4.0 mi.
Biking	Western	17	Hio Fire Road	Easy	4.0 mi.
Biking	Eastern, Carriage Roads	18	Witch Hole Pond & Paradise Hill	Easy	4.4 mi.
Biking	Western	19	Seal Cove Pond–Western Mountain Loop	Easy	5.0 mi.
Biking	Western	20	Long Pond Fire Road	Easy	5.5 mi.
Biking	Eastern, Carriage Roads	21	Amphitheater Loop	Moderate	5.5 mi.
Biking	Eastern, Carriage Roads	22	Aunt Betty Pond Loop	Moderate	6.0 mi.
Biking	Eastern, Carriage Roads	23	Eagle Lake Loop	Moderate	6.0 mi.
Biking	Eastern, Carriage Roads	24	Day Mountain	Moderate	8.0 mi.
Biking	Eastern, Carriage Roads	25	Jordan Pond–Bubble Pond Loop	Moderate	9.0 mi.

ELEVATION	ESTIMATED HIKING/ BIKING TIME	FEATURES	PAGE
1,500 ft.	4 hrs.	A relatively long hike over open ledges to the summit of Mount Desert Island's highest mountain. Great views during most of this hike.	85
350 ft.	1.25 hrs.	A relatively easy ride to a forty-foot waterfall and a visit to Upper Hadlock Pond. Great for families.	94
100 ft.	1 hr.	An easy ride for the family on a dirt road in prime bird-watching habitat.	97
350 ft.	1.25 hrs.	An easy ride past beaver ponds and bogs to great views of Hulls Cove and Frenchman Bay. A great trip for families.	102
150 ft.	1.25 hrs.	An easy ride through a boreal forest frequented by moose.	105
250 ft.	2 hrs.	An easy ride on a dirt road to a secluded cove on Long Pond. Maybe you'll spot a moose.	107
350 ft.	2 hrs.	A moderate ride through an enchanting evergreen forest past streams lined with pink-granite stones. Great for families.	112
300 ft.	1.5 hrs.	A moderate ride with views of Sargent Mountain and Eagle Lake and the chance to see beaver.	115
350 ft.	2 hrs.	A great ride for families through rich woodlands, with good views of Eagle Lake.	120
500 ft.	2.5 hrs.	A moderate ride up a mountain to great views of the ocean and the islands to the south.	123
500 ft.	2.5 hrs.	A moderate ride next to the spectacular scenery of Jordan and Bubble ponds.	126

SPORT	SECTION	TRIP #	TRIP	DIFFICULTY	DISTANC
Biking	Eastern, Carriage Roads	26	Giant Slide Loop	Difficult	8.5 mi
Biking	Eastern, Carriage Roads	27	Around the Mountain Loop	Difficult	12.0 mi
Paddling	Eastern	28	Little Long Pond	Easy	1.25 m
Paddling	Western	29	Echo Lake	Easy	1.5 mi
Paddling	Eastern	30	Jordan Pond	Easy	2.5 mi
Paddling	Western	31	Long Pond South End	Easy	3.0 mi
Paddling	Western	32	Seal Cove Pond	Easy	4.5 mi
Paddling	Eastern	33	Northeast Creek	Moderate	5.0 mi
Paddling	Eastern	34	Eagle Lake	Moderate	4.0 mi
Paddling	Western	35	Long Pond North End	Strenuous	7.5 mi
Kayaking	Ocean	36	Mount Desert Narrows	Difficulty depends on weather conditions	6.0 mi

ELEVATION	ESTIMATED TIME	FEATURES	PAGE
600 ft.	2.5 hrs.	A challenging ride over rushing mountain streams to fantastic ocean and mountain views.	132
1,000 ft.	4 hrs.	This ride has it all: waterfalls, mountain and ocean views, and seven major bridge crossings.	135
N/A	1 hr.	A short and easy paddle on one of Mount Desert Island's most picturesque ponds.	144
N/A	1 hr.	A short paddle beneath towering cliffs, with a chance to see peregrine falcons.	148
N/A	2 hrs.	A pleasant paddle on an incredibly scenic pond.	151
N/A	2 hrs.	A paddle beneath the steep cliffs of Beech and Mansell Mountains on the quiet end of Long Pond.	154
N/A	2.5 hrs.	A paddle on the westernmost pond, with good opportunities to see waterfowl and bald eagles.	156
N/A	2.5 hrs.	A quiet paddle on a narrow creek through extensive wetlands and prime wildlife habitat.	161
N/A	3 hrs.	A moderate paddle on a beautiful lake with mountain views and wild shorelines.	167
N/A	4 hrs.	A long and popular paddle that explores the wooded coves of Mount Desert Island's biggest lake.	170
N/A	3 hrs.	A relatively sheltered paddle in shallow waters, with the chance to see an eagle's nest and possibly seals and porpoises.	177

SPORT	SECTION	TRIP #	TRIP	DIFFICULTY	DISTANCE
Kayaking	Ocean	37	Frenchman Bay and the Porcupine Islands	Difficulty depends on weather conditions	6.5 mi
Kayaking	Ocean	38	Sutton & Bear Islands	Difficulty depends on weather conditions	6.0 mi.
Kayaking	Ocean	39	Somes Sound	Difficulty depends on weather conditions	7.5 mi.
Kayaking	Ocean	40	Seal Cove to Pretty Marsh	Difficulty depends on weather conditions	10.0 mi.

ELEVATION	ESTIMATED TIME	FEATURES	PAGE
N/A	3 hrs.	An exciting paddle around the beautiful and wild Porcupine Islands.	182
N/A	3 hrs.	A moderate paddle past a remote light-house and a sea arch with great views of the mountains of Acadia.	191
N/A	4 hrs.	A paddle in the only fiord in the eastern U.S. with views of tall oceanside cliffs and good wildlife watching.	197
N/A	7 hrs.	A paddle on the "quiet" side of Mount Desert Island filled with wooded shoreline, beautiful islands, and bountiful wildlife.	202

4

hiking in acadia

HIKING THROUGH ACADIA'S forests to its storied rocky coast or its bare mountain summits has been a popular activity since the mid-1800s. With more than 100 miles of maintained trails providing access to almost every corner of the park, it is possible to explore ocean cliffs, rocky gorges, quiet mountain ponds, and wide-open granite mountaintops with spectacular views of forest and ocean. During a hike in Acadia, you may spot bald eagles and peregrine falcons flying overhead, deer and beaver feeding in and around ponds, or loons and harbor seals swimming in the Atlantic. While most of Acadia's trails are short, creative trip planning can make for some enjoyable extended hiking. This chapter suggests fifteen hiking loops that are, in our opinion, some of the most scenic in the park. For some trips we have combined several trails into one hike. For others, we have included walks on the park's carriage roads and dirt fire roads, as well as the park loop road. A complete listing of trails can be found in appendix A.

Hiking Times and Trail Ratings

Our hiking times are estimates based on our experience as average thirty-something hikers carrying fifteen to thirty pounds of gear.

Obviously these times can vary based on the weather, the physical fitness level of your group, and how much gear you stuff into your pack. While we think these times are useful for planning a trip, your hiking times will undoubtedly vary from ours. We have used the National Park Service's system for rating trails, using a scale of *easy, moderate, strenuous,* and *ladder. Easy* trails are suitable for families with kids of any age. *Moderate* and *strenuous* trails can be fun for older children who have experience hiking steep and rocky trails. Expect a strenuous trail in Acadia to be like climbing a very steep staircase with large and uneven steps. *Ladder* trails have at least one section of climbing iron rungs that are driven into granite cliffs. It is exactly like climbing a ladder on the side of a mountain. These can be challenging and fun trails, but they are also frightening for small children or people with a fear of heights. It is also illegal to bring a dog on a ladder trail.

Safety and Etiquette

Its mild summer climate makes Acadia an enjoyable and relatively safe hiking destination. Of course, bad weather or poor planning can spoil any hiking adventure. Before heading into Acadia's backcountry, consider the following tips:

- Select a trip that is appropriate for everyone in the group. Match the hike to the abilities of the least capable person in the group.

- Plan to be back at the trailhead before dark. Determine a turn-around time and stick to it—even if you have not reached your goal for the day.

- Check the weather. Wet weather can make Acadia's granite very slick, and high winds and pelting rain can make the summits an uncomfortable place to be. Trails with iron rungs and ladders should be avoided in the rain as they become very slippery and dangerous when wet. Weather phone is 207-667-8910.

- Bring a pack with the following items:

  Water—one or two quarts per person depending on the weather and length of the trip

Food—Even for a short hike, it is a good idea to bring some high-energy snacks like nuts, dried fruit, or snack bars. Bring a lunch for longer trips.

Map and compass

Extra clothing—rain gear, sweater, hat

Flashlight

Sunscreen

First-aid kit

Pocketknife

Binoculars for wildlife viewing

- Wear appropriate footwear and clothing. Hiking shoes should be waterproof and provide good ankle support. Wear wool hiking socks and comfortable, sturdy hiking boots that give you good traction and support. Bring rain gear even in sunny weather, since unexpected rain, fog, or wind is possible at any time in Acadia. Avoid wearing cotton clothing which absorbs sweat and rain, making for cold, damp hiking. Polypropylene, fleece, silk, and wool are all good materials for keeping moisture away from your body and keeping you warm in wet or cold conditions.

   In addition to practicing the no-impact techniques described in this book's introduction, it is also a good idea to keep the following things in mind while hiking:

- Try not to disturb other hikers. While you may often feel alone in the wilderness, wild yelling or cell phone usage will undoubtedly upset another person's quiet backcountry experience.

- When you are in front of the rest of your hiking group, wait at all trail junctions. This avoids confusion and keeps people in your group from getting lost or separated from each other.

- If you see downed wood that appears to be purposely covering a trail, it probably means the trail is closed due to overuse or hazardous conditions.

- If a trail is muddy, walk through the mud or on rocks, never on tree roots or plants. Wearing waterproof boots will keep your feet comfortable, and by staying in the center of the trail you will keep the trail from eroding into a wide "hiking highway."

For the most part, Acadia is not a frightening place to be. Cool, quiet forests and tranquil ocean views are the norm. When hiking, expect an enjoyable time and keep your senses tuned to your surroundings. Every one of the trips in this chapter passes through two or more different natural habitats, adding variety to every outing. Don't expect to see eagles and bears and moose on every hike. However, by paying attention to details such as a rare alpine flower on Saint Sauveur, the jack pines on Cadillac, or the salamanders in a forested wetland, you can finish a hike with a satisfying sense of wonder.

The following hikes will take you from the shores of Ship Harbor to the summit of Cadillac Mountain. You will encounter forests shaped by fire and man and nature. You will hike through valleys and over hills created deep within the Earth before being pushed up by earthquakes and scoured by glaciers. Eagles, falcons, and hawks will soar over head, and warblers will fill the forest with bird song. If you have visited Acadia before, hopefully we have thought of some new and interesting hikes that you have yet to try. If you are new to the park, you should find these trips to be a great way to explore this special place.

Flat and Easy Walks

While many of Acadia's trails consist of steep hikes with rough footing, a few trails are flat, easy, yet worthwhile destinations. In midsummer, these trails do attract the crowds; however, early mornings and evenings tend to be less crowded than the middle of the day.

SHORE PATH. This 1.5-mile path conveniently starts in downtown Bar Harbor. It begins on the shoreline at the pier of the Bar Harbor Inn, next to the parking lot at the municipal pier. From the path, you can look out over the harbor at Bar Island and the Porcupine Islands as well as the Schoodic Peninsula. You will also get a good view of the most impressive homes in Bar Harbor. The path ends at Hancock Street, which will lead you back to Main Street.

OCEAN TRAIL. This trail (which is also part of the Gorham Mountain hike, trip #5 in this chapter), is an easy walk from Sand Beach to Otter Point. It provides an up-close experience with the shoreline of Acadia over the course of about two miles. There are cobble beaches and tide pools to explore, as well as Thunder Hole and Otter Cliffs. The soothing sounds, smells, and sights of the Atlantic Ocean are so captivating that you hardly notice the nearby Park Loop Road.

JORDAN POND SHORE TRAIL (APPENDIX A). The 1.5 miles of this trail on the east side of Jordan Pond are flat and have relatively good footing. Look for mergansers and loons on the pond as well as peregrine falcons on the cliffs of Penobscot Mountain. This is an especially good destination for children. Please note that the portion of this trail on the west side of Jordan Pond has extremely difficult footing and is rated as a *moderate* hike.

JESSUP PATH (APPENDIX A). Close to Bar Harbor, this trail is almost a mile long. A hike on the Jessup Path is an easy walk past the beaver ponds of the Great Meadow and through hemlock and mixed hardwood forests. It also passes by Sieur de Monts Spring, home of the Abbe Museum of Native American History, the Wild Gardens of Acadia, and the Nature Center.

WONDERLAND TRAIL. Located between Seawall Campground and the Ship Harbor Trail on Maine Route 102A, the Wonderland Trail is a gravel fire road that takes you to a cobble beach in about 0.5 mile. From the beach, you can see the Duck Islands to the southeast and Great Cranberry Island to the northeast. This is a good place to bring kids for beach and tide-pool exploration.

SHIP HARBOR NATURE TRAIL. See trip #1 below.

Ship Harbor Nature Trail

NPS Rating: **Easy**

Distance: **1.3 miles round-trip**

Elevation Gain: **25 feet**

Estimated Time: **30 minutes**

A flat, easy hike to pink-granite outcrop-pings with views of Blue Hill Bay, several islands, and the Atlantic Ocean. A great destination for families with small children.

The Ship Harbor Nature Trail is an easy self-guided nature walk of 1.3 miles. Brochures detailing the natural and human history of this part of Acadia are available at the trailhead. This trail leaves Seawall Road 1.5 miles from Seawall Campground and gives hikers the opportunity to enjoy ocean views from the western side of Mount Desert Island and to see tidal currents at work as Ship Harbor empties into the Atlantic, only to be filled back in a few hours later.

The trail is basically a figure eight with numbered signposts that correspond to descriptions in the nature-walk brochure. To follow the brochure in order, always stay to the left at trail intersections. The trail leaves the parking area and immediately enters a forest of red and white spruce. The footpath is wide and flat with a few roots and boulders to contend with, but generally easy. The trail stays in the forest until the 0.6-mile mark, where it hits pink-granite boulders and ledges at the ocean. These ledges are a good place to watch for harbor seals and seabirds as well as to explore the tide pools, looking for urchins and sea stars. Great Gott Island, Great Duck Island, and other islands can be seen to the south and west.

The trail turns right and hugs the shoreline, which brings you to Ship Harbor. Thirty-foot granite cliffs topped with spruce make a typical Maine coast scene across the harbor. As the tides change, water rushes through the narrow inlet that leads to the harbor. The harbor is eight feet deep at high tide but is almost completely emptied of water at low tide, revealing several acres of mud flats and providing feeding opportunities for shorebirds. While in the forest, keep your eyes open for great horned owls, which nest in the area.

The trail meets up with itself a few hundred yards from the parking area. Turn left here to return to the trailhead.

Directions

From Maine Route 102 in the town of Southwest Harbor, turn left onto Maine Route 102A. Follow 102A for 4.7 miles. The Ship Harbor Nature Trail parking area will be on your left.

Flying Mountain

> **NPS Rating: Moderate**
> **Distance: 1.2 miles round-trip**
> **Elevation Gain: 275 feet**
> **Estimated Time: 45 minutes**
>
> **A short hike to good views of the waters surrounding the entrance of Somes Sound.**

FLYING MOUNTAIN stands as a sentinel at the southern end of Somes Sound, jutting out into the water at a point that almost closes off the entrance to the sound. At 284 feet tall, Flying Mountain is more a hill than a mountain, but it provides good views for a small amount of effort. This hike loops over the mountain and over to Valley Cove, a protected tongue of water that laps up against 500 vertical feet of rock known as Eagle Cliff. For only forty-five minutes of work, this hike has a lot to offer.

Start this hike on the Flying Mountain Trail, which begins on the west side of the Fernald Cove parking area. The trail, marked with blue blazes, climbs moderately through a pure spruce forest. The soil here is thin, and erosion has made the trail difficult to follow at first. Please do your part to prevent further erosion by seeking out the blazes and keeping to the intended footpath. You will reach the summit fairly quickly, 0.3 mile from the parking lot. There are views of the south end of Somes Sound and out to Greening, Sutton, and Bear Islands as well as the Cranberries. Cadillac and Norumbega Mountains are also visible across the sound.

After continuing past the summit, a side path leads to the right to an overlook with more views of the sound and the large houses of Northeast Harbor. The Flying Mountain Trail leads to the left and then descends steeply to Valley Cove. Valley Cove is a place where you can explore tide pools and gaze up at the steep walls of Eagle

Flying Mountain and Somes Sound as seen from Eagle Cliff.

Cliff. This cove is one of the safest places on Mount Desert Island for boats to drop anchor in big storms, as Flying Mountain extends into Somes Sound far enough to prevent large storm swells from making their way into the cove.

The trail follows the shoreline of the cove all the way to Man o' War Brook and the Acadia Mountain Trail. However, for this hike, look for a path on the left just after climbing a set of wooden and gravel steps. Turn left on this path and then left again when it reaches a gravel fire road in a few yards. Follow the fire road through a mature forest of spruce and cedar. The parking area is 0.6 mile from Valley Cove.

Directions

From the intersection of Maine Routes 102 and 198 in Somesville, follow Route 102 south for 5.4 miles to Fernald Point Road. Turn left (west) on Fernald Point Road. The Fernald Cove parking area is on the left, 0.9 mile from Route 102.

Great Head and Sand Beach

NPS Rating: **Moderate**

Distance: **1.8 miles**

Elevation Gain: **200 feet**

Estimated Time: **1 hour**

A beach walk followed by a wooded climb to the 145–foot cliffs of Great Head, which overlook the Atlantic Ocean.

THIS HIKE STARTS at Sand Beach and climbs to the outlooks along the cliffs of Great Head. Great Head is a peninsula of granite, basalt, and sedimentary rock that juts out into the ocean just to the east of Sand Beach. The cliffs are as high as 145 feet and are a dramatic spot for looking at the wildlife plying the waters below. This loop hike returns to Sand Beach, which is composed of small grains of quartz and pieces of clamshells, blue mussel shells, and green sea urchins.

From the Sand Beach parking area, walk down the stairway that leads to Sand Beach. Walk east across the beach, which is about 300 yards long, to the beginning of the Great Head Trail. A stream cuts through the beach just before the trail. Depending on the tide and the season, the stream can be completely dry or a couple of feet deep. Be prepared to ford the water, as there is no bridge. The current is not strong, so the crossing is easy, but you will want to wear waterproof boots or sport sandals because the bottom is rocky. The stream can be an interesting place to study the rocks that exist beneath the beach, as the water tends to carry the sand here to the ocean. Pink-granite, dark basalt, and brownish sedimentary rocks give the stream a multicolored presence.

The Great Head Trail begins by climbing a short stretch of granite steps, at the top of which is an old millstone. Turn right here and start a moderate climb over granite slabs. Keep an eye open for blue

Sand beach as seen from the Great Head Trail.

trail blazes painted on the rocks, as the footpath is not always obvious. The hike reaches what seems like the high point of the trip before descending to the right into the woods to an overlook with views of Sand Beach, Gorham Mountain, and the Beehive.

From this overlook, the trail follows the coast to the left and gradually climbs over rocky cliffs before reaching the high point of Great Head, marked by the stone foundation of an old teahouse. The house was part of the estate of Louisa Satterlee, who received Great Head and Sand Beach as a present from her father, J. P. Morgan. The teahouse was destroyed in the fire of 1947, and the Morgan property was donated to the park two years later. Great Head is the highest point on the coast of Mount Desert Island. The entire walk over these cliffs is out in the open, with the sights and sounds of the ocean on the right. Open ocean is due south, while the mouth of Frenchman Bay and the Schoodic Peninsula are to the east. To the west are Otter Cliffs, probably named for otterlike sea minks that could be seen here until they went extinct in the mid-nineteenth century. The rocky shoal between Great Head and Otter Cliffs is called Old Soaker and is a favorite hangout for seabirds. The cliffs are a good place to sit and watch for porpoises, seals, gulls, terns, guillemots, and common eider ducks. In the fall and winter, common loons can be seen here as well.

From the top of Great Head, follow the trail north, then northwest, as it descends back into a forest of spruce. At the next trail junction, continue straight as the forest changes into a mix of white birch, aspen, and balsam fir. About 0.5 mile from Great Head, the trail reaches a junction with a narrow dirt service road. Turn left onto the service road, which seems much more like a woodland path than a road. In 0.3 mile, the road completes the Great Head loop at the millstone seen at the beginning of the hike. To finish your hike, go down the stairs to Sand Beach and walk back to the west end of the beach.

Directions

From downtown Bar Harbor, drive south on Maine Route 3 for 2.1 miles and turn right at the Sieur de Monts entrance to the Park Loop Road. Follow the signs for Sand Beach. The Sand Beach parking area is on the left, 3.25 miles south of the Sieur de Monts entrance. You will need to pay a fee to enter this part of the park.

Trip #4

The Bubbles

> **NPS Rating: Strenuous but short**
> **Distance: 1.6 miles**
> **Elevation Gain: 550 feet**
> **Estimated Time: 1.5 hours**
>
> **A short but irresistible climb to the summits of Jordan Pond's distinctive mountains.**

THE BUBBLES are two well-rounded granite hills that stand at the northern end of Jordan Pond, home to loons and mergansers. Their shape and location are so distinctive, it is hard to imagine Jordan Pond without them. At 768 feet and 872 feet, they are far from being the tallest mountains in the park, but they do provide good views of Jordan Pond and the taller surrounding peaks. South Bubble is also home to perhaps the most well known rock in the state of Maine: Bubble Rock, perched precariously over the steep eastern slope of the mountain, is a perfect example of a glacial erratic.

This hike starts at the Bubble Rock parking lot, which is about 1.1 miles south of Bubble Pond on the Park Loop Road. From the parking lot, follow the Bubble-Pemetic Trail west for a short distance to a junction with the North Bubble Trail and the Jordan Pond Carry Trail. Go straight on the North Bubble Trail. The footpath is wide and level as it passes through one of the few true northern hardwood forests on the island. Birch and American beech dominate. Search the forest floor for beechnuts, a favorite food of bear, turkey, and other animals. With the demise of the American chestnut, which was decimated by a fungus earlier in this century, beechnuts became an even more important food source for the animals of eastern North America. Now the American beech is being attacked by the combination of a fungus and a scale introduced by the importation of European beech trees. Without the natural defenses necessary to

Enjoying the views of Jordan Pond from South Bubble.

fight off this threat, it is possible that the American beech could go the way of the American chestnut.

The trail turns left and climbs up a set of stairs to a junction with the South Bubble Trail. From here the summit of South Bubble is 0.3 mile to the left, while the summit of North Bubble is 0.3 mile to the right. For this hike, stay to the right on the North Bubble Trail, which soon begins a steep climb over granite ledges. Scree walls (small rock walls) built by the park's trail crew line the trail in an attempt to keep hikers on the footpath. Like most trails in Acadia, this one is heavily used. It is very important to stay on the trail in order to assure that the surrounding vegetation remains healthy.

Views begin to open up as thick forest gives way to pitch pines and blueberry bushes. The summit is reached 0.6 mile from the parking lot. The view takes in Jordan Pond and the surrounding group of Mount Desert's highest peaks—Cadillac, Pemetic, Penobscot, and Sargent.

To go to South Bubble, head back down the North Bubble Trail toward the parking lot. At the junction with the South Bubble Trail, turn right. The trail is fairly level for 0.1 mile, until a trail junction

the northern hardwood forest

As a result of the 1947 fire, much of the forest on the eastern side of Mount Desert Island is a mosaic of forest types. A few pockets of forest in the park, however, can be labeled as "northern hardwood forest," which is a forest where the predominant trees are American beech, yellow birch, and sugar maple. Before the fire, small stands of northern hardwood forests were interspersed among the dominant boreal forest. The northern hardwood forest is a transition forest that grows in a climate between the boreal forests to the north and the oak-hickory forests to the south. For this reason, you will often find species from these other forest types present in a northern hardwood forest. On the trail up the Bubbles, you may see trees like white and red pines, red spruce, paper birch, eastern hemlock, or northern red oak, but you will soon notice that the forest is dominated by American beech, yellow birch, and sugar maple. Beech trees have smooth, gray bark and pointed, oval leaves. Birch trees also have pointed, oval leaves, but their bark can be white, gray, or brown and is usually rough or peeling off the trunk like paper. Maple trees have a deep, furrowed, brownish-gray bark and leaves with five deep, long-pointed lobes (think of the Canadian flag).

The understory of this forest is populated by striped maple, a favorite food of moose, and hobblebush, with its broad round leaves and showy white flowers. Wildflowers include the pink lady-slipper, painted trillium, and wood sorrel. White-tailed deer, red squirrels, porcupines, and snowshoe hares are common in a northern hardwood forest, as are the yellow-bellied sapsucker, American redstart, black-throated blue warbler, brown creeper, and hermit thrush. It is the red, yellow, and orange foliage of the northern hardwood forest that is responsible for northern New England's spectacular fall foliage displays.

where going straight will bring you down to the northern end of Jordan Pond. Turn left for a moderate 0.2-mile ascent to the summit of South Bubble. Although lower than North Bubble, this summit has better views of Jordan Pond.

Bubble Rock, which lies just to the east of South Bubble's summit, is the most conspicuous example of a glacial erratic on Mount Desert Island. Glacial erratics are rocks carried by glaciers and dropped far from their place of origin. They are easily identifiable by the fact that they are made of a different type of rock than their general surroundings. Bubble Rock is made of a coarse-grained white granite which contrasts markedly with the pink granite of the Bubbles and the other peaks on Mount Desert Island. Bubble Rock most likely came from Lucerne, forty miles to the northwest. Another erratic from Lucerne, Balance Rock, can be seen from the Shore Path in Bar Harbor. Estimated to weigh between eight and twelve tons, Bubble Rock is often described as being about the size of a living room.

To return to the car, retrace your steps down the South Bubble Trail, the North Bubble Trail, and the Bubble-Pemetic Trail.

Directions

From the Acadia National Park Visitor Center, drive south on the Park Loop Road for 6.3 miles. Be sure to continue straight at the intersections marked Sand Beach and Cadillac Mountain. The Bubble Rock parking area will be on your right.

Gorham Mountain and Ocean Trail

NPS Rating: Moderate, then easy

Distance: 3.5 miles round–trip

Elevation Gain: 500 feet

Estimated Time: 2 hours

A moderate hike up to wide–open views of the ocean, followed by a walk along the dramatic coastline between Sand Beach and Otter Cliffs.

THIS HIKE makes the climb up Gorham Mountain from the Park Loop Road at a parking area opposite Monument Cove. A short detour explores the caves on the Cadillac Cliffs Trail before reaching the summit and its views out over the Ocean Drive section of the Park Loop Road. After descending the north ridge of Gorham Mountain, the hike follows an easy footpath along Ocean Drive and passes Thunder Hole. This hike's moderate grades and relatively accessible views make it a good trip for families with young children.

From the parking area, the Gorham Mountain Trail enters a forest of paper birch and red spruce, but quickly reaches a forest of pitch pine spread out among the ledges of pink Cadillac granite. At 0.3 mile, the Cadillac Cliffs Trail goes to the right. If you are not up for some rough footing or a short but steep ascent, continue straight on the Gorham Mountain Trail. Otherwise, turn right and follow the 0.5-mile-long Cadillac Cliffs Trail.

The Cadillac Cliffs Trail meanders around and under modest, fern-covered cliffs and caves which were once at sea level. Huge boulders have broken off the cliffs and created a jumbled trail of tunnels and "lemon squeezers," places where the trail squeezes between large pieces of granite. If you have a big pack, you may need to take it off to get through these narrow passages. In addition to challenging hiking, the cliffs also create a cool and moist microclimate where ferns and mosses grow thick. On a hot summer day, this is a good place to stay cool and study some of Acadia's woodland flora.

After the last big set of boulders, the trail turns left and climbs quickly to rejoin the Gorham Mountain Trail. Turn right to hike over open ledges to the summit of Gorham Mountain in 0.4 mile. While only 525 feet above sea level, Gorham Mountain is less than half a mile from the waters of the Atlantic Ocean. The views of Ocean Drive, Otter Cliffs, and Sand Beach are excellent, as are the views of Champlain, Dorr, and Cadillac Mountains.

To resume this trip, continue north on the Gorham Mountain Trail as it descends gently into a forest of mixed hardwoods. The hardwoods here grew up out of the ashes of the great fire of 1947. It is now difficult to imagine this area as the charred, treeless plain it was fifty years ago, but the fire here burned so hot that the ground was actually sterilized in some places, and it was many years before these trees recolonized the area. As the trail descends, an unofficial and unmaintained trail leaves the Gorham Mountain Trail on the right. Continue straight on the Gorham Mountain Trail and avoid the unmaintained trail, which the Park Service is trying to let fade back into the forest from disuse.

The trail reaches a junction with the Bowl Trail 0.7 mile from the summit. Turn right here and follow the Bowl Trail 0.5 mile to the Park Loop Road. (For a longer trip, combine this hike with the Bowl-Beehive Loop, trip #6.) Cross the Park Loop Road and turn right on a gravel path known as the Ocean Trail.

The Ocean Trail follows the Ocean Drive section of the Park Loop Road for the entire mile from here to the Monument Cove parking area. The Ocean Trail provides the park's best access to Mount Desert Island's famed pink-granite coastline. During this walk, you can scramble over smooth granite ledges and explore the cobble beaches of Newport and Monument Coves, all while watching and listening to the surf making landfall in typical Maine fashion. Herring and great black-back gulls are common and are used to getting handouts from lunching tourists. Of course, feeding wildlife is prohibited in Acadia and is not a good idea anywhere, as it is dangerous to the health of the animals and potentially to people as well. Eider ducks and double-crested cormorants cruise the waters, feed-

Cadillac granite ledges along Acadia's famed Ocean Drive.

ing on fish, crustaceans, and mollusks. Occasionally a bald eagle will fly overhead. Eagles, which feed on fish as well as carrion such as dead deer and seals, nest on several islands in the area.

The biggest attraction along the Ocean Trail is Thunder Hole, a narrow cleft in the granite shoreline. When the waters of the rising tide hit this hole in the rock just right, a giant splash of water hurtles skyward, emitting a thunderous crash and soaking any visitor who happens to be standing in the wrong spot (or the right spot, depending on your point of view). While it is rather tame most of the time, chances are good that Thunder Hole will be booming if you visit near high tide on a windy day. Tides are usually listed in local papers such as the *Bar Harbor Times*, *Acadia Weekly*, and the National Park Service's *Beaver Log*. You can also buy official tide charts at local bookstores.

Just beyond where the Ocean Trail reaches the parking area is Monument Cove. Take a few minutes to hike down to this cove filled with melon-sized cobbles of granite. These fascinating globe- and egg-shaped rocks have been smoothed and shaped over time by constantly rolling and grinding against each other as the waves wash over them. As time goes on, these cobbles will become smaller and small-

leave the snakebite kit at home

An eastern garter snake, *Thamnophis sirtalis sirtalis*, suns itself on a carriage road.

If poisonous snakes put the fear of God into you, you can rest easy, because Mount Desert Island has no resident poisonous snake species. However, there are five species of nonpoisonous snakes that call Acadia National Park home. The snake most often encountered while hiking in Acadia is the familiar garter snake, which likes to sun itself on trails and carriage roads. This two-foot-long snake

er, eventually becoming a pebble beach. For more than 300 years, cobbles from Maine's beaches were harvested and used for ships' ballast, building materials, and cobblestone streets. Cobbles are now understood to be an important part of the environment, however, and should be left on the beach. The Gorham Mountain parking area is directly across the Park Loop Road from Monument Cove.

is easily identified by its three lateral stripes, which vary in color from green to yellow to brown. It most often eats frogs, toads, salamanders, fish, and earthworms but will occasionally eat small mammals and birds.

The other snakes that live in the park are the red-bellied snake, ringneck snake, smooth green snake, and northern milk snake. *Red-bellied snakes* are small, usually less than a foot in length, and have a plain red belly and a brown back. They are common in mountainous areas but also are found near sphagnum bogs. *Ringneck snakes* are usually ten to fifteen inches long and have a yellow belly, a dark back, and a golden ring around their neck. They are secretive and live in forests. *Smooth green snakes* are twelve to twenty inches in length and are plain bright green above with a plain white or pale yellow belly. Gentle snakes, they prefer uplands and feed on spiders and insects. *Northern milk snakes* are the largest of Acadia's snakes. They are gray or brown, with three rows of reddish brown, black-bordered blotches on their back and sides. In some parts of the country, milk snakes can reach six feet in length, but northern milk snakes rarely grow to be more than three feet long. Like ringneck and red-bellied snakes, northern milk snakes feed on small rodents, amphibians, slugs, insects, and worms and fill an important niche as predators in woodland, wetland, and grassland habitats. In turn, snakes are preyed upon by hawks, owls, and herons, and occasionally by coyotes, skunks, raccoons, and even bullfrogs.

Directions

From downtown Bar Harbor, drive south on Maine Route 3 for 2.1 miles and turn right at the Sieur de Monts entrance to the Park Loop Road. Follow the signs for Sand Beach. The Gorham Mountain parking area is on the right, 4.4 miles south of the Sieur de Monts entrance. You will need to pay a fee to enter this part of the park.

The Beehive and the Bowl

NPS Rating: Ladder

Distance: 1.3 miles round–trip

Elevation Gain: 450 feet

Estimated Time: 1 hour

A challenging climb up iron rungs to spectacular views, and a visit to a quiet and beautiful mountain pond.

THE CHALLENGING NATURE of this hike up the Beehive makes this one of the more popular hikes in the park. The fact that it is just across the road from Sand Beach and has good views probably adds a bit to its popularity as well. The Bowl is a beautiful pond nestled between the Beehive and Champlain Mountain and is one of two ponds in the park that are accessible only by foot (Sargent Pond is the other).

CAUTION: This hike is very steep and traverses the cliffs of the Beehive using iron rungs and ladders. This hike is very dangerous in wet weather. People who have a fear of heights should consider climbing the Beehive from the Bowl instead of up the Beehive Trail. It is not a recommended hike for people with small children, and those with older children should consider hiking it without kids first to determine if it is an appropriate hike for the family.

Begin this hike on the Bowl Trail, which is across the Park Loop Road from the Sand Beach parking area. The Beehive Trail is the first trail junction, 0.2 mile from the road. Turn right to follow the Beehive Trail toward the 350-foot cliffs of the Beehive. Like most of the mountains on Mount Desert Island (as well as many of the islands surrounding it), the Beehive has a gradual-sloping north face and steep cliffs on the south face. Glaciers during the last ice age created this landscape feature. The pressure of the ice caused water to fill the

Climbing the iron ladders of the Beehive Trail.

cracks on the south face of the peaks. The rock weakened as the water went through repeated cycles of freezing and thawing. As the glacier moved forward, it sheared off these weakened pieces of granite, creating the cliffs.

Designed and built by Rudolph Brunnow, the man who built the Precipice Trail on Champlain Mountain, the Beehive Trail quickly rises to meet the cliff wall and begins to climb almost straight up. The iron rungs and ladders alternate with stretches of granite ledges. Views of the Atlantic Ocean, Sand Beach, and Champlain Mountain get better and better as you climb, but be sure of your footing before you look back over your shoulder! While strenuous, the climb up the Beehive is relatively short, and most hikers can finish the 0.5-mile hike to the summit in about thirty minutes. The views of the ocean are good, but the view toward the interior of the island is one of the prettiest mountain views in the park. While looking over the Bowl toward Dorr and Cadillac Mountains, you see no sign of man—no Park Loop Road, no carriage roads, no power lines.

To hike down to the Bowl, a small 9.5-acre pond, follow the Beehive Trail northwest, away from the cliffs. A side trail leads left back to the Bowl Trail but bypasses the Bowl. Continue straight on the Beehive Trail to reach the Bowl, a good example of a glacial tarn, which is a deep, typically circular lake that forms when an alpine glacier melts. The Bowl is a quiet place with a unique view of Champlain Mountain. To finish the hike, follow the trail to the left, along the southern end of the pond. In the middle of a set of wooden puncheons built to protect the boggy shoreline, the Bowl Trail comes in from the left. Turn left on the Bowl Trail and follow it 0.6 mile back to the Park Loop Road.

Directions

From downtown Bar Harbor, drive south on Maine Route 3 for 2.1 miles and turn right at the Sieur de Monts entrance to the Park Loop Road. Follow the signs for Sand Beach. The Sand Beach parking area is on the left, 3.25 miles south of the Sieur de Monts entrance. The Bowl Trail is across the road from the parking area. You will need to pay a fee to enter this part of the park.

Beech Mountain

> NPS Rating: **Moderate**
>
> Distance: **2.0 miles round-trip**
>
> Elevation Gain: **700 feet**
>
> Estimated Time: **1.5 hours**
>
> **An enjoyable hike over rocky ledges to the summit of Beech Mountain and excellent views.**

THIS HIKE BEGINS at the southern end of Long Pond and makes its way up 700 feet of granite ledges to the fire tower atop Beech Mountain. Due to its relatively easy access and its good views, this is perhaps the most popular summit on the western side of Mount Desert Island. A longer walk down the open south ridge of Beech Mountain makes for a less steep return trip filled with good views.

From the parking area, follow the Beech Mountain West Ridge Trail along the eastern shore of Long Pond. The trail stays near the shore of the pond for 0.3 mile and passes two private residences along the way. Please respect these residents' privacy. After passing the second house, the trail turns right and begins climbing the relatively steep west ridge of Beech Mountain. The trail quickly reaches open granite ledges populated by white pines and scrub oak. Views begin to open up across Long Pond to Mansell Mountain.

The trail reaches the Beech Mountain Loop Trail 0.9 mile from the parking area. Turn right on this trail for a 0.1-mile hike to the summit. The summit of Beech Mountain is only 849 feet above sea level, but, like most peaks on Mount Desert Island, it is treeless, making for excellent views in all directions. The fire tower is not currently manned, as small planes are now used to patrol for fires. While you can't currently climb the tower, the summit still has excellent views of Somes Sound, Cadillac Mountain, Sutton and Greening

Islands, the Cranberry Islands, Isle au Haut, and all of the western mountains.

To return to your car, look for a trail that heads south. This is the Beech Mountain South Ridge Trail. This trail descends moderately through a forest of spruce that opens up regularly to provide more good views to the south past Southwest Harbor and out to the Atlantic Ocean. The views finally end as the trail enters a thick forest of tall spruce. The trail descends steeply here, using switchbacks and stone steps to ease the hiking. You will reach a trail junction 0.6 mile from the summit, marking the end of the Beech Mountain South Ridge Trail. Turn right on the Valley Trail for a 0.4-mile forested walk back to the parking area at Long Pond.

Directions

From the center of Southwest Harbor, go west on Seal Cove Road. Take the first paved road on the right, Long Pond Road. Follow Long Pond Road through a residential area until it ends at the south end of Long Pond. There is a small parking area to the right of the water-pumping station.

Trip #8

Huguenot Head and Champlain Mountain

NPS Rating: Moderate, with one short, strenuous section

Distance: **3.3 miles**

Elevation Gain: **1,100 feet**

Estimated Time: **2.5 hours**

A classic Acadia hike up steep pink granite to spectacular mountain and ocean views.

CHAMPLAIN MOUNTAIN is a popular wildlife-viewing spot due to its pair of nesting peregrine falcons. This is also one of the best places to view Frenchman Bay while visiting Mount Desert Island. The Beachcroft Trail makes a moderate ascent from the west and offers distinctive views of the Tarn and Dorr Mountain from Huguenot Head. This trail is a good alternative to the east face's Precipice Trail, a steep climb up iron rungs. The Precipice Trail is usually closed for much of the summer so that hikers do not disturb the nesting falcons. By combining the Beachcroft Trail with the Bear Brook Trail and the Park Loop Road, it is possible to have a varied hike above treeline, watch for eagles and falcons, and visit an active beaver pond.

This hike starts on the east side of Route 3, across the road from the north end of the Tarn, a glacial pond nestled below the cliffs of Dorr Mountain. Look for a set of granite stairs and a wooden sign marking the Beachcroft Trail. George Dorr had the Beachcroft Trail built in 1915, using stones from the base of the mountain as the material for the 1,482 steps that ease the climb. The first few hundred yards of the trail follow a sidewalk-like stretch of skillfully laid granite through a deciduous forest. The trail then rises quickly above the trees on switchbacks built into the steep face of Huguenot Head. At 0.4 mile, the trail reaches the southwestern shoulder of Huguenot Head, passing within 150 yards of the summit. This open granite ledge provides views of Dorr Mountain, the Tarn, and the Atlantic Ocean.

The trail drops back below the trees for 0.1 mile before beginning the climb to the summit of Champlain Mountain. The next section of the hike is the most difficult. A short, steep climb over rocks and through the trees brings you to a prime example of a pitch pine forest. Due to its open nature, a pitch pine forest looks like few others in New England. The widely spaced trees grow on exposed granite ledges, accompanied only occasionally by prostrate shrubs like lowbush blueberry and mountain cranberry. The trees themselves seldom grow to more than twenty feet in height and are gnarled and twisted by constant exposure to high winds. The open aspect of the forest makes it possible to see the summit of Cadillac Mountain, now visible directly behind Dorr Mountain.

The climb through the pines to the summit of Champlain is over smooth but steep granite. This part of the hike can be very slip-

Fragrant waterlilies fill a beaver pond below Champlain Mountain and Huguenot Head.

pery when wet, so exercise caution in rainy and foggy conditions. The Beachcroft Trail ends at the summit, 0.8 mile from Route 3. Champlain's open, rocky peak is a good place to watch for wildlife and follow the boat traffic in Frenchman Bay. During the summer, the peregrine falcons are often conspicuous, with the chicks loudly announcing the return of either parent to the nest. In addition to the falcons, bald eagles and other raptors frequent the thermals around Champlain Mountain. With a good pair of binoculars, it is also possible to spot harbor porpoises, harbor seals, and minke whales plying the waters of Frenchman Bay. The views of the bay are breathtaking, as you sit 1,058 feet above sea level while less than a mile from the water. From here, you can see the Porcupine Islands and Bar Harbor to the north, Egg Rock and the Schoodic Peninsula to the northeast, the Cranberry Islands to the south, and the other mountains of Mount Desert Island to the west.

To begin your descent, look for the Bear Brook Trail at the summit cairn. Follow the trail north, toward Bar Harbor and the Porcupine Islands. This trail has good views to the east and north as it descends moderately over smooth granite ledge. It stays on open ledge for most of its mile-long traverse of Champlain Mountain's north ridge and enters the forest shortly before ending at the Park Loop Road.

Turn left and follow the Park Loop Road. You will soon come to an active beaver pond with views of both Huguenot Head and Champlain Mountain. The beaver are most active at night, but you can often see them from the road at dawn and dusk. This is also a good spot to look for warblers, phoebes, and flycatchers and to photograph the abundant waterlilies.

At 0.75 mile from the Bear Brook Trail, turn left toward Sieur de Monts Spring. Turn left again in about 200 yards. In 300 more yards, turn right on Route 3 for a short walk to the parking area.

Directions

This hike begins at the Tarn parking area, 2.2 miles south of Bar Harbor on Maine Route 3. Across Route 3 from the parking area look for a granite staircase marking the beginning of the Beachcroft Trail.

impressive speed: the peregrine falcon

The peregrine falcon is about the size of a crow, but it has the speed of a Corvette. A peregrine regularly attains speeds in excess of 100 miles per hour while diving to catch and kill its prey in flight. Even in regular flight, this awesome predator reaches speeds of 60 miles per hour. While flying, a peregrine looks like a typical falcon, with long, pointed wings and a long tail. The bird has a white or buff-colored breast, a slate-gray back, a small head made distinctive by long gray "sideburns," and yellow legs. It feeds on other birds ranging in size from small songbirds to large ducks.

By the mid-1960s, the falcon was considered extinct in the eastern United States. Hunting caused much of its downfall, but the ingestion of chemical pesticides accelerated its extinction by making it nearly impossible to reproduce successfully. The peregrine was declared an endangered species in 1973. Acadia National Park began participating in a peregrine-reintroduction program in 1984. The park released twenty-two hand-raised chicks into the park between 1984 and 1986. In 1987 adult peregrines began returning to the park, and in 1991 peregrines successfully fledged chicks in Acadia for the first time since 1956.

The program has been such a success that, depending on the year, two or three pairs of peregrines now nest in the park, where they seek out small ledges on high cliffs. The nest sites are consistently on Champlain Mountain, Jordan Cliffs on Penobscot Mountain, and on Beech Mountain. The park usually closes any hiking trails in nest areas if the nests are active.

The best opportunity to observe peregrines is on Champlain Mountain during the spring and summer. From the parking area for the Precipice Trail, it is possible to view the birds on the cliffs above with a spotting scope or a good pair of binoculars. (The Precipice Trail is closed while the birds are nesting.) The National Park Service often stations a volunteer in the parking area to answer questions and to help visitors locate the birds. It is also possible to see the birds soaring above the cliffs from the summit of Champlain Mountain, which can be climbed via the Beachcroft or Bear Brook Trail during nesting season.

To help protect and promote conservation of the peregrine falcon, Acadia National Park asks interested visitors to do the following:

- Learn the characteristic field marks and behaviors of peregrines so you can make a positive identification when you see one in the park.

- Report any peregrine sightings to a park information station.

- Keep away from areas where peregrines are nesting. Avoid observing the birds from a location higher than the nest. Adult peregrines generally won't tolerate people above them and may dive at intruders, particularly if they are defending a nest or chicks.

Pemetic Mountain and Bubble Pond

NPS Rating: Strenuous to start, then moderate and easy

Distance: 4.1 miles round-trip

Elevation Gain: 950 feet

Estimated Time: 2.5 hours

A strenuous hike to some of Mount Desert Island's most spectacular views.

AT 1,234 FEET, Pemetic Mountain is the fourth highest on Mount Desert Island and affords some excellent views of Cadillac Mountain, Jordan Pond, and the Atlantic Ocean. Beginning and ending at Bubble Pond, a picturesque glacial pool nestled between Pemetic and Cadillac Mountains, this hike climbs the northeast face of Pemetic via the Pemetic Mountain Trail. The long hike above treeline on the south ridge of Pemetic is nicely complemented by an easy walk along the carriage road on the western shore of Bubble Pond.

The Pemetic Mountain Trail starts at the south end of the Bubble Pond parking area. After crossing the carriage road, follow the Pemetic Mountain Trail to the right. The trail to the left is the Cadillac West Face Trail. The signs in the area near the pond can be confusing, as the Pemetic Mountain Trail is sometimes marked as the Pemetic Northeast Face Trail. Be assured that any trail marked Pemetic in this area is the Pemetic Mountain Trail. The trail quickly crosses back over the carriage road before starting its climb to the summit.

The trail climbs moderately through a forest of mixed hardwoods and conifers before it becomes a steep climb through a forest of pure hemlock. Due to the thick hemlock canopy, the forest floor

From this aerial view, Pemetic Mountain is bordered by Eagle Lake, Jordan Pond, and Bubble Pond.

here is devoid of undergrowth except for spruce saplings and the occasional striped maple. The climb stays steep and the footing gets rougher as the elevation increases.

The trail crosses a few open ledges with views of Cadillac Mountain. Lowbush blueberry and sheep laurel are common through here. After going in and out of the trees several times, the trail leaves the forest for good at its junction with the Bubble-Pemetic Trail, 1.1 miles from the trailhead. The Bubble-Pemetic Trail is to the right and leads to the Bubble Rock parking area. Follow the Pemetic Mountain Trail, which turns left, climbs over open ledge, and reaches the summit of Pemetic Mountain in another 0.1 mile.

From the summit of Pemetic, which is the Abenaki Indian word for "gently sloping land," there are views in all directions. To the northeast are Bubble Pond and Cadillac Mountain. To the south are the Atlantic Ocean and the Cranberry Islands. Jordan Pond is directly below the mountain to the west, and the summits of Penobscot and Sargent Mountains rise up directly behind the pond. Eagle Lake is to the north.

walking the
carriage roads

All signs on the carriage roads are made of wood, with yellow-painted lettering.

Acadia's system of carriage roads have perhaps the best road surface of any crushed-gravel road in the world. They were built by John Rockefeller Jr. in the 1920s and 1930s in order to give walkers and horse-drawn carriages a means to explore the backcountry of Acadia without resorting to the noise and pollution of cars. They were designed to follow the contours of the landscape in such a way that they blend into the mountainsides. They comprise several different layers of stones topped with an eight-inch crown of crushed gravel. This creates an extremely well drained surface and makes them ideal for biking and horseback riding. Hikers looking to explore the backcountry of the park via easy grades and good footing will find the carriage roads an excellent alternative to the steeper and rougher hiking trails. All of the carriage roads are open to hikers, and any of the trips in the "Biking in Acadia" chapter would also make worthwhile hikes. In fact, by combining the carriage roads with hiking trails, you can make some interesting loop hikes instead of the usual out-and-back hiking trip.

Of course, while walking on the carriage roads you need to be aware that bikes and horses will be sharing the road with you. It is important to note that hikers and bikers are required always to yield the right of way to horses. While near horses, try to remain still and quiet. Bike riders should yield to walkers and not ride too fast. By following these simple rules, everyone can enjoy the carriage roads safely. Also note that one reason the carriage roads are in such good shape is that they are closed during the wet spring season, even to hikers. Usually there are signs to indicate that the roads are closed, but in early spring or during wet weather you should check road status at the visitor center.

Continue south on the Pemetic Mountain Trail, which is marked by cairns and blue blazes on the bare rock. The south ridge of Pemetic is gently sloping exposed granite, making for an extended walk with views in all directions. The views end at 1.9 miles, where the West Cliff Trail comes in from the right. Follow the Pemetic Mountain Trail left into the trees. The trail makes a short, steep descent before becoming a moderate footpath through a northern hardwood forest.

At 2.2 miles, the trail intersects the Pond Trail. Turn left onto the Pond Trail, which makes an easy descent of 0.3 mile to a carriage road. Follow the carriage road left for 1.6 miles back to the Bubble Pond parking area. Along the way, the carriage road follows the western shore of Bubble Pond. Views across the pond are of the steep west slope of Cadillac Mountain, which includes a large boulder field that rises from the southeast corner of the pond. While on the carriage road, remember that you are now sharing the trail with horses and bikes.

Directions

From the Acadia National Park Visitor Center, drive south on the Park Loop Road for 5.2 miles. Be sure to continue straight at the intersections marked Sand Beach and Cadillac Mountain. The Bubble Pond parking area will be on your left.

Acadia and Saint Sauveur Mountains

NPS Rating: Strenuous

Distance: 3.7 miles round-trip

Elevation Gain: 1,050 feet

Estimated Time: 3 hours

A strenuous hike to the best views of Somes Sound, the only fiord on the East Coast of the United States.

ACADIA and Saint Sauveur Mountains form the western wall of Somes Sound, providing a symmetrical counterpart to Norumbega Mountain on the east side of the sound. Although these peaks are both under 700 feet in height, this is a strenuous hike that starts at around 150 feet and drops back down almost to sea level between Acadia and Saint Sauveur. Both the summit of Acadia Mountain and the ledges of Eagle Cliff offer excellent views of the sound.

The Acadia Mountain Trail begins with a set of stone steps directly across the road from the parking area. At 0.1 mile, the Saint Sauveur Trail leads to the right. You will be returning via this trail in a few hours. At this point, turn left to continue on the Acadia Mountain Trail, which meanders through a forest of pine and spruce with an understory of blueberries and sheep laurel. At 0.2 mile, the trail crosses a dirt fire road and then begins climbing steeply over granite ledges and stone stairs.

The trail quickly reaches its first reward, an area of open ledges with views to the south and west of Echo Lake, Beech Mountain, and Saint Sauveur Mountain. At 0.8 mile from the parking area, the trail reaches Acadia Mountain's summit, a beautiful flat area of pitch pine, blueberry, and prostrate juniper. The trail continues east over granite,

Blueberry bushes and pitch pines line the Acadia Mountain Trail.

in and out of pine, to a point where the mountain drops almost straight down to Somes Sound. From here, you get excellent views of the eastern mountains and the whole of Somes Sound, its deep waters bordered by steep mountains, making it the only fiord on the East Coast of the United States. The sound was carved by the Wisconsin Glacier between 15,000 and 25,000 years ago. The water in the sound reaches depths of almost 200 feet.

To continue on this hike, follow the Acadia Mountain Trail to the right as it descends very quickly through beautiful pitch pine forest. At 1.5 miles, the trail levels out at Man o' War Brook. A side trail leads left to where the brook cascades over rock directly into Somes Sound. During the seventeenth and early eighteenth centuries, when Down East Maine was hotly contested territory between the French and British, Mount Desert Island was a dangerous place to visit for ships of either side. According to legend, this made Somes Sound a haven for pirate ships, which would sail up next to the cascade at Man o' War Brook to fill up with fresh water.

Soon after the brook is a trail junction. Take the right fork, heading toward the Man o' War Brook Fire Road and Saint Sauveur Mountain. In another 100 yards, the fire road leaves the trail to the right and the Flying Mountain Trail leads left to Valley Cove. Continue straight on what is now called the Valley Peak Trail. From here, the trail climbs steeply through a mixed conifer forest of white pine, red pine, cedar, spruce, and fir before reaching the open ledges of Eagle Cliff. Eagle Cliff rises 500 feet straight up from Valley Cove, a very protected part of the sound where boats often drop anchor to wait out bad storms. From here, you get a good view of Flying Mountain and the estates of Northeast Harbor across Somes Sound.

At a trail junction on the cliff, turn right to head toward the summit of Saint Sauveur. In another 0.1 mile, you will reach a second trail junction. Turn right again for a fifty-yard walk to the wooded summit of Saint Sauveur, which was known as Dog Mountain before becoming part of the national park. The forest here is a fairly thick stand of pitch pine, while blueberry bushes fill in the understory and turn a spectacular fire-engine red in late fall.

From the summit it is 1.3 miles back to the parking area on Route 102. The rest of the hike is a moderate descent of the north ridge of Saint Sauveur. Just 0.3 mile below the summit, the Ledge Trail enters from the left. Continue straight here and at the next trail junction as the trail makes it way through a rocky forest of pine, cedar, and

the lowly juniper

Common juniper (*Juniperus communis*) is the most widely distributed coniferous tree in the world and can grow to be more than twenty feet tall. Common juniper can be found from central Arizona north to Alaska and east across North America and northern Eurasia. On the wind-beaten rocky outcroppings of Acadia's coast and mountaintops, it rarely grows more than two feet tall, but it is conspicuous because of its sharp-pointed, scaly leaves and its whitish blue berries.

Creeping juniper (*Juniperus horizontalis*), another variety, has been given the nickname "Bar Harbor juniper" by gardeners who have made it one of the most cultivated native shrubs of New England. If you have a low-lying juniper in your front yard or garden, it is probably creeping juniper. Common on Mount Desert Island, creeping juniper is difficult to distinguish from common juniper, but it generally has a soft blue foliage as opposed to common juniper's brighter green. It rarely grows to be more than one foot tall but will spread out up to ten feet in all directions.

The berries of both plants are actually cones. Their sweet aroma will be familiar to martini drinkers, as juniper berries are a main ingredient of gin. Wildlife enjoy the berries as well, especially grouse and white-tailed deer.

spruce. As the trail flattens out, it reaches a junction with the Acadia Mountain Trail. From here, the parking area is 0.1 mile to the left.

Directions

The parking area for the Acadia Mountain Trail is on the west side of Maine Route 102, 3.3 miles from the intersection of Routes 102 and 198 in Somesville.

Trip #11

Penobscot and Sargent Mountains

> **NPS Rating: Strenuous**
> **Distance: 5.2 miles round-trip**
> **Elevation Gain: 1,300 feet**
> **Estimated Time: 3.5 hours**
>
> **A strenuous hike to two of Acadia's highest peaks, with long periods of hiking on open ledges with spectacular views.**

THE CLIFFS of Penobscot Mountain rise steeply from the western shore of Jordan Pond and provide habitat for one of Acadia's nesting pairs of peregrine falcons. This hike provides an alternative to the Jordan Cliffs Trail, which is often closed due to the nesting falcons. Sargent Mountain is the second highest peak on Mount Desert Island, and its flat, wide-open subalpine summit provides some of the island's best views of Somes Sound, the Cranberry Islands, and the western mountains.

This hike starts on the Penobscot Mountain Trail, which is located behind and to the left of the Jordan Pond House. The trail crosses a carriage road in about fifty yards. Cross the stream on the other side of the carriage road where there is a trail junction. The trail to the left is the Asticou Trail. This hike continues straight on the Penobscot Mountain Trail, which you will follow for 1.6 miles to the summit of Penobscot Mountain.

The trail rises and falls gently through the mixed hardwood and conifer forest to the west of Jordan Pond. After crossing another brook, the trail begins a steep ascent up a well-built set of rock steps. These steps are a good example of how proper trail maintenance can prevent severe erosion on a trail that receives a lot of use. Just before crossing another carriage road, the Penobscot Mountain Trail turns left at its junction with the Jordan Cliffs Trail. After crossing the car-

Hiking the subalpine plateau on Sargent Mountain, Acadia's second highest Peak.

riage road, the trail makes a very steep ascent up the cliffs of Penobscot Mountain. There are a few iron rungs on this section of the hike as the trail squeezes through narrow cracks in the granite cliff face.

The steep climb ends at about 0.5 mile from the Jordan Pond House. Here the trail emerges from the trees and turns sharply right in order to make a moderate ascent of the south ridge of Penobscot Mountain. The walk up the south ridge is over open granite ledges with good views of most of the mountains in the park and of the Atlantic Ocean. The environment is subalpine with prostrate trees and plants from the heath family like sheep laurel and rhodora. Low-bush blueberries are very common along this trail.

Looking north from the summit you will see Sargent Pond and the summit of Sargent Mountain, second only to Cadillac Mountain in height. Cadillac Mountain is to the east, beyond Pemetic Mountain. The summit is a good place to watch for ravens and hawks riding the thermals of air warmed by the sun-baked granite peaks. You should be able to spot the peregrines if they are nesting on Jordan Cliffs. The small but swift-flying sharp-shinned hawk can also be seen here. Hawk watching in Acadia is particularly good in the fall on a sunny day that follows several days of storms. After hunkering down in the wet weather, the hawks are eager to find thermals and ride the winds out of the northeast.

To continue the hike, take the Sargent Pond Trail, which heads north from the summit cairn and descends quickly to the col between Penobscot and Sargent Mountains. At this col, the Deer Brook Trail enters from the right. Continue to the left on the Sargent Pond Trail, which soon reaches Sargent Pond. Sargent Pond is fairly typical of ponds in the boreal forests of Maine—a bowl of water surrounded by spruce forests with blueberry bushes and rhodora clinging to its banks. From the pond, the trail rises moderately to a junction with the Sargent Mountain South Ridge Trail.

Turn right on the Sargent Mountain South Ridge Trail. From here, the trail ascends very gradually for 0.8 mile to the summit of Sargent Mountain. This part of the hike is reminiscent of the Tableland plateau on Maine's Katahdin, although at a much lower elevation. The summit of Sargent is surrounded by an extensive area of relatively flat, open terrain filled with sedges, wildflowers, and stunted versions of spruce, cedar, and birch. On the way to the summit, two more trails come in from the left. Continue straight at these junctions to keep on track for the summit cairn. The views from the summit are excellent.

To return to the Jordan Pond House, walk back down the Sargent Mountain South Ridge Trail to the Sargent Pond Trail and turn left. After passing by Sargent Pond again, the trail rises to meet the Deer Brook Trail. Turn left on the Deer Brook Trail, which goes down toward Jordan Pond. This trail descends steadily and has very rough footing over wet rocks and tree roots. The trail follows a stream, which overflows onto the trail after heavy rains.

After 0.5 mile, the trail reaches a carriage road. Turn right on the carriage road for an easy 1.5-mile walk back to the Jordan Pond House. Shortly after leaving the Deer Brook Trail, the carriage road passes through a boulder field below Jordan Cliffs. There are good views of the pond and the Bubbles from here. The rest of the walk is through northern hardwood forest. At the only intersection, stay to the left.

Directions

From the Acadia National Park Visitor Center, drive south on the Park Loop Road for 7.3 miles. Be sure to continue straight at the intersections marked Sand Beach and Cadillac Mountain. The Jordan Pond parking area will be on your right.

cairns

Cairns, like this one on the West Ledge Trail, are important markers that direct hikers in inclement weather. Building your own cairns can confuse other hikers and disrupt the fragile environment, so please leave the cairn building to park trail crews.

Cairns are conical-shaped piles of rocks used to mark hiking trails above treeline. With Acadia's open summits, cairns are numerous and play an important role in keeping hiking traffic confined to the intended trails. This in turn helps to prevent erosion of what little soil exists above treeline and to prevent the destruction of important plants and animals that need the rocks for shelter. Cairns are also an important safety feature on trails, as they help keep hikers from getting lost, particularly in bad weather.

The cairns in Acadia seem to take on a life of their own, as they tend to grow over time—and even reproduce!

Many park visitors find it irresistible to add a rock to a cairn or build their own. This is a problem for two reasons: First, trail maintainers build cairns to direct hiking traffic along specific routes. Adding a cairn can work against this route building, increase trail erosion, and get hikers lost. Second, moving rocks above treeline disturbs delicate microhabitats that exist because of the soil and moisture that collect around the rocks. The flora and fauna that survive in these microhabitats usually perish when the rocks are removed.

Park naturalists ask that as you visit Acadia, admire the construction of cairns, but please leave them as you find them.

The Western Mountains: Mansell and Bernard

NPS Rating: Strenuous, with ladders on the Perpendicular Trail

Distance: 4.2 miles round-trip

Elevation Gain: 1,350 feet

Estimated Time: 3.5 hours

A strenuous hike to the highest peaks on the western side of Mount Desert Island.

THIS IS A HARD HIKE with few views. It is a great chance, however, to enjoy an uncrowded hike through a mature spruce forest that was untouched by the fire of 1947. This hike starts at the southern end of Long Pond and climbs Mansell Mountain via the Perpendicular Trail, which features an amazing stretch of stone staircases. Unlike the rest of the higher peaks on Mount Desert, the summits of both Mansell (949 feet) and Bernard Mountain (1,071 feet) are wooded and have no views.

From the parking area at the southern end of Long Pond, follow the western shore of Long Pond on the Long Pond Trail, which starts behind the pumping station. After 0.2 mile, turn left on the Perpendicular Trail. This trail rises quickly, angling over a boulder field on the east face of Mansell. The 704 stone steps built by the Civilian Conservation Corps in 1933 and 1934 give the trail a spiral-staircase look. The craftsmanship of this stretch of trail is excellent and rivals that of the Ladder Trail on Dorr Mountain. From the boulder field, views open up of Long Pond, Southwest Harbor, and the Cranberry Islands.

The trail levels off for a while as it works its way through a mixed forest dominated by spruce and cedar. The trail resumes its steep climb and shortly before the summit of Mansell reaches an overlook with perhaps the best views of the hike. A sign marks the short path on the right that will take you to a granite ledge high above Long Pond. From here, there are good views of Beech Mountain; Cadillac Mountain; the towns of Southwest Harbor, Bass Harbor, and Bernard; the Cranberry Islands and the Atlantic Ocean.

From here, the wooded summit of Mansell is reached after 0.1 mile of gradual climbing. The trail goes west, through a spruce forest that tops the west ridge of Mansell. At junctions with the Mansell Mountain Trail and the Razorback Trail, continue hiking straight. The trail crosses a granite ledge that affords views across Great Notch to Bernard Mountain, as well as views west and north of Blue Hill Bay, Pretty Marsh, and Bartlett Island. After the Razorback Trail, the trail descends steeply for 0.3 mile into Great Notch, a narrow passage between the summits of Bernard and Mansell. From here, the Great Notch Trail leaves to the left and descends quickly to the Cold Brook Trail and eventually the south end of Long Pond. The Long Pond Trail leaves to the right and makes a gradual and lengthy descent to the western shore of Long Pond.

This view of Bass Harbor Marsh and Western Mountain can be seen from near the beginning of the Hio Fire Road.

a forest and a
wetland in one?

wetlands and forests have both received considerable attention in recent years as vital habitats for sustaining the health of our planet, increasing species diversity, and providing a natural filtering system for drinking-water supplies. The forested wetland is a combination habitat often overlooked by scientists and amateur naturalists alike. Forested wetlands are usually small areas of forest, an acre or two in size, that have standing water for only part of the year. In Acadia National Park, trees such as the northern white cedar grow in these wetlands, and the ground is often covered with sphagnum moss.

While it can look like the rest of the forest on the surface, a forested wetland is a bonanza of biodiversity which provides habitat for a disproportionate number of threatened and endangered plants and animals. They are a good place to look for unusual wildflowers like orchids in the spring and summer, and they are the most likely place in Acadia to find uncommon amphibians such as the four-toed salamander. Common plants include skunk cabbage, starflower, and partridgeberry. Common birds in a forested wetland include cedar waxwings, hermit thrushes, and northern saw-whet owls. Like other wetlands, forested wetlands are also important for regulating water flow in a forest and helping to recharge ground-water supplies.

Forested wetlands can be found throughout the park, especially on the western side of Mount Desert Island. They are common along the Long Pond, Western Mountain, and Hio Fire Roads.

To continue this hike, go straight (west) and begin the steep climb to the summit of Bernard, which is 0.6 mile from Great Notch. After the steepest part of the climb, an overlook on the left has limited views to the east and south of Mansell Mountain, Southwest Harbor, and the Atlantic Ocean. Shortly after this overlook, the trail crosses the wooded Knight's Nubble before descending 0.1 mile to Little Notch and a junction with the Sluiceway Trail. Continue straight on what is now called the Bernard Mountain South Face Trail and make a short but steep climb to the Bernard Overlook, which has limited views north and west to Bartlett Island and over Blue Hill Bay to Blue Hill.

Like Mansell, the summit of Bernard Mountain is a viewless spruce forest, thick and mossy but also quiet and secluded. The Bernard Mountain South Face Trail makes a gradual descent through this forest, which is one of the highest spruce forests on the coast of Maine. From the summit to the Western Mountain Fire Road, it is 1.7 miles. At the only trail junction (with the West Ledge Trail), turn left to stay on the Bernard Mountain South Face Trail. As the trail descends, the forest becomes increasingly diverse as hardwoods and pines fill the spaces not occupied by spruce. At times the trail is steep, but the footing is good. After crossing a stream, the trail ends at a parking area on Western Mountain Road.

Hike up the road for a short distance to where another road leads to the left. Take this left, and you will soon find yourself in a cul-de-sac. On the right side of this cul-de-sac look for a sign marking the Cold Brook Trail, which leads east toward the southern end of Long Pond. This trail is a relatively flat trail through mixed forest. Continue straight at intersections with the Razorback and Mansell Mountain Trails. The Cold Brook Trail ends at the Long Pond Trail on the southern shore of Long Pond, completing the loop you started several hours ago. From here, the parking area is 0.1 mile to the right.

Directions

From the center of Southwest Harbor, go west on Seal Cove Road. Take the first paved road on the right, Long Pond Road. Follow Long Pond Road through a residential area until it ends at the south end of Long Pond. There is a small parking area to the right of the pumping station.

Peak–Baggers' Delight:
Bald Peak, Parkman Mountain, Gilmore Mountain, and Sargent Mountain

NPS Rating: **Strenuous**

Distance: **4.0 miles round–trip**

Elevation Gain: **1,500 feet total**

Estimated Time: **3.5 hours**

A difficult hike over four peaks, including Sargent Mountain, Acadia's second highest point.

WITH THE POTENTIAL to summit four peaks in less than four hours, this hike can be tiring but enjoyable. Starting on Maine Route 198 north of Northeast Harbor, this hike loops up and over Bald Peak and Parkman, Gilmore, and Sargent Mountains. Sargent, at 1,373 feet, is the second highest peak on the island and has one of the more interesting summits, with a large plateau-like area full of subalpine vegetation like mountain sandwort, mountain cranberry, and alpine club moss. While lower than Sargent, the other three peaks on this hike all have open summits with good views. The return trip from the summits follows the cool waters of Maple Spring as it courses down the southeast flank of Sargent Mountain through a forest with large trees and a small gorge.

Begin this hike on the Hadlock Brook Trail, which starts on the eastern side of Route 198, directly across the road from the Norumbega Mountain parking lot. Hike past the junction with the Parkman Mountain Trail and then turn left onto the Bald Peak Trail 0.3 mile from the road. The Bald Peak Trail crosses a carriage road and ascends moderately through a forest of cedar and spruce. After crossing a second carriage road, the trail climbs more steeply, breaking out of the trees and quickly providing views of Norumbega Mountain, Upper Hadlock Pond, and the islands at the mouth of Somes Sound.

More steep hiking brings you to the summit of Bald Peak, 0.8 mile from the parking area. The great views here are similar to those you will have on Parkman and Gilmore Mountains. The other peaks on this hike are visible to the north and east, while Penobscot and Cedar Swamp Mountains are to the east and south. The views do not end with the surrounding peaks, however, as on a clear day you can see beyond Mount Desert Island and its environs to Isle au Haut, Blue Hill, and the Camden Hills to the west.

After enjoying the views, Parkman Mountain is next. Follow the trail northwest and down into the col between Bald Peak and Parkman Mountain. The descent is steep but only 0.1 mile long. At 0.2 mile from Bald Peak, turn right on the Parkman Mountain Trail for the short hike to the summit of Parkman. From here, follow the trail east toward Sargent Mountain. The trail descends moderately, then steeply, through a forest of spruce and birch, and comes to the low point between Parkman and Gilmore in 0.3 mile. Here the trail crosses the Giant Slide Trail before making a short but steep climb to the summit of Gilmore Mountain.

You can soak up more of the same great views on Gilmore before continuing toward Sargent Mountain. Follow the Grandgent Trail, which heads north from the summit for a short distance before turning east and descending moderately into a mixed forest of spruce, cedar, birch, and maple. You soon come to the col between Gilmore and Sargent. After crossing a brook, the Grandgent Trail is not well marked but continues to the left, following the brook. Unofficial and unmaintained trails go straight and to the right here, making it a somewhat confusing area. As long as you follow the brook to the left, the trail's blue blazes will become obvious and you will get to Sargent Mountain.

The climb up Sargent on the Grandgent Trail is steep and the footing is rough in places, but the forest here is interesting with its mixture of spruce, fir, cedar, and hardwoods. The entire hike from Gilmore to Sargent feels wilder than other areas on Mount Desert Island, because it is a relatively difficult place to reach by Acadia

the subalpine zone

New Hampshire's White Mountains and Maine's Katahdin are well known for their alpine zones of rare flora and fauna. While Acadia's mountains are not high enough to harbor a true alpine zone, many summits have a distinct subalpine zone that shares characteristics with the higher mountains of New England. Trees are stunted and look more like shrubs. Common in more-northerly climates, herbaceous plants like mountain sandwort and mountain cranberry share the few pockets of soil with low-lying heathers, grasses, and sedges.

This subalpine zone occurs at much lower elevations than the alpine zones of Katahdin or Mount Washington due to Acadia's exposed location on the Atlantic Ocean. On some peaks, it is as low as 500 feet above sea level. A constant barrage of ocean winds and winter storms makes it difficult for trees and other plants to grow as they would in a more sheltered environment. While you will find red spruce, northern white cedar, paper and yellow birch, and balsam fir in Mount Desert Island's subalpine habitats, they will rarely grow to be more than a few feet high. Lowbush blueberries and mountain cranberry are common and provide important sustenance for migrating birds in the fall. This is also the only habitat in the park where you can find alpine club moss, mountain sandwort, or alpine blueberry.

Enjoy hiking through this rare environment, and help protect it by staying only on marked trails.

National Park standards. As the Grandgent Trail emerges from the trees, more views of Somes Sound and beyond appear. The summit of Sargent Mountain is attained 0.7 mile from Gilmore Mountain.

The summit of Sargent is surrounded by an extensive area of relatively flat terrain filled with sedges, wildflowers, and stunted versions of spruce, cedar, and birch. The views from the summit are excellent. Over the Bubbles and Jordan Pond is Cadillac Mountain to the east. Somes Sound and the western mountains are to the west. Somes Sound, with mountains on both sides and a V-shaped bottom that is 200 feet deep, is the only fiord on the entire East Coast of the United States. On clear days you can see as far as Isle au Haut, twenty miles to the southwest, and the Camden Hills.

For the return trip, turn right (south) on the Sargent Mountain South Ridge Trail. It is an almost flat walk above treeline for 0.3 mile to a trail junction, where you should turn right onto the Maple Spring Trail. The Maple Spring Trail descends moderately over open granite ledges for the first 0.3 mile before entering the forest for the rest of the hike. Rocks and tree roots make the footing on this trail rough for most of its length, creating a longer hike than you would expect. The trail is one of the few in the park that follow a stream, often crossing it during the descent. At 1.2 miles below the summit of Sargent, the trail passes the Giant Slide Trail. Continue straight on the Maple Spring Trail as it enters a small but beautiful gorge before crossing under an attractive stone bridge which carries a carriage road. In this area, the trail is lined with large white pines, hemlocks, and cedars.

The Maple Spring Trail dead-ends into the Hadlock Brook Trail. Turn right for the final 0.4 mile to the parking area on Route 198.

Directions

For this hike, park at the Norumbega parking area on Routes 198/3, 1.5 miles north of Northeast Harbor. The Hadlock Brook Trail is directly across the street.

Dorr Mountain, the Gorge, and Sieur de Monts Spring

NPS Rating: Strenuous, with a few ladders

Distance: 4.0 miles round-trip

Elevation Gain: 1,200 feet

Estimated Time: 4 hours

A difficult hike to spectacular views, a narrow gorge, and quiet forests.

THE FIRST LEG of this hike is very steep, gaining 1,100 feet in about a mile. The Ladder Trail's continuous series of stone steps makes much of the climb relatively simple, although strenuous. After reaching the summit of Dorr Mountain, this hike loops around the north ridge of Dorr, descending through a picturesque gorge that separates Dorr from Cadillac. The hike meanders through the forest near historic Sieur de Monts Spring before returning to the parking area near the Tarn.

From the south end of the Tarn parking lot, begin your hike by following the trail that skirts the north end of the Tarn, a pond gouged out by glaciers during the last ice age. After crossing the outlet of the Tarn, turn left onto the Tarn Trail, which follows the west side of the pond. The trail traverses the bottom of a large field of granite boulders plucked off the east face of Dorr Mountain by glaciers. Luckily for hikers, the builders of this trail managed to build an almost sidewalk-like trail through the boulder field using granite they found among the rubble.

Shortly after the Tarn Trail leaves the shore of the pond, turn right on the Ladder Trail. From here, it is 0.9 mile to the summit of Dorr. The Ladder Trail is so named because of three sets of iron ladders which are used to scale particularly steep sections of the trail.

The cliffs of Dorr Mountain and the Tarn as seen from Huguenot Head.

However, the trail might have been more appropriately named the "Hike of 1,000 Stairs." While the ladder sections of this trail are very short, there is a seemingly endless proliferation of impressive stone steps, which were built in 1893 and restored by the Civilian Conservation Corps in the 1930s.

The trail rises quickly through a mixed forest of paper birch, yellow birch, beech, oak, white pine, big-tooth aspen and maple. After squeezing through a very narrow passage between a large boulder and the cliff face, the trail continues over iron ladders and stairs into a forest of pitch pine and scrubby red oak. The stairs end for good once the trail meets up with the Dorr Mountain Trail, where you should turn left. The trail climbs up steep granite slabs (avoid these in wet weather) during the next 0.3 mile, and the views really start to open up, with Frenchman Bay visible over Huguenot Head and Champlain Mountain.

Just below the actual summit, the trail reaches a junction with the Dorr Mountain Notch Trail and the Dorr Mountain North Ridge Trail. Turn left to walk the final few hundred yards to the summit. Cadillac Mountain looms directly to the west and seems almost close enough to touch. Otter Creek and the Cranberry Islands are now visible, as is all of Frenchman Bay and the Schoodic Peninsula. At 1,270 feet, Dorr Mountain is the third highest peak on the island.

For the next part of the hike, return to the trail junction just north of the summit. Turn left onto the Dorr Mountain Notch Trail. The trail descends steeply 0.2 mile over Cadillac pink-granite boulders to the gorge between Cadillac and Dorr Mountains. Once the trail levels off, the A. Murray Young Path goes south, while the Gorge Path goes north to the Park Loop Road. Turn right onto the Gorge Path.

The Gorge Path takes an interesting route through the narrow, rocky gorge separating Dorr and Cadillac Mountains. The trail passes under steep cliff walls and descends moderately along a stream and past small cascades. The footing can be rough, but much of the trail has flat rocks strategically placed to improve the hiking. The trail crosses the stream often and sometimes coincides with the stream. Waterproof your boots before this hike! While the forest in here consists mostly of mixed hardwoods, there are also some impressive hemlocks that somehow survived the fire of 1947.

About a mile from the Dorr Mountain Notch Trail, the Gorge Path levels off and the Hemlock Trail enters from the east. Turn right onto the Hemlock Trail, which will lead you to Sieur de Monts Spring. After briefly rising to meet the Dorr Mountain North Ridge Trail, the Hemlock Trail runs into an old dirt service road, which is now used as a hiking trail from Sieur de Monts Spring. Turn right on the road and then right again 0.3 mile later onto the Jessup Path, which is not marked by a trail sign. If you reach the Sieur de Monts parking area you have gone too far. At a Park Service nature center building, the trail forks. Stay to the right. The trail crosses a road and a bike path, which both lead to the Abbe Museum, before continuing through the woods to the Tarn. When you reach the Tarn, you have completed the loop. Turn left and head up the path to return to the Tarn parking area.

Directions

This hike starts at the parking area on the west side of Maine Route 3, just past Sieur de Monts Spring at the north end of the Tarn, 2.2 miles south of Bar Harbor.

Cadillac Mountain

NPS Rating: **Moderate**

Distance: **7.0 miles up and back**

Elevation Gain: **1,500 feet**

Estimated Time: **4 hours**

A relatively long hike over open ledges to the summit of Mount Desert Island's highest mountain. There are great views during most of this hike.

THIS IS THE ONLY TRIP in the hiking section of this book that is not a loop hike. However, the south ridge of Cadillac Mountain, with its open forests of pitch and jack pine, is worth experiencing twice in the same day. This hike starts on Maine Route 3 near the entrance to Blackwoods Campground and makes a moderate, enjoyable climb to Cadillac's busy summit over a leisurely 3.5 miles. While the summit may not be the wildest spot in the park, with its gift shop and parking lot full of tourists, the south ridge of Cadillac is relatively quiet and full of excellent views.

The Cadillac South Ridge Trail starts on the north side of Maine Route 3, about fifty yards west of the entrance to the Blackwoods Campground. It is legal to park on the shoulder of the highway. The first mile of this hike rises gently, then moderately, through a forest predominated by white pine and spruce. At the 1-mile mark, a spur path leads 0.1 mile to the right to an overlook called Eagle Crag, which has good views of Otter Creek and the Atlantic Ocean. This is a worthwhile destination for families staying at the campground who are not up for the full hike to the summit.

The spur path loops around to reconnect with the main trail after a total of about 0.2 mile. Turn right to head toward the summit. Almost immediately, the hike enters a forest of pitch pine spread

Lowbush blueberry grows in the rock crevices on the summit of Cadillac Mountain.

over granite ledge, taking on an open, airy feeling. The occasional boulder among the gnarly and twisted trees contributes to the forest's look of a grown-up Japanese bonsai garden. Of course, this is a real forest, and wind and water are the gardeners. From here there are good views of the island and the surrounding waters for most of the way to the summit. The trail then passes though one of the few pockets of jack pine on the island just before it makes a short descent to the Featherbed.

The Featherbed is a boggy area 2.3 miles from the trailhead. This is one of the highest wetlands in the park. The trail crosses the Canon Brook Trail, which leads east to Dorr Mountain and west to Jordan Pond. Continuing straight on the Cadillac South Ridge Trail, the hike soon reaches its steepest climb. A trail junction 0.5 mile below the summit marks the Cadillac West Face Trail, which leads west to Bubble Pond. At this point, the trail nears the summit road before making its final ascent toward the summit.

Shortly before reaching the summit, the trail descends into a thick spruce-fir forest, which stands in marked contrast to the open pine forest of the last 2.5 miles. This forest grows in an area protected from the strong summit winds, and it collects just enough soil and water to allow the spruce-fir forest to thrive. The trail crosses a fire road and reaches the summit parking area just below the actual summit, which is marked by a set of interpretive signs describing the views extending in all directions of Frenchman Bay, the Schoodic Peninsula, the islands to the west, and even Katahdin 115 miles to the north.

Sixteen species of hawks, eagles, and falcons live in or migrate through Acadia. In the fall, Cadillac Mountain's location and elevation make it an excellent spot to watch for migrating raptors, especially when the wind is out of the north. Check with the park visitor center for information about hawk-watching programs run by park naturalists throughout September and early October.

To complete your hike, walk back down the trail to your car.

Directions

The trailhead for the Cadillac South Ridge Trail is just west of the entrance to Blackwoods Campground on Maine Route 3, 5.6 miles south of Bar Harbor.

twisted pines

While hiking on Cadillac Mountain and most of the other rocky summits in Acadia, you will encounter beautiful stands of pitch and jack pine. Although these pines will grow to be as tall as seventy feet in ideal conditions, they usually top out at twenty or thirty feet in the exposed environment of Acadia's mountains. Harsh winds twist the trunks into gnarled, stunted, surreal shapes which make for a fascinating forest to hike through. The lack of fertile soil also creates an "open" forest, making it quite common to have good views out past the trees, even when they are thirty feet tall. It is relatively easy to tell these pines apart by studying their needles. A pitch pine has four-inch needles in bundles of three, while the jack pine's one-inch needles come in bundles of two.

In Acadia, pitch pine is the more common of the two, but it is most often associated with the sandy pine barrens of southern New England and New Jersey. Jack pine is less common in Acadia, as it is a more northerly species that lives primarily in Canada. Both species are highly resistant to fire, and jack pine actually depends on fire to heat open its cones and release its seeds. Without fire, both species would gradually be replaced by hardwoods. In Acadia, pitch and jack pines colonize granite ledges where there is little soil and where they are usually joined by an understory of blueberries, sheep laurel, and sometimes scrubby oaks.

Pitch pines, *Pinus rigida*, colonize rocky ledges throughout Acadia.

5
biking in acadia

DURING MUCH OF THIS CENTURY, the Rockefeller family has donated large amounts of time, money, and land in an effort to make Acadia and Mount Desert Island a nature paradise for future generations to enjoy. Perhaps the greatest Rockefeller legacy is the network of carriage roads John Rockefeller Jr. had built during the 1920s and 1930s. These roads were built originally so that walkers and horse-drawn carriages could enjoy the island's backcountry without the disturbing noise and pollution of automobiles. Horses and walkers still use the carriage roads, but now these roads get most of their traffic from bicycle riders. The roads follow easy grades and blend into the contours of the hills in a way that makes them seem a natural part of the landscape, and their crushed-gravel surface makes an excellent base for riding. Built by local craftsmen, the roads traverse a series of intricate stone bridges which cross streams, gorges, and the Park Loop Road and provide visitors with the greatest viewing pleasure possible. With no single-track mountain-bike trails to speak of (bikes are not allowed on hiking trails), Acadia is not a place for hard-core extreme mountain-biking. However, the carriage roads, as well as the dirt fire roads on the western side of the island, provide an excellent way to experience the park on two wheels. Trips range from flat, one-hour rides through mature spruce forest to steep, half-day climbs with spectacular views of the surrounding peaks, lakes, and bays.

Biking the carriage roads is a wonderful way to explore the natural beauty of Mount Desert Island's eastern district. Fifty-seven miles of these roads take you to the scenic splendor of places like Jordan Pond, Eagle Lake, and Day Mountain. Passing through a variety of natural habitats, they create the opportunity for extensive nature study and wildlife watching. Magnificent bridges provide views of waterfalls and mountain vistas, and the roads make occasional climbs to reveal stunning views of the Atlantic Ocean and the rest of Maine. The western part of the island, with its cool, quiet boreal forests can be explored on a series of dirt fire roads. These fire roads are a great way to see the natural habitats of Mount Desert Island as they were before the great fire of 1947.

Trip Times and Ratings

Our trip times are based on our experience as average bike-riders. They do not include much time for breaks, so if you plan to take in much of the scenery, your times may be longer. Obviously, these times can vary based on the weather, the physical fitness level of your group, and how much gear you bring with you. While we think these times are useful for planning a trip, your trip times undoubtedly will be different from ours. Trip ratings vary based on the length of the trip and the elevation gain. Most trips in Acadia are fairly short and easy from a road-biking standpoint, but the elevation gains can make a trip seem much longer.

Safety and Etiquette

Its mild summer climate makes Acadia an enjoyable and relatively safe biking destination. Of course, bad weather or poor planning can spoil any biking adventure. Before heading into Acadia's backcountry, consider the following tips:

- Select a trip that is appropriate for everyone in the group. Match the ride to the abilities of the least capable person in the group.

- Plan to be back at the trailhead before dark. Determine a turn-around time and stick to it even if you have not reached your goal for the day.

- Check the weather. Acadia's carriage roads and fire roads are safe places to be during wet weather, but riding can be less enjoyable in a steady rain or when there are strong winds. Give yourself more time to stop in the rain, as wet brakes do not work as well as dry ones.

- Bring a pack with the following items:

  Water—One or two quarts per person depending on the weather and the length of the trip

  Food—Even for a short trip, it is a good idea to bring some high-energy snacks like nuts, dried fruit, or snack bars. Bring a lunch for longer trips.

  Map

  Extra clothing—rain gear, sweater, hat

  Flashlight

  Sunscreen

  First-aid kit

  Pocketknife

  Basic bike-maintenance tools and a spare inner tube

- Wear appropriate footwear and clothing. Legwear should be tight fitting: loose pants can get stuck on pedals and in the gears of a bike, causing nasty accidents. Bring rain gear even in sunny weather, since unexpected rain, fog, or wind is possible at any time in Acadia. Avoid wearing cotton clothing, which absorbs sweat and rain, making for cold, damp riding. Polypropylene, nylon, fleece, silk, and wool are all good materials for keeping moisture away from your body and keeping you warm in wet or cold conditions.

In addition to practicing the no-impact techniques described in this book's introduction, it is also a good idea to keep the following things in mind while bike-riding:

- Call the Park Service to confirm that the carriage roads are open. In the spring, the roads are often closed because they are too wet to handle traffic of any kind. It can cost thousands of dollars to repair one tire rut, so if the roads are closed, please stay off them.

- Bikes are not permitted on hiking trails or on the carriage roads to the south of Jordan Pond and east of the Stanley Brook Road.

- Always wear a helmet.

- When on paved roads or the dirt fire roads where cars are allowed, wear bright colors and follow the same rules of the road you follow while driving a car.

- Ride slowly and in control—and be able to stop quickly. Gravel surfaces are loose, and quick stops are dangerous.

- Do not obstruct the road by riding (or resting) three or four abreast.

- Yield to hikers.

- Yield to horses and walk your bike past them. Sometimes they can get spooked by a bicycle speeding past them.

- When passing, politely inform the person you are passing by saying, "On your left," or, "On your right."

- Try not to disturb other bike-riders and hikers. While you may often feel alone in the wilderness, wild yelling or cell phone usage will undoubtedly upset another person's quiet back-country experience.

- When you are ahead of the rest of your group, wait at all road junctions. This avoids confusion and keeps people in your group from getting lost or separated from one another.

Maple Spring—Hadlock Brook Loop

> **Rating: Easy**
>
> **Distance: 4.0 miles**
>
> **Elevation Gain: 350 feet**
>
> **Estimated Time: 1.25 hours**
>
> **A relatively easy ride to a forty–foot waterfall and a visit to Upper Hadlock Pond.**

THIS TRIP may be short, but it packs in views of the Cranberry Islands, rides through sweet-smelling spruce forests, and a visit to one of Acadia's biggest waterfalls. The carriage roads on this ride pass over Maple Spring and Hadlock Brook on two of the magnificent granite bridges that are synonymous with Acadia's carriage-road system. Except for one short steep section, the grades are reasonable and the pedaling easy. The trip finishes with a ride along the afternoon-sun-soaked eastern shore of Upper Hadlock Pond, which provides a good habitat for a variety of waterfowl.

From the Parkman Mountain parking area, follow the sign that points toward post #13. At post #13 turn left for a steep climb through a beautiful spruce forest. To the south Upper Hadlock Pond and the Cranberry Islands come into view shortly before reaching post #12 at 0.4 mile from the parking area. This is the steepest part of this trip. At post #12, turn right. At 0.8 mile, you come to the Hemlock Bridge, which rises high above Maple Spring, a beautiful pine- and hemlock-lined stream that tumbles down to Upper Hadlock Pond from just below the summit of Sargent Mountain. Only a hundred yards or so beyond the Hemlock Bridge is Waterfall Bridge, with its single arch spanning Hadlock Brook. Like many of the bridges on the carriage roads, viewing turrets entice you to stop and soak in the sights and

Waterfall Bridge overlooks Hadlock Brook as it tumbles forty
feet over pink Cadillac granite.

sounds of nature. To the left of the bridge, Hadlock Brook tumbles forty feet over Cadillac granite, carrying the soothing sounds of rushing water past the bridge to the valley below.

Beyond Waterfall Bridge, the carriage road parallels the south ridge of Cedar Swamp Mountain, making a long, gradual descent that will have you wishing all biking were this easy. As you coast through the dark green of a spruce forest, the calls of chickadees and nuthatches fill the air as the pungent smell of the North Woods wafts over you. Just before reaching post #19 at 2.2 miles, you pass through a grove of northern white cedar. Named arborvitae, Latin for "tree of life," the northern white cedar's bark and foliage is high in vitamin C. Tea made from northern white cedar foliage was used to prevent scurvy in the men of French explorer Jacques Cartier in 1535. The tree was introduced as an ornamental in Europe the following year. It tends to grow in wet, acidic soils covered with a thick layer of sphagnum moss, creating a forested wetland that is the ideal habitat for rare orchids. Birds that live in a cedar stand include northern saw-whet owls, alder flycatchers, hermit thrushes, cedar waxwings, Canada warblers, and black-throated green warblers.

At post #19 turn right, and then turn right again at post #18. A fairly level ride brings you to Upper Hadlock Pond at 3.0 miles. In the afternoon, the sun shines on the eastern shore of the pond, which is only a few yards to the west of the carriage road. It is a peaceful spot to take a break and watch for the ducks that live on the pond. Norumbega Mountain rises steeply beyond the west side of the pond, its thick spruce-fir forest looking like an impenetrable covering. As the road makes its way around the northern end of the pond, it crosses a small stream over a modest bridge made of large granite blocks. While not as large or dramatic as the taller and longer bridges of the carriage-road system, this small bridge and others like it display the same intricate craftsmanship. After the bridge, the road begins a 150-foot climb back to post #13. Turn left at this intersection to complete your journey.

Directions

For this trip, park at the Parkman Mountain parking area on Routes 198/3, 1.8 miles north of Northeast Harbor.

Trip #17

Hio Fire Road

Rating: Easy

Distance: 4.0 miles

Elevation Gain: 100 feet

Estimated Time: 1 hour

An easy ride for the family on a dirt road in prime bird-watching habitat.

THE HIO ROAD is an unused dirt fire road near Seawall Campground that traverses a spruce-fir forest near a large bog called the Big Heath. Birds more common in Canada than coastal Maine inhabit the woods along this road, which is relatively flat and has a good riding surface for most of its length. Although there are a few very short rough spots, kids will enjoy this trip. Since it is short, you can take your time with this trip, watching and listening for birds, exploring vernal pools for frogs and salamanders, and enjoying flora like rhodora, bog laurel, and skunk cabbage. You can also add a short ride to the Atlantic Ocean at Seawall.

This trip is an out-and-back trip that can be started either from Maine Route 102 or from the group camping area in Seawall Campground. This description assumes you will start from Route 102. From the east side of Route 102, the Hio Road starts out near Bass Harbor Marsh, which has excellent views of Bernard, Mansell, Beech, and Acadia Mountains. The road immediately enters the spruce-fir forest that will be the dominant feature for the entire ride. This forest attracts northern bird species such as boreal chickadees, gray jays, black-backed woodpeckers, and spruce grouse. At 0.8 mile, you cross a small stream that flows through a northern white cedar swamp toward the Big Heath. In April skunk cabbage is the first herbaceous (nonwoody) plant to appear in large quantities, sprouting through a layer of fuzzy green sphagnum moss.

Skunk cabbage is common in the sphagnum-covered forested wetlands along the Hio Fire Road.

The Big Heath is one of Acadia's largest bogs. Bogs usually form in glacial depressions that were at one time lakes or ponds. Over time the lake fills with accumulated plant material that decays at a very slow rate. What results is a layer of peat that can be as deep as forty feet and often floats on top of water. For this reason, bogs are a less-than-pleasant place to walk through. If you attempt to pass through a bog, consider yourself lucky if all you lose is a boot or two. This slowly decaying plant material creates a highly acidic and nutrient-poor environment that makes it difficult for plants to survive. Insectivorous plants such as sundew and pitcher plants survive there by trapping insects and consuming their nutrients. Other plants that tend to grow in bogs are evergreen shrubs such as Labrador tea, sheep laurel, bog laurel, and orchids. Black spruce, larch, and white cedars are the types of trees that usually manage to survive in the acidic soil of a bog. Birds you might find in the Big Heath include Lincoln's sparrow, northern waterthrush, and palm warblers.

Two miles from Route 102, you reach the end of Hio Fire Road. Through the gate is the group camping area at Seawall Campground. From this end of the campground it is about a 0.4-mile ride over pavement to the Atlantic Ocean. There is a picnic area on a natural sea wall overlooking the ocean. The ten-foot-high cobblestone sea wall is impressive as it winds its way along the coast for about a mile.

Directions

From Southwest Harbor, follow Maine Route 102 south. At the intersection with 102A, bear right to stay on 102. In another 1.4 miles, the Hio Fire Road will be on your left, just before crossing the Bass Harbor Marsh.

moose and bears in acadia?

Aside from the gray seals and whales that swim in coastal waters, moose and black bears are the largest mammals in Maine. Most visitors to Acadia hope to see at least one of these animals. While very common on the mainland in Maine, both moose and bears are relatively rare on Mount Desert Island. Nonetheless, they do exist, and you can often see moose tracks and droppings while biking the fire roads of Acadia. While hiking the thick forests of Acadia's western mountains, finding bear tracks and scat can be an exhilarating, if somewhat frightening, experience. Knowing these animals inhabit the park is exciting enough for most people, but a few visitors a year do catch a fleeting glimpse of these large omnivores.

Black bears can grow to be six feet long and weigh up to 450 pounds in Maine. They are primarily vegetarian and will quickly become habituated to human foods if given the chance. A habituated bear is a dangerous bear and might attack people, so if you see one, do not approach or feed it. If you are camping in bear country, keep a clean camp and store food either in the trunk of your car or in a bear-proof container, or hang the food from a tree. While bears are not known to visit campgrounds in Acadia, it is still a good idea to keep a clean camp so that raccoons, skunks, and other animals do not become a nuisance. There are estimated to be around fifteen black bears living on the western side of Mount Desert Island. They are seen very rarely, but if you are in a blueberry patch at harvest time, keep your eyes open for signs of bears. While black bears rarely attack people, mothers will fiercely protect their cubs. If you see a bear on a trail, do not run, but back away slowly. Most likely the bear will leave on its own.

The moose is the largest land animal in the state of Maine, weighing as much as 1,200 pounds. It is dark brown

Less numerous in Acadia National Park than in other parts of Maine, moose inhabit the boreal forests on the western side of Mount Desert Island.

with paler legs. Males sport huge, flattened antlers, and females, while generally smaller than males, are still as big as a horse. The moose is the largest member of the deer family, and it is generally less timid than its more common relative, the white-tailed deer. While a moose is not as intimidating as a black bear, it can be dangerous nonetheless. Give a moose a good distance, and if one approaches you, quickly back away. It eats aquatic plants, woodland shrubs, and even tree bark in winter. Like the black bear, it primarily inhabits the western side of Mount Desert Island, but it can be found in any part of the park where swamps and bogs meet forest.

Witch Hole Pond and Paradise Hill

> **Rating: Easy**
>
> **Distance: 4.4 miles**
>
> **Elevation Gain: 350 feet**
>
> **Estimated Time: 1.25 hours**
>
> **An easy ride past beaver ponds and bogs to great views of Hulls Cove and Frenchman Bay. A great trip for families.**

WITCH HOLE POND is a beautiful remote lake surrounded by colorful bogs and filled with beaver lodges. This bike ride takes you past more beaver activity than any other trip in this book. We saw numerous dams and lodges as well as recent tree cuttings. A great view from Paradise Hill also reminds you the ocean is only a few thousand feet away. This is an easy trip with only a few short gradual climbs, making it a perfect choice for families with small children. It is also very convenient to downtown Bar Harbor, as you can ride your bike to the carriage road from town. Of course, this easy access does draw the crowds in midsummer, so you may want to get an early-morning start on this trip in order to enjoy the peacefulness of Witch Hole Pond.

Begin your trip by crossing Duck Brook Bridge, an impressive triple-arch structure built in 1929. The views from the bridge of Duck Brook and Acadia's mountains are especially spectacular in the fall. Stone steps lead down from the bridge to Duck Brook, where the sound of the rushing stream can make it seem as though you are miles from civilization. Once you cross the bridge, turn right at post #5 to make your way toward Witch Hole Pond. After 0.7 mile and a short gradual uphill section, you will come to a beaver pond with a

Paradise Hill has good views of Frenchman Bay.

small dam and lodge. Beavers are most active at night, but you can sometimes catch a glimpse of them in the early morning.

In the spring, this is a good place to listen for the drumming of ruffed grouses. The seventeen-inch-long ruffed grouse is the common partridge in New England, and it is well suited to Acadia's mixed woodlands. To attract females, a male will perch on a favorite "drumming log" and beat its wings in an accelerating drum roll. This drumming sounds like a distant helicopter or tractor engine starting up. The beaver pond is also an ideal breeding area for insects, which attract all kinds of small songbirds such as swamp sparrows and fly-catchers. This seemingly small and insignificant pond bustles with activity on a warm, sunny day.

After about a mile from Duck Brook Bridge, Witch Hole Pond appears on your left, with views of Youngs and McFarland Mountains providing a backdrop for the pond. You will see that beavers have dammed the inlet to the pond, creating an extensive marshy area to the right. Witch Hole Pond itself has at least three large beaver lodges which are as tall as six feet. With the marsh and pond both surrounded by bogs and mixed woodlands, this is a good place to look for the large variety of ducks that can be seen in Acadia, such as mallards, black ducks, wood ducks, and blue-winged teals. Witch Hole Pond is also big enough to support a good population of fish, which draw both ospreys and fly-fishermen.

After passing between Witch Hole Pond and the marsh, the carriage road comes to post #3. Turn right to head up Paradise Hill. At this point, it is possible to turn left to avoid the extra mile required to summit Paradise Hill, but the views of Hulls Cove and Frenchman Bay are well worth the extra effort. The climb up to the summit is gradual and relatively short, about 0.4 mile from post #3. From the summit, you can see beyond the deep blue waters of Frenchman Bay toward the hills of the Schoodic Peninsula and the rest of eastern Maine. As you loop back toward Witch Hill Pond, continue straight at post #1 (turning to the right would take you to the park visitor center). You return to Witch Hole Pond at post #2, where you will want to turn right and explore the bogs surrounding the southern end of the pond. Stunted spruce and white pine attempt to grow in the acidic soil, which is held together by sphagnum moss.

A long but very gradual uphill section brings you through more mixed woodlands peppered with beaver activity. Just before reaching post #4, you come upon Halfmoon Pond on your right, which has a small beaver lodge in its center. There are good views here of Youngs Mountain. At post #4, bear to the left for the final mile of this trip. Sheep laurel and rhodora are common on the roadside here. Both plants have beautiful pink blossoms in late May and early June. At post #5, turn right to cross over Duck Brook Bridge and return to your car.

Directions

From the intersection of Route 3 and West Street in Bar Harbor, head west on the West Street Extension for 0.7 mile, where you should turn right on Duck Brook Road. The parking area is on the right in 0.6 mile.

Seal Cove Pond–Western Mountain Loop

> **Rating: Easy**
> **Distance: 5.0 miles**
> **Elevation Gain: 150 feet**
> **Estimated Time: 1.25 hours**
>
> **An easy ride through a boreal forest frequented by moose.**

THE SYSTEM of fire roads around Acadia's western mountains provides about ten miles of bike-riding opportunities. The roads are all similar in character: dirt and gravel auto roads that pass through a dark yet enchanting boreal forest. Views are nonexistent, but that only adds to the feeling of wilderness in what could pass for Maine's North Woods. This trip begins and ends at Seal Cove Pond, which is home to herons, loons, and bald eagles. The rest of the trip loops through tall spruce and past biologically interesting cedar bogs. This is an easy trip that leaves plenty of time for a paddle on Seal Cove Pond or a hike up the West Ledge Trail, which provides almost instant views of Blue Hill Bay and the Atlantic Ocean. Cars are allowed on this road, and while traffic is light, you still need to observe the rules of the road.

From the Seal Cove Pond parking area, ride up the hill on Western Mountain Road. This short, steep section is the hardest climb of the trip. In this area, the road passes through a small stand of hardwoods, with beech and maple trees lining small rushing streams. By the time you reach the West Ledge Trail, the makeup of trees begins to change as you enter the boreal forest. The West Ledge Trail leads 1.6 miles to the summit of Bernard Mountain (hiking only). This strenuous trail makes a great side trip, as it leads hikers to the island's best views of Blue Hill Bay.

Continue straight on Western Mountain Road until you reach an intersection at 0.7 mile. Turn right, following the sign that points to

Seal Cove. At 1.2 miles you will reach another intersection, where you should turn left (turning right will lead you to a dead end in only a few hundred yards). Just before reaching Seal Cove Road at 1.6 miles, you enter a stand of tall red spruce and the forest takes on a primeval feel. Keep your eyes open for moose! At Seal Cove Road, turn left.

The hard dirt surface of Seal Cove Road makes for easy riding. Despite being a dirt road, Seal Cove Road is a popular road for those driving between Southwest Harbor and Seal Cove. Ride single file for safety. The road passes through more spruce forest, although some deciduous trees like birch and downy serviceberry have taken over the disturbed areas along the road. Common along streams, downy serviceberry, with its showy white flowers, was nicknamed "shadbush" by early colonists because it blooms at the same time shad swim upstream to spawn. At 2.0 miles, a small family cemetery from the nineteenth century can be seen among the trees on the left. When visiting the cemetery, remember to follow the Leave No Trace ethics discussed in this book's introduction, and "leave what you find."

At 3.1 miles you will reach another intersection, where you should turn left to return to Western Mountain Road. At 3.5 miles turn left again, following the sign for Seal Cove Pond. (To extend your trip by about 3 miles, you can turn right here for an out-and-back trip to Gilley Field and the trailheads for hiking trails up Bernard and Mansell Mountains.) At 4.1 miles the boreal forest is interrupted on the left by a northern white cedar bog, with its carpet of sphagnum moss hosting such hardy plants as partridgeberry and starflower. Sphagnum wetlands like this add a boost to the biodiversity of Acadia, providing habitat for rare orchids and uncommon animals such as the four-toed salamander.

At the next intersection, go straight to complete the final 0.7 mile back to Seal Cove Pond.

Directions

From Maine Route 102 in Southwest Harbor, drive east on Seal Cove Road. After 3.5 miles, turn right on a dirt Park Service road. After 0.4 mile there will be a sign for Western Mountain Road. Turn right. After another 0.5 mile, there will be a sign for Seal Cove Pond. Follow this sign to the left. You are now on Western Mountain Road. The road ends at Seal Cove Pond in another 0.7 mile.

Long Pond Fire Road

Rating: **Easy**

Distance: **5.5 miles**

Elevation Gain: **250 feet**

Estimated Time: **2 hours**

An easy ride on a dirt road to a secluded cove on Long Pond.

LONG POND is the largest body of fresh water on Mount Desert Island. On a calm day its deep blue waters reflect the rounded shapes of Acadia's mountains in mirrorlike fashion. The pond itself is a busy place in summer, with motorboats and jet skis sharing the water with canoes and kayaks (see trips #31 and #35). This trip on one of Acadia's dirt fire roads brings you to a secluded cove on the bay formed by the pond's Southern Neck peninsula. Thick evergreen forests line the entire length of the road, adding to the feeling of seclusion on Mount Desert Island's "quiet side." This trip also has good wildlife-viewing opportunities, as it visits a boggy beaver pond and passes through some of the island's best moose habitat.

Begin your trip on the Long Pond Fire Road, just south of the Pretty Marsh Picnic Area. This dirt road is open to cars during the summer and fall, but traffic is light. It is a fairly level ride for the 1.8 miles to Long Pond, with a only a few short ups and downs. The forest is boreal, dominated by spruce and fir. There are a large number of small, boggy areas where northern white cedar or alders grow. Vernal ponds, temporary pools of water where amphibians breed, are also common, making this an interesting trip in spring. Pickerel and wood frogs make use of these small vernal pools to mate and lay eggs. Softball-sized clumps of gelatinous eggs can be found floating free in the pools or attached to sticks or other debris. You will cer-

The Long Pond Fire Road takes bike riders to this scenic vista of Long Pond.

tainly hear the calls of these frogs as you pedal your way toward Long Pond. Smaller egg clumps are probably those of salamanders that also use small temporary pools of water to breed.

From the shore of Long Pond, you get good views across the water to Cadillac Mountain. The bay to your right is formed by the peninsula of land called Southern Neck. The bay on the left is formed by Northern Neck. All of the shoreline on the Southern Neck side of the pond is part of Acadia National Park, making it seem much wilder than most of the pond, which is home to many summer cottages. Mallards, loons, and mergansers are common on the lake, and ospreys and bald eagles often soar high above it looking for fish. Northern white cedar bogs are common along this part of the shoreline, with sphagnum moss carpeting the forest floor and pitcher plants surviving in the nutrient-poor soil by capturing and digesting insects.

After leaving the shoreline of Long Pond, the fire road soon reaches a fork, where you should bear right. Still in a forest of spruce and fir, you are experiencing the forested island much as it was before the forest fire in 1947. This part of the island, with its thick forest peppered with bogs, is home to many of the moose in the park. Moose are about six feet tall and can weigh as much as 1,200 pounds. Only males have antlers, which can be as big as six feet across. They are not terribly dangerous, but it is a good idea not to approach moose, as they have been known to trample people when angry. If you see a moose and it puts its ears back or starts to move toward you, just move back and it will probably leave you alone. If you do not see moose around Long Pond, you are still likely to see their tracks in the road. Look for prints shaped like deer hooves but much larger, between three and six and a half inches in length.

At 2.5 miles, a road on the right leads about 100 yards to Duck Pond, a small, boggy pond that appears to have been flooded by beaver at one point in time. The sun-bleached trunks of scores of long-dead spruce stand in much of the pond, which is bordered by rhodora and blueberry shrubs. Pitcher plants and sundews grow from the bed of sphagnum moss that lines the shore. This is a good place to watch birds, with the pond and forest edge joining to form a habitat where you can see warblers, flycatchers, wrens, sparrows, wood ducks, hawks, and even bald eagles perching in the tall white pines circling the pond.

At 3.5 miles, the Western Trail (hiking only) leads to the summits of Mansell and Bernard Mountains on the left. In another 100

the boreal forest

Before the great fire of 1947, most of Mount Desert Island was covered by a spruce-fir, or boreal, forest. The boreal forest is the northernmost forest ecosystem in the world, circling the globe across northern North America, Europe, and Asia. It is characterized by a dominance of evergreen trees, usually spruce and fir or jack pine. Other species such as hemlock, white pine, and red pine are also found here, and birches, poplars, and aspens populate disturbed sites. In New England, the boreal forest is usually comprised of white spruce and balsam fir. In Acadia, red spruce and balsam fir make up the inland boreal forest, while white spruce is more common close to the ocean. The 1947 fire destroyed 17,000 acres of boreal forest on the eastern half of Mount Desert Island.

The boreal forest is a dark place, often preventing the growth of an understory of smaller trees or shrubs. Thin, acidic soil, a product of recent glaciation and a slow rate of decomposition, also prevents many plants from taking root. Some common plants that do manage to grow beneath the canopy of evergreens include partridgeberry, bunchberry, wood sorrel, and starflower. The most common mammals in the boreal forest are red squirrel, porcupine, beaver, snowshoe hare, and moose. (The boreal forest is so readily identified with the moose that it is sometimes

yards, turn left at the T intersection. The road continues through spruce-fir forest and cedar swamps, passing by Seal Cove Pond on the left and Hodgdon Pond on the right at 4.1 miles. At 4.4 miles, turn left onto the narrow paved road, which leads to Route 102 at 4.5 miles. Turn right on 102 to ride the final mile of the trip. Maine 102 is not an extremely busy road, but it is narrow and the shoulder is soft, so you will need to be cautious while riding this final stretch.

called the "spruce-moose" forest. Moose are not common on Mount Desert Island, but it is in the forests of spruce and fir that you are most likely to encounter them.) Other mammals that live in the boreal forest are fishers, pine martens, and lynx. Lynx no longer live in Acadia, and it is rare to see fishers and pine martens. Birders flock to Acadia's boreal forest to see gray jays, boreal chickadees, and finches like crossbills, pine grosbeaks, and pine siskins. Spring brings colorful migrants like Blackburnian, bay-breasted, yellow-rumped, and Cape May warblers.

Spruce and fir trees are remarkably well adapted to survive the long winters of the high latitudes. Their conical, "Christmas tree" shape sheds the heavy snows of winter so that their branches are not damaged by heavy snow. The short growing season makes it inefficient to grow new leaves every year, so they grow needles that stay on the tree year-round and go dormant during the winter. The needles are protected by a thick wax on the outside and a sugary fluid on the inside which acts much like an antifreeze, preventing frost damage. The way needles are arranged on the tree has been shown to prevent windchill and evaporation, and actually helps keep the trees warmer in winter. The needles can quickly begin photosynthesizing in the spring when temperatures rise.

The best places to experience the boreal forest in Acadia are on the western side of the island on Mansell and Bernard Mountains, around Long Pond, and near Seawall Campground.

Directions

Head south on Maine Route 102 in Somesville. Turn right at the flashing yellow light onto Pretty Marsh Road/Route 102. After 4.9 miles, park at the Pretty Marsh Picnic Area, which will be on your right. The Long Pond Fire Road is on the east side of the road about 0.1 mile south of the picnic area.

Trip #21

Amphitheater Loop

> Rating: **Moderate**
>
> Distance: **5.5 miles**
>
> Elevation Gain: **350 feet**
>
> Estimated Time: **2 hours**
>
> **A moderate ride through an enchanting evergreen forest with streams lined with pink-granite stones.**

THE AMPHITHEATER is a narrow valley that is walled in by the steep sides of Penobscot and Cedar Swamp Mountains. Its cool streams and forests are the perfect place to escape summer's heat, and the carriage roads rise just high enough above the trees to give you good views of the ocean. This trip takes you from the Brown Mountain Gatehouse on Route 198 around the southern end of Cedar Swamp Mountain and into the Amphitheater before heading south along the west side of Penobscot Mountain. Like all of the carriage roads, this piece of Mr. Rockefeller's work features gentle grades, majestic bridges, and sweeping curves that seem to melt into the hillsides.

From the south end of the parking lot just north of the gatehouse, pedal up the fire road, which leads about fifty yards to the carriage road. At post #18, turn right and make your way through the forest of tall red spruce. The road climbs quickly to post #19 (0.3 mile), where you should take another right. After about a mile, views begin to open up to the south. In the fall, hardwoods in the foreground create a beautiful contrast to the dark green spruce that cover the hills between you and the Cranberry Islands. The forest is so thick that it hides any signs of civilization, despite the fact you are looking past Maine Route 3 and the town of Northeast Harbor.

The road makes a gentle descent below the trees where it reaches post #20 at 1.3 miles. Turn left toward the Amphitheater. The road

Taking a break on Hemlock Bridge, built in 1924.

makes a graceful left turn toward Cedar Swamp Mountain in order to hug the contour of the mountain. In the forest above the road are car-sized boulders covered in green, gray, and brown lichens. The ride eventually turns into a downward coast until you reach the Amphitheater Bridge at 1.8 miles. Built in 1931, the Amphitheater Bridge is 235 feet long, the longest in the carriage-road system. Turrets are used as viewing platforms for looking at the small waterfall, which is part of Little Harbor Brook. The bridge's single arch was built in order to frame the waterfall from below. Characteristic of his love for nature, Rockefeller insisted that a 20-foot pine and a 20-foot hemlock both be left standing after construction.

The bridge sits at the head of the Amphitheater, which was named for its shape. The steep walls of Cedar Swamp and Penobscot Mountains rise above and around the northern end of the valley, which gradually widens as it falls toward the ocean. Apparently the early visitors who named the Amphitheater pictured giants sitting on the sides of the mountains watching some grand event out on Bear Island. As you continue south on the carriage road, you can get a look back at the mountains that form the Amphitheater. The road falls slowly through a mosaic forest of white pine, spruce, maple, beech, and birch. At 2.5 miles turn right at post #21, and turn right again at post #22 in another 0.5 mile. To the left of post #22 the carriage road enters private property where bikes are not allowed.

At 3.2 miles, the road parallels and soon crosses Little Harbor Brook, a small but beautiful stream lined with pink Cadillac granite. The small bridge that crosses the brook is a peaceful place to listen to birdsong and rushing water as you rest up for the steep climb that follows. The climb continues until you reach post #20 at 4.2 miles. During the climb, you get views of the east side of Cedar Swamp Mountain, which you traversed at the beginning of the trip. Looking at the mountain, it is impossible to discern where the carriage road travels. Once at post #20, turn left to retrace your route back to the parking area. Turn left again at posts #19 and #18 to complete the 5.5-mile loop.

Directions

For this trip, park at the Brown Mountain Gatehouse parking area on Routes 198/3, 0.5 mile north of Northeast Harbor.

Trip #22

Aunt Betty Pond Loop

Rating: Moderate

Distance: 6.0 miles

Elevation Gain: 300 feet

Estimated Time: 1.5 hours

A moderate ride with the chance to see beaver and views of Sargent Mountain and Eagle Lake.

THIS TRIP begins at the northern end of Eagle Lake. It quickly veers away from the lake to visit Aunt Betty Pond and Gilmore Meadow, both of which offer good opportunities to see wildlife. A steep climb through cool evergreens is rewarded with a downhill coast to the western shore of Eagle Lake, with its stunning views of Cadillac Mountain, Pemetic Mountain, and the Bubbles. This trip can easily be combined with the Eagle Lake Loop (trip #23) or the Giant Slide Loop (trip #26).

If you park on the north side of Route 233, turn left on the carriage road, which soon passes under Route 233. Go straight at post #6. If you park on the south side of Route 233, go right on the carriage road and turn left at post #6. From either direction, about 100 yards past post #6, turn right at post #9 to head toward Aunt Betty Pond. The road makes a moderate climb to views of Cadillac, Pemetic, and Sargent Mountains before heading downhill for more than a mile on its way to Aunt Betty Pond. At 2.4 miles from the parking area, you reach the pond, which is surrounded by the dark green of spruce and the light green of white pine. There are at least two active beaver lodges in the pond; they can be seen on the shore opposite the carriage road. Since beaver are nocturnal, your best chance of seeing them is at dawn or dusk.

Kids find the carriage roads relaxing.

At 2.8 miles, you reach post #11 and Gilmore Meadow. Gilmore Meadow is formed by a small stone dam at the bridge to the left of post #11. A narrow, meandering channel can be seen in the center of the meadow as tall grasses fill in the rest of this freshwater wetland. Lincoln and swamp sparrows, sedge and marsh wrens, flycatchers, and warblers all feed on the insects that proliferate here in spring and summer. There is also an excellent view to the south of Sargent Mountain, the second tallest mountain in Acadia. Turn left at post #11 for a short downhill before beginning a steep climb that crosses several streams and tops out at post #10, 3.9 miles from the parking area.

Turn left at post #10 and again at post #8. The carriage road heads moderately downhill until it reaches the western shore of Eagle Lake, which it follows for the remainder of the trip. At 110 feet deep, Eagle Lake is one of the deepest lakes on Mount Desert Island, and its cold water provides the ideal habitat for cold-water fish like salmon and trout. Loons, mergansers, and cormorants ply the lake's surface looking for fish. Bald eagles and ospreys fish from the tall spruce and pines circling the lake, and belted kingfishers can be heard chattering away between attempts at catching fish.

At 6.0 miles you reach post #6 and the end of your trip.

Directions

From the intersection of Route 3 and Route 233 in Bar Harbor, take Route 233 west toward Cadillac Mountain. There are two parking areas for the carriage road in 2.1 miles, one on the right and one on the left.

white-tailed deer facts

North America's most common deer, white-tailed deer, can be seen almost anywhere in Acadia National Park. However, they are seen most often at the edges of forests, in fields, or next to roads, where they emerge from the woods from dusk to dawn. Places such as the field near Seawall Campground and the roads near Sand Beach are a good place to watch them as they eat grass, twigs, shrubs, and herbs. Sharp-eyed nature watchers might also catch a glimpse of them during the day while hiking or riding bikes through the forest. They love to eat acorns, so they often can be found in the hardwood forests on the island that include northern red oak. The Giant Slide carriage road travels through one of these hardwood forests. In the winter, white-tails prefer mature conifer forests where snow depths remain low.

White-tailed deer grow to be between three and three and a half feet tall at the shoulder, with males weighing as much as 400 pounds and having antlers that measure twelve to thirty inches across. Their antlers branch off from a main beam as opposed to those of mule deer, which branch as symmetrical forks at each division. Females weigh between 50 and 250 pounds and do not have antlers. White-tailed deer are named for the pure-white underside of their tails, which are raised in alarm when they are frightened. In addition to their white tails, they have a tawny coat with white on the throat and inside the ears. Fawns are born in early spring and have white spots. Twins are common, and occasionally triplets are born. White-tailed deer are the most widely distributed deer in the New World, with thirty-eight subspecies inhabiting all but four U.S. states and ranging from southern Canada to Peru.

Like most deer on the East Coast, the white-tailed deer in Acadia are hosts to deer ticks, which carry Lyme disease. Deer ticks can pass this disease to humans, so it is important to check your entire body for these small ticks after hiking or walking in woods or grassy fields. The nymph stage of the deer tick is very small, about the size of your smallest freckle, so check carefully. Lyme disease is a debilitating disease that affects the nervous system. However, if treated early, it can be cured. Symptoms include a red bull's-eye-shaped rash at the bite site, followed by flu-like symptoms such as fever and achy joints. If you experience these symptoms and you suspect you were bitten by a deer tick, have your doctor test you for Lyme disease. If you test positive for the disease, antibiotics are used to cure it.

Eagle Lake Loop

> **Rating: Moderate**
>
> **Distance: 6.0 miles**
>
> **Elevation Gain: 350 feet**
>
> **Estimated Time: 2 hours**
>
> **A great ride for families through rich woodlands, with good views from Eagle Lake.**

EXCEPT FOR ONE LONG, gradual uphill stretch, this ride is relatively easy on the legs. It begins at the northern end of Eagle Lake, with its spectacular views of Cadillac and Pemetic Mountains. This trip circles the lake in a counterclockwise direction in order to complete the climb up the west side of Conners Nubble at the beginning of the trip. This makes for an easy ride for the rest of the loop. While the views from higher up are limited on this trip, the mixture of beautiful forests makes for a very scenic ride. As with Witch Hole Pond, Eagle Lake is very accessible to Bar Harbor and can be crowded during busy weekends, but the lake's undeveloped shoreline gives it a good wilderness character.

To park on the north side of Route 233, turn left on the carriage road which soon passes under Route 223. Go straight at post #6. To park on the south side of Route 223, go right on the carriage road and turn left at post #6. About 100 yards past post #6, stay to the left at post #9. The carriage road makes a long and steady ascent for much of the 2.1 miles to post #8. The forest alternates between tall spruce, tall white pine, and mixed hardwoods, occasionally providing views through the trees down to Eagle Lake. Eagle Lake is the second biggest lake on the island after Long Pond, and its deep, cold waters provide good habitat for salmon and trout. Osprey can often be seen circling above the lake while hunting for fish. In the forest, you are more likely to see and hear chickadees, juncos, and thrushes, and the noisy chattering of red squirrels. When you reach post #8, you have completed most of the climbing on this trip. Stay to the left and enjoy the ride back down to the shoreline of the lake, first through sweet-smelling spruce forest and then through a stand of large maple and beech.

As you round the southern end of the lake, you will notice that the forest opens up. Tall hemlocks grow here, shading the ground so well that very little light reaches the forest floor, making it hard for shrubs and small trees to grow. The eastern hemlock is one of the more beautiful conifers in the Northeast, with its rich brown bark and feathery green-and-white needles. A hemlock's needles are flat and soft like those of a fir tree, but they are much shorter, only about half an inch in length. Unlike fir trees, which live only 70 to 100 years, eastern hemlocks can live to be 400 years old and grow to be seventy feet tall. They often grow in pure stands in cool, moist valleys and ravines like the one at the southern end of Eagle Lake. These pure stands are often pockets in the midst of a larger northern hardwood forest, creating an edge habitat within the forest that has a higher number of species than the habitat away from the edge.

Dawn at Eagle Lake. Cadillac and Pemetic Mountains are in the distance.

Approximately 3.8 miles from the parking area, you will come to post #7. Stay to the left and continue through a marshy area where the trees are smaller and closer together and views open up toward Cadillac Mountain. In the spring, you can hear wood frogs making their *quack*-like mating call here. They are hard to find with their brown coloring, but if you scan the small vernal pools near the road for moving shapes about two inches long you should find some. After crossing a stream lined with white birch and sugar maples, the carriage road makes a short ascent before it makes a fairly level return to the parking area. Beautiful stone retaining walls line the Cadillac Mountain side of the road. Just before the parking area, a mosaic forest of hardwoods and softwoods provides a good opportunity to look for pileated woodpeckers and yellow-bellied sapsuckers.

Directions

From the intersection of Route 3 and Route 233 in Bar Harbor, take Route 233 west toward Cadillac Mountain. There are two parking areas for the carriage road in 2.1 miles, one on the right and one on the left.

Trip #24

Day Mountain

Rating: Moderate
Distance: 8.0 miles
Elevation Gain: 500 feet
Estimated Time: 2.5 hours

A moderate ride to great views of the Atlantic Ocean and the islands to the south and west of Mount Desert Island.

DAY MOUNTAIN is the only peak in Acadia that you can climb via the carriage roads. When John D. Rockefeller Jr. was having the carriage roads constructed, he originally decided against building them over mountaintops. He agreed to this road because Day Mountain is a relatively small peak, 583 feet tall, and it was possible to build the road so that it was not visible from any other peaks. Bikers visiting Acadia National Park are glad he made this decision. This trip is an enjoyable one, as you climb above the trees to sweeping vistas of the open Atlantic and the islands to the south and west of the park.

Begin this ride by heading east on the carriage road next to the Jordan Pond Gatehouse, across the Park Loop Road from the Jordan Pond House. Rockefeller had the prominent New York architect Grosvenor Atterbury design the Jordan Pond Gatehouse, which was constructed in the early 1930s. It was designed along the lines of a European hunting lodge in the French Romanesque architectural style. Another gatehouse was built near Lower Hadlock Pond outside of Northeast Harbor. These gatehouses were built to provide a place for attendants to live while manning the gates that would allow carriages in but not automobiles. The gatehouses are no longer occupied, and the gates are left closed except for Park Service maintenance vehicles.

Day Mountain is the only summit that can be climbed via the carriage road system. The Cranberry Islands are in the distance.

The first 0.25 mile is a nice downhill coast before the road begins a long, gradual ascent. After passing above Wildwood Stables, the carriage road reaches post #17 at 1.2 miles. Turn right and cross the Triad-Day Bridge. Completed in 1940, this was the last of the carriage-road bridges to be built. Across the bridge, you will come to post #37. Turn right to circle around the west side of Day Mountain. You will need to watch your speed on a long downhill stretch here in order to maintain control and avoid accidents with horses or other bikes. At 1.8 miles you will reach post #38, where you should continue straight through a forest of spruce, fir, birch, and maple. From post #38, the road begins its gradual ascent toward the summit of Day Mountain. On your left you will see a low but beautiful retaining wall made of bowling-ball-sized boulders of pink granite.

At 2.5 miles, turn left at post #36 to ride the final 1.5 miles up to the summit. As you gain elevation, spectacular views open up of the Atlantic Ocean to the east and the Cranberry Islands to the south. The climb is steady but moderate, and long stretches of the carriage road are well above the trees, so the views are constant while you ride. At 3.7 miles you will reach the summit, which has excellent views to the south of the Cranberry Islands, Duck Island, Isle au Haut, and the western mountains. With its quiet woods and good views, Day Mountain is a great place for a picnic lunch.

Return down the carriage road to post #36, where you should turn left. You will have to watch your speed again on the descent, as there are many tight corners. Between post #36 and post #37 are more good views of the Atlantic before you drop down for good into the shade of the cool forest. When you reach post #37, you are back at the Triad-Day Bridge, which spans the Park Loop Road. Cross the bridge and turn left at post #17. About 100 yards past post #17, take the right fork in the road, as the left fork is used as an access from Wildwood Stables. From here, retrace your route back to the Jordan Pond House.

Directions

From the Acadia National Park Visitor Center, drive south on the Park Loop Road for 7.3 miles. Be sure to continue straight at the intersections marked Sand Beach and Cadillac Mountain. The Jordan Pond parking area will be on your right. The carriage road for this trip begins next to the Jordan Pond Gatehouse, across the road from the Jordan Pond House.

Jordan Pond–Bubble Pond Loop

Rating: Moderate

Distance: 9.0 miles

Elevation Gain: 500 feet

Estimated Time: 2.5 hours

A moderate ride next to the dramatic scenery of Jordan and Bubble Ponds.

JORDAN POND is arguably the most scenic pond in Acadia National Park, with its deep blue waters reflecting the steep cliffs of Penobscot Mountain and the graceful curves of the Bubbles. Bubble Pond is smaller and more intimate, with dramatic scenery of its own as the steep west face of Cadillac Mountain rises above its eastern shoreline. This is one of the longer rides in the carriage-road system, but its grades are never steep. For this reason it makes a great day trip for a family with older children who are comfortable spending the day on bikes. Of course, following your ride you can recharge your system with tea and popovers at the Jordan Pond House.

Begin this trip by turning onto the carriage road across the street from the Jordan Pond Gatehouse. Turn right at post #16 and go straight at post #15. At 0.3 mile, a small bridge crosses the outlet to Jordan Pond as the carriage road climbs up to post #14 at 0.5 mile, where you should continue straight. The road continues its upward trek through a mixed forest until Jordan Pond and the Bubbles come into view at 1.25 miles. The road crosses a huge rock slide where giant boulders line the steep east face of Penobscot Mountain.

George Dorr, the first superintendent of Acadia National Park, feared that constructing a road through such a treacherous rock slide was a risky proposition. John Rockefeller Jr. and his contractor man-

Bubble Pond was created by glaciers during the last ice age between 15,000 and 18,000 years ago.

aged to assure Dorr that no one would get hurt, and they were allowed to proceed. The views from this stretch of the carriage road are fantastic. The pond is about 150 feet below the road, and you can see the Bubbles as well as the entire south ridge of Pemetic Mountain. You can also look straight up at Jordan Cliffs, home to one of Acadia's nesting pairs of peregrine falcons.

As you re-enter the forest, you are rewarded with a crossing of Deer Brook Bridge. This bridge, with its pair of tall, narrow arches, gives you a close-up view of Deer Brook as it cascades in a waterfall over large slabs of pink granite. The Deer Brook Trail, on the south side of the bridge, makes its way up to Sargent Pond and Sargent and Penobscot Mountains (see trip #11). After the falls, the ride levels out as you pass the north end of Jordan Pond and head toward Eagle Lake. At 2.5 miles, turn right at post #10. At 2.7 miles, turn right again at post #8. At this point you are about 500 feet up to the west of Eagle Lake behind a small peak called Conners Nubble. At 3.2 miles, you cross a hiking trail that you can use to walk quickly up to the summit for a nice view of Eagle Lake.

After passing Conners Nubble, the road makes a long descent to the southern end of Eagle Lake, which is surrounded by thick spruce forest. This forest is a great place to look for finches such as red crossbills, white-winged crossbills, pine siskins, and common redpolls. Except for redpolls, all these finches breed in the park, but their numbers are highly variable. These finches of the boreal forest tend to migrate in waves depending on the severity of the weather and the abundance of the seed crop, so their numbers in any one area can change greatly from year to year.

At 4.5 miles, turn right at post #7 to ride toward Bubble Pond. You will cross the Park Loop Road at 4.8 miles and pass by the northern end of Bubble Pond. You then cross a bridge that seems to cross nothing but forest. The bridge was built to cross the Park Loop Road, which was subsequently relocated because it passed too close to the pond. Bubble Pond Bridge was constructed of compressed rock, as opposed to the granite blocks used for the rest of the bridges in the park. After crossing the bridge, the road turns left and follows the shoreline of Bubble Pond. Pemetic Mountain rises steeply to the west. Across the pond to the east is the steep west face of Cadillac Mountain. Cedar and paper birch grow on the shoreline as well as on the ledges on Cadillac. During the spring and fall migrations, you can see hawks, eagles, falcons, and vultures riding the thermals above Cadillac. Turkey vultures are known to use the huge boulders at the southeastern end of the pond as a resting spot. They blend in well with the gray rocks, so you may need binoculars to spot them.

As the road continues past the pond, it passes through a variety of forest types: spruce-fir, northern hardwood, cedar. In the northern hardwood forest, you will notice irregularly shaped and dying beech trees which are infected with a blight that is a combination of a fungus and a scale and was introduced by European beech trees imported in the nineteenth century. While bad for the trees, the blight does benefit the insects that feed on the dying trees as well as the woodpeckers and flickers that feed on the insects. Nonetheless, the loss of a large number of American beech trees would be devastating to the forest animals that depend on beechnuts for food. Scientists are still unsure as to the long-term effects of this blight on the beech forests of North America.

After rounding the southern end of the Triad, go straight at post #17 (7.7 miles). The road then climbs for 0.5 mile as it traverses the west side of the Triad behind Wildwood Stables to views of the Cranberry Islands. From here it is an easy coast back down to the Jordan Pond Gatehouse.

Directions

From the Acadia National Park Visitor Center, drive south on the Park Loop Road for 7.3 miles. Be sure to continue straight at the intersections marked Sand Beach and Cadillac Mountain. The Jordan Pond parking area will be on your right. The carriage road for this trip begins across the street from the Jordan Pond Gatehouse.

acadia's mosaic forest

Mosaic is a term Acadia's naturalists use to describe much of the forest on the eastern half of Mount Desert Island. It is a forest with a high diversity of tree species that does not fit into the normal forest-habitat categories, e.g., northern hardwoods or boreal. This mosaic forest came about after the great fire of 1947. Before the fire, a boreal forest of red spruce and balsam fir covered most of the island. The thick canopy of the spruce and fir trees made it nearly impossible for other trees to grow. With the spruce-fir canopy gone, sun-loving trees such as birch, aspen, and maple were able to take root. White pine also grew quickly, while spruce and fir saplings sprouted from the stumps of trees killed in the fire. The result is a forest that is part boreal, part northern hardwoods.

With a new forest of deciduous trees, Acadia became a different place. Visually, Acadia now experiences the brilliant fall foliage displays that make New England famous. Wildlife concentrations are also different. Beaver, which eat birch and aspen, are much more common in the park now compared to fifty years ago. Their presence has created an increase in wetland habitats which in turn has attracted more river otters. These additional wetlands nur-

A northern hardwood forest in fall as seen from South Bubble.

ture fish, crayfish, and amphibians that attract not only otters, but also birds such as great blue herons and king-fishers. The forest itself provides good habitat for a myriad of songbirds, including yellow warblers, scarlet tanagers, and northern orioles, as well as pileated wood-peckers and ruffed grouse. White-tailed deer numbers are up, as they feed on acorns and the twigs of young birches and aspens.

Giant Slide Loop

Rating: Difficult

Distance: 8.5 miles

Elevation Gain: 600 feet

Estimated Time: 2.5 hours

A ride over rushing mountain streams to spectacular ocean and mountain views.

THIS TRIP BEGINS with a long ride over relatively flat terrain to the northwest of Parkman and Sargent Mountains. It then visits a beautiful meadow with views of the mountains before beginning a long and steep climb up the north side of Sargent Mountain. The 600-foot climb is well worth the effort, though, as views open up all the way to the Camden Hills, thirty miles away. With wetlands, streams, and several different forest types, this trip also provides excellent opportunities for nature study.

Starting at the Parkman Mountain parking area, follow the carriage road to the left, away from post #13. The 3.3 miles to post #11 is almost all downhill, following a gentle grade through a dark green evergreen forest. The road crosses several small streams tumbling down from Sargent and Parkman Mountains. As you get closer to post #11, wetlands begin to appear on the left and the forest changes, with deciduous trees such as northern red oak, maple, and birch taking over the flat valley floor. Northern red oak is the northernmost oak in the eastern United States, and its range extends well into Quebec and Ontario. While it is most often associated with the oak-hickory forests to the south and west of Maine, in northern New England and Canada northern red oak can be found in northern hardwood forests. Like most oaks, it can grow to be tall and stately, producing bumper crops of acorns every three or four years.

lichens

Lichens are usually the first organisms to colonize bare rock after glaciers, fire, rock slides, or other events remove the layers of soil that sustain plant growth. Lichens that grow on bare rock are called crustose lichens and cling closely to the rock, looking more like a discolored section of rock than a living organism. Crustose lichens are common on Acadia's ledges and subalpine summits as well as on rocks along the carriage roads. Foliose lichens grow more upright, look more plantlike, and will colonize rocks after crustose lichens. They can also be found on trees and buildings.

Lichens come in a wide variety of shapes and colors, making it difficult to believe they are related to one another in any way. What makes a lichen a lichen? Lichens are actually two plants in one: a fungus and an alga. Their relationship is one of mutualism, as one can not survive without the other. The alga photosynthesizes light, producing food for the fungus, which provides the means for the alga to stay rooted to a rock or tree. Crustose lichens are flat and come in colors like black, gray, brown, green, yellow, and orange.

Foliose lichens vary widely in shape. In Acadia, you can find foliose lichens such as rock tripe, a black or dark brown leafy lichen that clings to rocks that are also covered in crustose lichens. British soldiers are foliose lichens that have red fruiting bodies at the end of green, scaly stalks and grow on rocks and mossy downed wood. Reindeer lichen is a silver-gray lichen that resembles many small deer antlers or tree branches.

Lichens are extremely durable plants, surviving in the harshest environments on Earth. They can survive long periods of drought, and some specimens are estimated to live as long as 4,000 years. However, they are not so tolerant of human-caused environmental degradation. They show a marked lack of tolerance for air pollution, dying off quickly in areas with air-quality problems. Acadia's lichens are in good shape except in areas where hiking trails cross bare rock, as they can not survive the constant impact of hiking boots.

At post #11, you reach Gilmore Meadow, a freshwater wetland with a great view of Sargent Mountain. The meadow, with its narrow meandering channel, surrounded by a wet, grassy swamp, is a great place to look for small birds such as sparrows, flycatchers, and warblers. Turn right at post #11 for a short downhill coast before beginning the steepest climb in the carriage-road system. The road enters a mixed evergreen and hardwood forest, passing through a grove of hemlocks as it makes several stream crossings over a series of uncharacteristic concrete and wooden bridges. At 4.4 miles you will reach post #10, where you should turn right.

The steep climb continues as you wind your way up the north face of Sargent Mountain. At 4.9 miles you reach Chasm Brook Bridge. Built in 1926, this bridge provides a welcome resting point where you can listen to the rushing water of Chasm Brook as it cascades over a forty-foot waterfall. The road continues up the mountain using switchbacks to make the climb more amenable. As you get higher, the hills of northern and eastern Maine come into view. Climbing still, Blue Hill and Acadia's western mountains appear to the west. At 6.3 miles the road crosses the Sargent Mountain North Ridge Trail, where the ride levels out.

As you round the north side of Parkman Mountain, you get wide-open views of Somes Sound and all of Maine to the west. The road stays in the open for much of its way down from Parkman Mountain. Pitch pines and white pines cling to the rock ledges amidst clumps of blueberry bushes and lichen. At 8.1 miles, turn right at post #12. Turn right again at post #13 at 8.4 miles. The parking area is on the left in another 0.1 mile.

Directions

For this trip, park at the Parkman Mountain parking area on Routes 198/3, 1.8 miles north of Northeast Harbor.

Around the Mountain Loop

Rating: Difficult

Distance: 12.0 miles

Elevation Gain: 1,000 feet

Estimated Time: 4 hours

This ride has it all: three waterfalls, mountain and ocean views, and seven major bridge crossings.

IT IS NOT CLEAR which mountain the person who named this loop had in mind, for it actually loops around six: Penobscot Mountain, Cedar Swamp Mountain, Bald Peak, Parkman Mountain, Gilmore Peak, and Sargent Mountain. It begins and ends next to the deep blue waters of picturesque Jordan Pond. For twelve miles, it rises and falls through almost every forest type in the park, passes steep cliffs and waterfalls, and climbs to dramatic views of the areas surrounding Acadia National Park. It is long by carriage-road standards and gains more elevation than any other loop in the park. Nevertheless, strong riders can still complete it in less than half a day. However, it is easy to spend the entire day studying the details of nature and soaking in the long-distance views.

Begin this trip by turning onto the carriage road across the street from the Jordan Pond Gatehouse. Turn right at post #16 and go straight at post #15. At 0.3 mile, a small bridge crosses the outlet to Jordan Pond, as the carriage road climbs up to post #14 at 0.5 mile, where you should turn left. A short but steep climb brings you to the modest West Branch Bridge with its single tall, narrow arch spanning a small stream tumbling down Penobscot Mountain. You continue to climb until 1.2 miles when you reach the 230-foot-long Cliffside Bridge, which has the style of a fortress from the Middle Ages. Two large viewing turrets invite you to look out at Pemetic and Day Mountains, as well as the Triad. Maples and other hardwoods dominate the foreground, while spruce and fir cling to the distant mountains.

As you round the southern end of Penobscot Mountain, you come to post #21, where you should continue straight toward the Amphitheater. The road gently rises through a mosaic forest, and views of the rounded ridges that make up the Amphitheater soon come into view. At 2.2 miles, you reach the head of the Amphitheater and the 235-foot-long bridge that crosses the small gorge there. Walking down a trail at the west end of the bridge will take you down to Little Harbor Brook, where you can look through the arch in the bridge to a small waterfall.

Continuing past the bridge, turn right at post #20 for a gradual climb up to views of the Cranberry Islands. As you ride toward post #19, notice the variety of lichens that grow on the rocks lining the road. Green target lichen grows in concentric rings. Brown-and-black rock tripe looks like lettuce gone bad clinging to the rocks. Reindeer lichen grows in bunches, its greenish white branches looking like antlers. It is actually eaten by reindeer and caribou in the arctic environments where they live. There are also large clumps of rhodora, an evergreen shrub that grows in bogs and other areas with acidic soils. When you reach post #19 at 3.6 miles, turn right.

At 5.0 miles you reach a pair of magnificent bridges that span Hadlock Brook and Maple Spring. Waterfall Bridge looks out at Hadlock Brook as it tumbles over forty feet of granite. Hemlock Bridge spans Maple Spring, which is lined with tall hemlocks and white pines. An enchanted-forest feeling creeps in as you ride over these intricate bridges through tall trees surrounded by the sounds of water and bird song. The road then climbs to views of Upper Hadlock Pond and the Cranberries at post #12 (5.5 miles). Turn right to begin one of the longest climbs in the carriage-road system.

The carriage road goes up for most of the next 1.8 miles, reaching an elevation of 800 feet. The road traverses the western shoulder of Parkman Mountain, rising through a forest of pitch pine on its way to extensive views to the west and north. Somes Sound, the only fiord in the eastern United States, can be seen just to the west of the road, with Acadia, Beech, and Bernard Mountains rising up to the west of the sound. As you get higher and round the northern end of Sargent Mountain, the wind gets a little stronger and the air a little colder. At this point, the views open up to include Mount Desert Narrows and northern Maine.

This section of the carriage roads on Parkman Mountian is part of both the Around the Mountain Loop and the Giant Slide Loop.

Once you pass the Sargent Mountain North Ridge Trail at 7.3 miles, you are rewarded with a long, winding, downhill coast that will take you back to Jordan Pond. It is easy to pick up a lot of speed on this stretch. Try to control your speed, because it is fairly likely that someone will be stopped on the road, hidden behind a curve. You will have good views of Eagle Lake on the way down. Notice how the forest is sharply demarcated between spruce-fir and paper birch. Spruce-fir forests dominated the island before the great fire of 1947. After the fire, pioneer species such as aspen, birch, and other hardwoods grew back in place of the spruce and fir. In this area, thin soil has made it hard for trees to return, and the paper birch that are growing are very thin and spindly. By identifying the different forest types, it is easy to see where the fire did its damage.

At 8.7 miles you cross a small bridge over Chasm Brook, which falls about forty feet over the rocks to the south of the bridge. At 9.2 miles, go straight at post #10. A slight incline brings you to another waterfall and the Deer Brook Bridge at 10.0 miles. The north end of Jordan Pond begins to come into view through the trees on the left. Continuing south, you will break out into the open as you pass

road trips

While bike-riding enthusiasts flock to Acadia's gravel carriage-road system, those who enjoy biking the pavement can find several enjoyable trips around the island. The following is a brief description of bike-riding trips on the roads in and around Acadia National Park.

- The Park Loop Road—19 miles. From Bar Harbor, take Kebo Road 1.2 miles to the Park Loop Road. The ride must be completed in a clockwise direction, since much of the road is one-way. This trip will take you to many of the park's highlights, including Champlain Mountain, Sand Beach, Otter Cliffs, and Jordan Pond.

- Schooner Head and Sand Beach—12 miles. This trip takes you from Bar Harbor to the Schooner Head Overlook's dramatic view of the Atlantic Ocean. It also visits Sand Beach, Ocean Drive, and the Tarn, a glacially carved pond beneath the steep cliffs of Dorr Mountain. Follow Route 3 out of town, and turn right onto Schooner Head Road. At the end of Schooner Head Road, the ocean view is a few hundred yards to the left. To the right is the Park Loop Road. Follow the Park Loop Road past Sand Beach and along Ocean Drive. At the end of Ocean Drive, turn right onto Otter Cliffs Road, which takes you back to Route 3. To complete your loop, turn right on Route 3.

- Western Side, Routes 102/102A—26 miles. Following Route 102 around the western side of Mount Desert Island gives you the opportunity to visit Long Pond, Bass Harbor Head Light, Seawall, Echo Lake, and the town of Southwest Harbor. From Somesville follow Route 102 south, turning right at the blinking yellow light. Route 102 basically loops around this side of the island. Pass the little town of Tremont and turn right onto 102A, heading toward Bass Harbor and Seawall. Just before reaching Southwest Harbor, you reconnect with 102, which you can follow north back to Somesville.

- Schoodic Peninsula—12 miles. From Route 186 in Winter Harbor, follow Moore Road south along the very scenic coastline of the Schoodic Peninsula. As you pass the picturesque scene of lobster boats in Bunker's Harbor and then Birch Harbor, turn left on Route 186 to return to Winter Harbor.

- Swans Island. An enjoyable, forty-minute ferry ride from Bass Harbor takes you to Swans Island. Its 16 miles of roads provide plenty of opportunity for spending your day exploring the hills and valleys of the island's 7,000 acres. Hockamock Head Lighthouse is probably the most popular attraction on the island, with rural countryside and ocean views making up the bulk of the scenery.

These road trips are a great way to get out of your car and see the island up close, but remember that you are sharing the road with cars which travel at speeds up to fifty-five miles an hour. Wear bright colors and follow the same rules of the road you follow while driving a car.

through a massive rock slide on the east face of Penobscot Mountain. Here you will have a great look at Jordan Pond, the Bubbles, and Pemetic Mountain. Looming above you are Jordan Cliffs. At 11.3 miles, bear left at post #14, which completes the loop. To finish your trip, stay to the left at posts #15 and #16.

Directions

From the Acadia National Park Visitor Center, drive south on the Park Loop Road for 7.3 miles. Be sure to continue straight at the intersections marked Sand Beach and Cadillac Mountain. The Jordan Pond parking area will be on your right. The carriage road for this trip begins across the street from the Jordan Pond Gatehouse.

6
quietwater paddling in acadia

EXPERIENCING ACADIA's quiet inland waters from a canoe or kayak is a great way to get a new look at the beauty of Mount Desert Island. From the grand vistas of Eagle Lake to the quiet comfort of Little Long Pond, all of these paddles are suitable for families and solo paddlers alike. These trips also provide excellent wildlife-watching opportunities: loons and ducks and occasionally bald eagles, ospreys, and river otters all can be spotted in Acadia's inland waters. While we did omit a few of the island's smaller ponds, this chapter is a fairly complete description of the quietwater paddling available in Acadia National Park. The following trips take you from serene paddles through waterlilies to dramatic cliffside paddling to meandering explorations in a bird-filled marsh.

Paddling Times and Distances

The distances listed on our trips basically assume you will follow the shoreline of the pond for most of the trip. Trips will be shorter in distance if you paddle directly from point A to point B and back, but we expect that most people will like to explore the shoreline for at least part of a trip to look for animals, flowers, and resting spots. Paddling times can vary widely based on paddlers' experience, physical conditioning, and curiosity. We have tried to come up with the time it would take a paddler of average strength and experience to complete these trips with only one short rest break to eat a snack. If you have a group of very curious paddlers, expect your trips to take a bit longer.

Safety and Etiquette

While paddling on Mount Desert Island is a fairly safe activity, cold and deep waters combined with regularly changing weather conditions require certain safety precautions. To ensure a safe and comfortable paddling experience, consider the following safety tips:

- Know how to use your canoe or kayak. Of course, lakes and ponds like those in Acadia are the perfect place for inexperienced paddlers to learn, but if you are new to the sport, you should at least have someone show you some basic paddling strokes and impress upon you how best to enter and exit your particular boat. New paddlers should consider staying close to shore until they are more comfortable with their paddling skills. Luckily, some of the most interesting aspects of the trips in this chapter are found close to shore.

- Turn around *before* the members of your party start feeling tired. Paddling a few miles after your arms are already spent can make for cranky travelers. All of the trips in this book start and end at the same location, so you can easily turn around at any time.

- Make sure everyone in your group is wearing a life jacket or personal flotation device (PFD). You are required by Maine law to have at least one PFD per person in your boat. We suggest that you actually wear them while paddling. It is very easy to tip a canoe accidentally and, with Acadia's ponds reaching depths of 150 feet, it just makes sense to wear a PFD at all times.

- Pay close attention to the winds. Winds as gentle as ten miles per hour can create some fairly large waves on all of the ponds on the island. Two- and three-foot waves are not unusual on Eagle Lake, Long Pond, and Echo Lake. We even paddled in one-foot waves on the fairly diminutive Jordan Pond. All of the ponds on the island run from north to south, making northerly or southerly winds even more problematic. Bring a windbreaker, as it can get cold in a canoe in the lightest of winds. Little Long Pond is probably your best bet on a windy day.

- Stay off the water if thunderstorms are nearby. Lightning is a serious danger to boaters. If you hear a thunderstorm approaching, get off the water immediately and seek shelter. For a current weather forecast, call the WDEA weather phone at 207-667-8910.

- Bring the following supplies along with you to make the trip more comfortable. Why not, when you don't have to carry them on your back?

  Water—One or two quarts per person, depending on the weather and length of the trip

  Food—Even for a short paddle, it is a good idea to bring some high-energy snacks like nuts, dried fruit, or snack bars. Bring a lunch for longer trips.

  Map and compass—And the ability to use them

  Extra clothing—Rain gear, wool sweater or fleece jacket, wool or fleece hat

  Flashlight

  Sunscreen and hat—You will be at the mercy of the sun on a clear day

  First-aid kit

  Pocketknife

  Binoculars—For wildlife viewing

In addition to the no-impact techniques described in this book's introduction, please keep the following things in mind while paddling:

- Give wildlife a wide berth. Lakes and ponds are much different from forests in that wildlife has less of an opportunity to hide from humans. The summer months see a lot of people in the water, and the ducks, herons, and loons waste a good deal of energy just swimming or flying away from curious boaters. If you spot wildlife, remain still and quiet and let the animals decide whether to approach you. Use binoculars if you want a closer view. In spring, steer well clear of loons nesting along the shore.

- Respect private property. Much of the land surrounding the waters of Acadia is private property. We have mentioned this fact in each of the trip descriptions, but take a map that shows the park boundaries. Do not land your boat on private property, and speak quietly when paddling near homes and cottages.

- Respect the purity of the water. Most of the ponds on Mount Desert Island are used for drinking water by the surrounding communities. If you need to relieve yourself, try to do so on land, at least 100 yards from the shoreline. Echo Lake is the only pond in the park where swimming is allowed.

- Sound carries a long way on the water, so try to keep your conversations quiet in order to not disturb other paddlers or nearby hikers.

You can thank the last ice age for your chance at quietwater paddling on Mount Desert Island. Ice sculpted the landscape into deep, cold-water ponds which reflect the rounded masses of pink granite that give Acadia its mountainous allure. Glaciers plowed through rock, creating cliffs that reach down to the water's edge on Long Pond, Jordan Pond, and Echo Lake. They created the deep waters of Eagle Lake, which remain cold enough throughout the year to support such cold-water fish as trout and salmon, which in turn support ospreys and bald eagles. The ice also left shallow depressions like Seal Cove Pond and Little Long Pond, which harbor marshes filled with wading birds and waterfowl, painted turtles and green frogs. Surrounded by enchanting scenery and abundant wildlife, you are sure to enjoy your time on the water!

Little Long Pond

> **Distance: 1.25 miles round-trip**
>
> **Estimated Time: 1 hour**
>
> **A short and easy paddle on one of Mount Desert Island's most picturesque ponds.**

LITTLE LONG POND, with its gently sloping lawns and beautiful views of Penobscot Mountain, is an easy and quiet place to paddle that is suitable for the entire family. While the pond is only about 0.5 mile long, it still provides a surprising amount of solitude during early-morning paddles. Owned by the Rockefellers, the pond and the surrounding lawns are open to the public and seem to have been landscaped for leisure. The lawns are an ideal spot to have a picnic, take a nap, and listen to the sounds of Mount Desert Island. You can also enjoy an easy walk around the pond on a wide, grassy path.

The route for this paddle is very simple. Put in at the southern end of the pond, along Maine Route 3. Paddle straight ahead for 0.5 mile to the north end of the pond and then return. Along the way, you will enjoy pink and white waterlilies and cattails hiding green frogs, mallards, and black ducks. The old boathouse on the eastern shore was built for John D. Rockefeller Jr. It is an impressive structure for such a small body of water. The marshlike northern end of the pond is home to an active beaver lodge. The beaver are nocturnal but may be seen during the early morning and the late afternoon swimming across the pond, carrying branches from a birch, maple, or willow tree. They store these branches underwater near their lodges and use them as food.

Beaver are not the only wildlife you might see here. Great blue herons wade near the shore, hunting for small fish, amphibians, and snakes. Belted kingfishers fly from tree to tree, making an occasional dive into the pond hoping to catch a fish. While on shore, watch

Canoeing in sight of Parkman Mountain on Little Long Pond.

and listen for the largest of New England woodpeckers, the pileated woodpecker. About the size of a crow, this bird is black and white with a bright red crest on its head, and makes a loud *kuk, kuk, kuk, kuk, kuk* call. This woodpecker excavates large, rectangular holes in trees as it searches for ants and termites to extract from the wood with its sticky tongue. Unlike the similar-looking, but extinct, ivory-billed woodpecker, the pileated woodpecker has adapted comfortably to second-growth forests near small towns, and it is now common in the woods of Maine.

Directions

From Bar Harbor, drive south on Maine Route 3 for 8.8 miles. Little Long Pond will be on your right. You can park on the wide gravel shoulder next to the pond.

frogs and turtles

While visiting the freshwater ponds, swamps, and streams in Acadia you may encounter frogs and turtles, from the diminutive spring peeper to the menacing snapping turtle. Seven species of frogs are known to live in Acadia. Five of those are relatively common: spring peeper, bullfrog, green frog, pickerel frog, and wood frog. The gray tree frog and leopard frog are less common. As many as six species of turtles live in the park, but only two, the snapping turtle and the eastern painted turtle, are common. While out there paddling or hiking near water, keep your eyes out for the following:

Spring peepers are more likely to be heard than seen. Considered chorus frogs but also exhibiting characteristics of tree frogs, spring peepers fill the night air in spring with their loud chorus of frog song. They prefer small, often temporary bodies of water near trees. These tiny frogs are less than an inch long and are usually brown or gray with a dark X on their backs.

Bullfrogs are the largest frogs in the United States, measuring from three and a half to six inches in length. They are either green or brown and gray with a green background. They can be found in lakes, ponds, bogs, and streams and have a voracious appetite, eating almost anything they can swallow, including small snakes.

Green frogs are smaller than bullfrogs, measuring two and a quarter to three and a half inches in length and tend to be greenish brown in color. In rare cases they may even be blue. Green frogs tend to like shallower water than bullfrogs, spending their time in brooks, small streams, and the edges of lakes and ponds.

Pickerel frogs are one and three-quarters to three inches in length and have square spots arranged in two parallel rows down their backs. They often have bright yellow or orange coloring on their hind legs. Pickerels prefer the clear, cold waters of sphagnum bogs, rocky ravines, and meadow streams.

Wood frogs are slightly smaller than pickerels but have an unmistakable "robber's mask," a dark patch around the eye. Wood frogs are generally brown, blending in well with leaf litter on the forest floor. They spend a lot of their time in moist woods, away from water.

Snapping turtles reach lengths of eighteen inches, weigh up to fifty pounds, and can live as long as 100 years. They are easily recognized by their large heads, beaklike mouths, long tails, and very rough, brownish-black shell. "Snappers" are voracious omnivores, eating small invertebrates, fish, reptiles, small birds, mammals, and vegetation. They will live in any permanent body of fresh water and spend a good deal of their time partially submerged in mud and shallow water. Luckily for swimmers, they tend to pull their heads in when underwater, letting people step on them and pass by unknowingly. On land, they will bite if harassed.

Eastern painted turtles are much smaller than snappers, measuring four to six inches in length, and are easily identified by their colorful red, yellow, and black shells. They commonly bask in small groups on rocks, riverbanks, and downed trees next to water with a muddy bottom and profuse aquatic vegetation, which is their favored food. They also eat insects, crustaceans, and small mollusks.

Frogs have been found recently throughout the United States with severe physical deformities, most commonly having extra sets of legs. Scientists have discovered that one cause of these deformities is a parasitic flatworm. While it has yet to be proven, scientists believe that pollution may be an additional cause. Breathing through their moist skin, all amphibians may be especially susceptible to acid rain, airborne pollutants such as mercury, and endocrine-system-disturbing chemicals like dioxin and PCBs. Acadia's frogs have yet to show these deformities, but if you happen to discover an individual with more than four legs you should report it to a park naturalist.

Echo Lake

> **Distance: 1.5 miles round-trip**
>
> **Estimated Time: 1 hour**
>
> **A short paddle below towering cliffs, with a chance to see peregrine falcons.**

ECHO LAKE is home to the AMC's Echo Lake Camp and Echo Lake Beach, the most popular place on the island to swim. At the southern end of the lake, Echo Lake Camp, with its comfortable tents, dining room, library, fireplace and hot showers, is a great place to bring the family for the week. Next to it is sandy Echo Lake Beach, with warm waters, lifeguards, and changing rooms. Echo Lake itself runs up against Beech Cliff and Canada Cliff, which both rise 150 feet straight up from the water's edge. The north end of the lake is fairly populated with cottages, and Route 102 runs next to the eastern shore for about 0.5 mile. For these reasons, this trip explores the southern end of the lake.

Put your boat in at Ikes Landing on the west side of Maine Route 102. There is plenty of parking in this lot, as Echo Lake is popular with both paddlers and motorboats. From the put-in, paddle your boat straight across the lake and then turn left to follow the shore toward the cliffs of Beech Mountain. Keep the shoreline on your right for the remainder of this trip. The cliffs of Beech Mountain are home to one of the three nesting pairs of peregrine falcons in the park. Point your binoculars skyward to search for these most efficient and speedy fliers. While they may hunt occasionally for ducks or other birds on Echo Lake, they often head out to the shorelines around Mount Desert Island to hunt for seabirds. Common loons also frequent Echo Lake. While not endangered, these birds have been declining in number for most of this century. It is against the law in the state of Maine to harass loons, so please do not approach them. Hearing their haunting call is just as exciting as seeing them up close.

Like most of the other ponds and lakes on the island, Echo Lake was created by glaciers during the last ice age. Carving out the lake to a depth of sixty-five feet, the ice also created the cliffs of Beech Mountain. Water ahead of the glacier filled cracks in the rock and froze. Freezing and thawing continued, weakening the granite until the glacier moved over the mountain and plucked boulders off the mountainside, creating the cliffs. The glacier also deposited the sand at the southern end of Echo Lake, creating Echo Lake Beach. The beach is popular with families, so pay attention for stray swimmers while paddling near the shore.

After paddling past the beach and the AMC camp, follow the shoreline north. As you paddle back toward the put-in, you will encounter about 0.5 mile of undeveloped national-park shoreline, where you can pull over for a private lunch or swim or a quiet moment to soak in the sounds and smells of the Maine Woods.

Paddling on Echo Lake.

echo lake camp

At the south end of Echo Lake, the AMC maintains Echo Lake Camp, a comfortable summer campground for families wishing to avoid the hustle and bustle of Bar Harbor. Accommodations are tents with board floors, beds, mattresses, pillows, and bedding. There is a shared bathhouse with hot showers as well as a library, recreation hall, dining room, and kitchen where your hosts will cook up your family-style meals. With access to Echo Lake outside your tent door, the camp provides rowboats, canoes, kayaks, and sailboats. Once a week the camp hosts a lobster picnic and clambake, and twice a week you have the opportunity to participate in trail maintenance.

Echo Lake Camp is usually open July 4 weekend through Labor Day. A one-week, Saturday-to-Saturday stay is required. The camp is not appropriate for children under four, and pets are not allowed. Despite these restrictions, tent space fills up quickly, so you will want to make reservations well ahead of time. For current prices and reservation information, contact the AMC at 617-523-0655.

Directions

From Somesville, drive south on Maine Route 102. At 2.7 miles from Pretty Marsh Road is a national-park sign on the right for Ikes Point. Turn right into the driveway, which leads to a parking area and the put-in.

Jordan Pond

> **Distance: 2.5 miles round-trip**
>
> **Estimated Time: 2 hours**
>
> **An easy paddle on one of the most scenic ponds in Maine.**

JORDAN POND has been a popular destination for visitors to Mount Desert Island ever since the first tourists started making their way to the island in the 1850s. One reason for this popularity is undoubtedly the Jordan Pond House, which has been serving afternoon tea at the south end of the pond since the 1870s. Of course, the incredible beauty of the area is just as big a draw. Jordan Pond, at 150 feet deep, is the deepest of Acadia's ponds and lakes, scraped out by the same glacier that gave the Bubbles their rounded appearance at the north end of the pond. The western side of the pond sits directly below Jordan Cliffs, a steep wall of granite on the east face of Penobscot Mountain. The long, sloping south ridge of Pemetic Mountain looms to the east. The pond is only about a mile long, making paddling trips here relatively short in duration. Of course that leaves plenty of time for tea and popovers at the Jordan Pond House.

The put-in for Jordan Pond is not at the teahouse but next to the Jordan Pond hiker parking area (located just to the north of the Jordan Pond House on the Park Loop Road). As you put in your boat on the eastern shore of the pond, you will be facing Penobscot Mountain and Jordan Cliffs. Blueberry bushes turn a fire-engine red in the fall on the side of Jordan Cliffs, which are home to one of Acadia's nesting pairs of peregrine falcons. As you paddle into the pond and turn to the right, you will be looking at one of the classic views in Acadia—Jordan Pond and the Bubbles. The Bubbles are a pair of rounded pink-granite peaks that are certainly bubble-like in shape. They are not particularly tall, reaching only 768 feet and 872 feet,

Adirondack chairs on the lawn of the Jordan Pond Teahouse.
Jordan Pond and the Bubbles are in the distance.

but they add a distinctive and beautiful look to the pond's horizon. Like most of the features on Mount Desert Island, the Bubbles were shaped by glaciers during the last ice age, their pink-granite composition being stronger than the surrounding rock, which was scraped away and deposited farther south.

Jordan Pond is home to both common loons and common mergansers in the summer. Female mergansers have rust-colored heads, gray backs, red bills and red feet, while the males have white bodies, black backs, and greenish black heads. Mergansers nest around Jordan Pond, either in tree cavities or on the ground. Unlike loons, which share parenting responsibilities, male mergansers abandon the females while they are incubating the eggs. Merganser chicks usually hatch by the Fourth of July, and those born in tree nests have to jump from the nesting cavity to the ground on their way to the pond. The female mergansers occasionally bring the fuzzy, cue-ball-colored chicks near the Jordan Pond Trail, which follows the shore for most of the pond.

As you paddle toward the northern end of the pond, the cliffs of South Bubble loom closer. The forest beneath the cliffs is a northern hardwood forest, filled with maples, birch, and beech that turn the mountainside a spectacular red, yellow, and orange in the fall. At the northern end of the pond is a small stream which is not navigable by canoe or kayak. The footbridge over the stream is for the Jordan Pond Shore Trail. If you feel like taking a short hike up South Bubble for an elevated view of Jordan Pond, park your canoe here. About fifty yards to the right of the footbridge is the South Bubble Trail, which leads 0.5 mile to the summit, a worthwhile side trip.

During the return trip the Jordan Pond House will be directly in front of you, while the hulking mass of Pemetic Mountain will be on your left.

Directions

From the Acadia National Park Visitor Center, drive south on the Park Loop Road for 7.3 miles. Be sure to continue straight at the intersections marked Sand Beach and Cadillac Mountain. The Jordan Pond parking area will be on your right.

Long Pond, South End

> **Distance: 3.0 miles round-trip**
>
> **Estimated Time: 2 hours**
>
> **A paddle beneath the steep cliffs of Beech and Mansell Mountains on the quiet end of Long Pond.**

THE SOUTHERN END of Long Pond is nestled between the dramatic cliffs of Beech and Mansell Mountains, granite walls hundreds of feet tall. This end of the pond is narrow (about 1,000 feet across) and quiet, as motorboats tend to stay at the larger, northern end of the pond. We found that we could not help but stop paddling from time to time to stare up at the mesmerizing cliffs and cedar-lined shoreline. At four miles long, this is the largest body of fresh water in the park and is home to loons, mergansers, and other waterfowl. Peregrine falcons nest on Beech Mountain and soar in the skies above the pond. Also known as Great Pond, Long Pond's shoreline has long been the home of summer cottages, much like the rest of Mount Desert Island, although here the homes are politely inconspicuous, often completely hidden from view.

The length of the pond and its north-south orientation can create some large waves at the southern end of the pond when the wind is out of the north. During north-wind conditions, the northern end of the pond is a better bet for paddlers (see trip #35). The pond is used as a water source for the town of Southwest Harbor, so take extra care not to pollute. Swimming is not allowed in any part of the pond. Also, try to arrive early because parking is limited to about six or seven cars, and hikers climbing Mansell and Beech Mountains also park here.

From the put-in at the end of Long Pond Road, begin your paddle by following the shoreline on your right. After passing a couple of private homes, you will be surrounded by Acadia National Park shoreline. The pond has a wild feeling here, as thirty-foot-high granite cliffs drop straight into the water. These cliffs are the western shoulder of Beech Mountain, one of the more popular hikes on the western side of Mount Desert Island (see trip #7). Eventually the cliffs recede and the forest comes down to the water's edge, with northern white cedars forming an impenetrable wall of green, their lower branches reaching out over the water to collect as much sunlight as possible. With cliffs and cedars everywhere, it is difficult to land a boat, even a small kayak, on this side of the pond.

As the terrain starts to flatten out, you will soon see a small cottage on the right bank. At this point, paddle over to the western shore of the pond for the trip back. The western side of the pond is also thick with cedars, but there are a few places to land a boat and take a break. If you hear voices, they probably belong to hikers on the Long Pond Trail, which follows the shoreline from here back to the parking area. The shoreline of Long Pond is a good place to look for mink near dusk and dawn as they hunt for fish, frogs, snakes, and mice. About the size of ferrets, mink can swim underwater up to 100 feet and will occasionally pop their heads up out of the water near a canoe, providing a pleasant surprise for the boat's occupants.

As you paddle south along the western shore of the pond, the 700-foot-high cliffs of Mansell Mountain will dominate your field of vision. At its narrowest point, the pond is only 700 feet across with cliffs on both sides. You can almost see the glacier squeezing through the huge granite mounds on either side of the pond, scraping clean the sides of the mountain and pushing the bits of rock and dirt it collects ahead into a terminal moraine, which is now the hill behind the parking area. You can thank the last ice age for providing you with the peaceful paddling and dramatic scenery. The cliffs end just prior to your return to the put-in.

Directions

From the center of Southwest Harbor, go west on Seal Cove Road. Take the first paved road on the right, Long Pond Road. Follow Long Pond Road through a residential area until it ends at the south end of Long Pond. There is a small parking area to the right of the pumping station.

Trip #32

Seal Cove Pond

Distance: 4.5 miles round–trip

Estimated Time: 2.5 hours

A paddle on the westernmost pond on Mount Desert Island, with good opportunities to see waterfowl and bald eagles.

LIKE THE REST of the ponds in Acadia, Seal Cove Pond is long and narrow and runs in a north-south direction. Geologically it is different from most of the other large ponds in the park, as it is shallow and marshy. It also lacks the dramatic scenery of Echo Lake or Long Pond, as there are no cliffs to speak of and Maine Route 102 runs along the western edge of the pond. However, there are plenty of reasons to paddle this pond. Its shallow waters provide a diverse habitat for waterfowl, making this an excellent spot to watch for ducks and wading birds. The eastern shore of the pond is densely forested and has some large spruce trees which provide good perches for bald eagles. There are also fewer boats here than in the rest of the park.

The drive into the pond on the narrow dirt road known as Western Mountain Road is perhaps the most remote drive on the island. This is a good place to watch for moose. The parking area at the end of the road is fairly small, so try to arrive early. From the put-in at the southeastern end of the pond, it is about 1.75 miles to the north end. However, before heading north take some time to explore the marshy southern end of the pond. Cattails, fragrant waterlilies, and pickerelweed creep in from the shoreline, providing hiding places for ducks, herons, and egrets. The small stream in the cove directly across from the put-in drains Seal Cove Pond into Seal Cove only 0.5 mile away. Seal Cove is a picturesque little harbor filled with sailboats and lobster boats and is worth a visit however. You will have to drive there, as the stream from Seal Cove Pond is not navigable.

Once you have explored the southern end of the pond, paddle past the put-in and toward the north end of the pond. Since the western shore is filled with houses, summer cottages, lawns, and driveways, the eastern shore is a much more interesting paddle. The eastern shore is also part of the national park, which makes it permissible to land your boat to take a break. The western shore and the island in the middle of the pond are private property. As you head north, the shoreline is less marshy than the southern end of the pond and it takes on a rocky, forested character. The bird life is still interesting, as loons and cormorants hunt fish in the deeper waters of the pond and bald eagles sit patiently in the trees waiting for a fishing opportunity. The forest is thick with cedar, fir, spruce, birch, and maple. It is as wild as it looks, as no roads or trails trespass between the pond and the summit of Bernard Mountain, more than a mile to the east.

Good views of Bernard Mountain can be had from the northwestern end of the pond. From here you can see a lush and uninterrupted forest that is home to moose and black bear, ruffed grouse, and black-backed woodpeckers. While black-backed woodpeckers are common winter visitors, a few also live year-round and breed on Mount Desert Island. Although quite tame, they are rarely seen, but the thick evergreen forest to the east of Seal Cove Pond is the type of habitat they prefer. Both sexes can be identified by their black backs, wings, and tails, and the fact that they have only three toes. Males have yellow caps. These birds feed by peeling the bark off dead and dying spruce trees and eating the underlying beetles and other insects. The boggy cedar-and-spruce woods at the northeast end of the pond are a good place to sit quietly and watch for these birds.

Directions

From Maine Route 102 in Southwest Harbor, drive east on Seal Cove Road. After 2.1 miles, turn right on a dirt Park Service road. After 0.5 mile there is be a sign for Seal Cove Pond. Follow this sign to the left. You are now on Western Mountain Road. In 0.8 mile follow the right fork in the road toward Seal Cove Pond. The road ends at the put-in in another 0.7 mile.

airborne enemies: bald eagles and ospreys

Bald eagles and ospreys are both conspicuous, but uncommon, residents of Acadia and the islands surrounding Mount Desert Island. While these large birds of prey are distinctly dissimilar in appearance, they share many common habits and habitats. These similarities often put them in close proximity to one another and occasionally result in battles for prey and territory. Ospreys catch fish more than 50 percent of the time they try, and they rarely eat anything else. On the other hand, bald eagles are less successful hunters and will feast on carrion every chance they get. They also follow and harass ospreys in an attempt to steal their catch. It was these habits that led Ben Franklin to observe, "I wish the bald eagle had not been chosen as the representative of our country. He is a bird of bad moral character; he does not get his living honestly. Besides he is a rank coward."

Although Ben Franklin may have disliked the habits of these huge birds, bald eagles are truly magnificent animals, soaring gracefully on thermals with an eight-foot wingspan and possessing beautiful and regal coloring. Adults mate for life and share in the parenting duties, raising broods of two chicks in huge nests that are used year after year. They nest in the tallest trees they can find—in Maine usually a white pine or spruce—near any large body of water that is sufficiently free of human disturbance. Older nests can weigh as much as a ton and will usually end up killing the trees in which they are situated. The birds do not grow their distinctive white tail and head feathers until they are four or five years old. Until that time, they are either mottled in appearance or have a completely brown coloring, resembling golden eagles. In Acadia they nest on the smaller islands around Mount Desert Island, but can be seen almost

Ospreys nest in and around Acadia National Park.

anywhere along the coast soaring high on thermals or perching on a tall tree where they can get a good view of their
surroundings. In winter, some birds will migrate south to
congregate with other birds in areas of open water and concentrated food. However, some birds do remain in the park
year-round.

Like bald eagles, the smaller ospreys prefer to nest in
tall trees near water in relatively wild areas. They are
somewhat more adaptable than eagles, often nesting closer
to civilization on telephone poles or other tall man-made
structures that give them an open view of the landscape.
They are also more likely to nest next to small ponds that
are rich in fish. Ospreys mate for life and, like eagles, both
parents raise the young. It is common to find eagles and
ospreys nesting in sight of each other, which results in constant aerial battles. While the birds seldom hurt each other,
ospreys will harass and dive at eagles flying in their vicinity.
Groups of ravens, peregrine falcons, and other birds of prey

will also harass eagles in order to get them to leave an area. These displays are quite exciting to watch and usually end with the eagle deciding to catch a thermal and fly to more-peaceful surroundings.

Bald eagle populations declined consistently from the time Europeans arrived in North America until the 1940s as a result of persecution by hunters, fishermen, and farmers. Ospreys, on the other hand, managed to escape some of this persecution because farmers believed their presence kept away smaller falcons, such as merlins and kestrels, which preyed on domestic fowl. After World War II, both birds met considerable peril due to the widespread use of the pesticide DDT and other pollutants. These chemicals do not kill the birds, but they are stored in the birds' fatty tissues and eventually reach a level that creates reproductive problems. Eggs laid by birds with high concentrations of DDT had thin shells which often ended up being crushed during incubation. Since DDT was banned, the birds' reproductive success has improved in most of the country, although Maine bald eagles are still losing an inordinate amount of chicks. It is speculated that this is due to the high amounts of chlorinated pollutants entering Maine watersheds as a result of the state's high concentration of paper-making facilities. Despite these problems, around 150 nesting pairs of bald eagles are now in Maine, and ospreys are relatively common in the state. The greatest threat to both birds is currently habitat loss.

It is possible to see bald eagles and ospreys in Acadia near the coast or one of the bigger lakes. Your best chance at seeing them is by getting out on the water, whether in a sea kayak or on one of the national-park nature cruises that leave from Bar Harbor. If you are kayaking, be aware that the Park Service prohibits the landing of any boat on an island with an active bald eagle, osprey, or seabird nest, and you should not approach within 0.25 mile of a nest. Check at the visitor center beforehand for a list of islands with active nest sites. These birds are very wary of people and will abandon a nest if disturbed often.

Trip #33

Northeast Creek

> Distance: **5.0 miles round-trip**
>
> Estimated Time: **2.5 hours**
>
> **A quiet paddle on a narrow creek through extensive wetlands and prime wildlife habitat.**

THIS IS THE ONLY paddling trip in this chapter that explores a moving body of water. Fortunately the current is negligible, as the creek drops a mere five feet from one end to the other. The meandering nature of Northeast Creek makes paddling here a completely different experience than canoeing one of Mount Desert Island's big glacial lakes or plying the waters of the wavy Atlantic in a sea kayak. Much of this trip is spent in the narrow channel of an extensive boggy area filled with wildlife and views of Acadia's mountains. Due to the open nature of the terrain for most of this paddle, windy days create some uncomfortable paddling here, but since this is an out-and-back trip, you can turn around and return to the put-in at any time.

To start this trip, park at the dirt parking area on the inland side of Maine Route 3, just east of the bridge that crosses the creek. A path descends the short hill leading to the put-in. The put-in area, as well as all of the land bordering the creek, is private property. Please tread lightly at the put-in area, and plan your trip so that you do not need to land your boat once you are beyond the put-in. This creek has a small tidal influence which is mostly confined to the portion of the creek on the Mount Desert Narrows side of the bridge.

Begin paddling on the inland side of the bridge and head toward the mountains. As you paddle south and east, you quickly leave the road and civilization behind. You are surrounded by private property, but you will only see one house and a few grassy lawns throughout your trip. The paddle makes its way through a mixed forest of maple, aspen, white pine, and oak. Keep your eyes open for

Northeast Creek is a quiet paddle, full of bird life.

white-tailed deer, black ducks, mallard ducks, and other waterfowl. You should watch also for the occasional large rock hidden just under the waterline for the first 0.75 mile.

After the creek turns sharply to the right, you leave the rocks and the woods behind. You have now entered Fresh Meadow, a boggy wetland of tall cattails, grasses and sedges. Here the vistas open up to include Cadillac and Sargent Mountains about 6 miles away to the south. Summer finds great blue herons hunting amid the cattails at the edge of the creek. The chatter of belted kingfishers can be heard on most days as they busily fly from perch to perch looking for fish. Lincoln's sparrows and swamp sparrows share the brushy surroundings with red-winged blackbirds and the occasional sedge wren.

About a mile from the put-in, Aunt Betseys Brook enters on the right. In most conditions, Aunt Betseys Brook is shallow and mucky and difficult to explore. This trip stays on Northeast Creek, which turns left and heads north for a short distance before resuming an easterly course. For the next mile, Northeast Creek continues to meander through Fresh Meadow and its marshy expanse. Quiet paddling in this remote section of the creek can pay off with a muskrat, beaver, or river otter sighting. Beaver and muskrats are vegetarians, eating young trees, shrubs, and other plants, while river otters feed on fish, frogs, salamanders, and snakes. Beaver and muskrats often swim at the surface of the water with their tails remaining underwater to be used as rudders. Otters, on the other hand, are more likely to be seen poking their heads out of the water in an attempt to get a better view of their surroundings.

After the creek flows past some higher land on the right bank, it turns right and heads due south for the final 0.5 mile of this trip. The creek narrows and becomes enclosed in an ever increasing crop of cattails as it again nears civilization and the houses along Crooked Road. While you can turn around at any point on this trip, the end effectively becomes the spot where you can no longer navigate the cattails.

Directions

From the Thompson Island Information Center, follow Maine Route 3 east for 2.5 miles to the bridge over Northeast Creek. A small dirt parking area is immediately after the bridge on the right. Neither the creek nor the parking area is marked by signs.

beaver: acadia's rodent corps of engineers

Beaver are common throughout much of North America as well as parts of northern Europe. They are a habitat-building species that cuts down trees and builds extensive dams, canals, and lodges, creating ponds and marshes critical to supporting a wide variety of flora and fauna. In Acadia National Park, beaver thrived after the fire of 1947, as hardwoods like birch and aspen repopulated burn areas that had previously been occupied by spruce and fir. The reshaping of Mount Desert Island by beaver has been extensive during the last fifty years, creating many more areas of shallow wetlands than existed previously. These new habitats have created more abundant food sources for many other animals, including the river otter, which feeds on fish, amphibians, and crayfish.

Beaver are the second largest rodents in the world, reaching lengths of three to four feet and weighing as much as 60 pounds. Only the capybara of South America, which can weigh more than 100 pounds, is bigger. Beaver fur is brown, soft, and shiny and was very popular for clothing from the 1600s through the 1800s, when beaver were hunted nearly to extinction. Beaver meat is edible, and they were a common food for both Native Americans and white settlers. Since being protected by the U.S. and Canadian governments, beaver have repopulated much of North America and are no longer considered a threatened species.

Beaver have perhaps the most unusual tail of all North American mammals. Shaped like a paddle, beavers' tails are about twelve inches long and six inches wide. Beaver use their tails as rudders while swimming and as props while standing on their hind legs, gnawing at tree trunks. To warn others of danger, beaver will slap the water with their tails, creating a very loud noise. Unsuspecting canoeists have been known to almost jump out of their canoe in fright after hearing a nearby beaver-tail slap. Aside from their tails, their most conspicuous feature is their large front teeth, which they use to gnaw on trees. Beaver have a total of twenty teeth, four strong incisors in front for gnawing and sixteen back teeth for chewing their food, which consists of the twigs, leaves, and roots of aspens, birches, willows, and other hardwoods.

Beaver re-engineer woodland habitats because their favorite food is on land, while they prefer to live in the water. Beaver will build a dam across a stream or the outlet of a small pond by cutting down trees and plastering the spaces in between logs and rocks with mud. They will "harvest" mud from the pond or stream bottom and carry it up to the dam with their front paws. Beaver dams can be more than 1,000 feet long and are often maintained for several years, sometimes by more than one family. The dams cause water levels to rise, flooding previously dry woodlands and making it possible for the beaver to swim to a larger number of food trees and shrubs. These new and larger ponds create ideal habitat for fish, amphibians, and invertebrates, which in turn attract large numbers of such birds as great blue herons, kingfishers, and ospreys. Smaller birds benefit as well, as they feed on the increased number of insects that breed in the new wetlands. Moose and deer come to browse on the shrubs that grow near the water's edge, and fox and coyote visit to feed on the large numbers of small birds and rodents. Without beaver, the forests of North America would be a much less diverse ecosystem.

Of course, beaver build more than dams. They will often build canals up to 700 feet in length so they can transport logs and branches in the water as opposed to carrying them over land. They also build tepee-shaped lodges out of sticks and mud. These lodges can be very large, sometimes rising 6 feet above the water. They are built either next to the bank of the pond or stream or as an island. A lodge serves as the home for an entire beaver family, which can vary in size from three to twelve members, although most families are smaller than six in size. There are several underwater entrances to a typical lodge, which has an open living chamber on a floor built four to six inches above the water level. In the winter beaver do not hibernate, but use their living chambers as a place to stay warm and dry, occasionally leaving the lodge to retrieve food cached nearby underwater. On large lakes or swift-moving streams, beaver will build a lodge by burrowing into a bank at the water's edge instead of building one out of sticks and mud.

As beaver flood more of their surroundings and kill more and more of the hardwoods, they may eventually run out of food. In this case, beaver either starve or make a dangerous journey over land in search of new food sources to exploit. As the beaver search for their new home, they may succeed at creating a brand-new wetland ecosystem miles from their original lodge. In the meantime, the wetland habitats they leave behind will continue to thrive until their dams give way and the water drains out. Of course, fertile land then results and the forest returns over time, probably to be flooded again by future generations of the original beaver families. In Acadia, beaver are most easily observed around dusk and dawn in Little Long Pond, Witch Hole Pond, and the beaver pond on the Park Loop Road just past the Bear Brook picnic area. Their handiwork can also be seen in the extensive wetlands near Sieur de Monts Spring and near Eagle Lake on the other side of Route 233.

Eagle Lake

> Distance: **4.0 miles round–trip**
>
> Estimated Time: **3 hours**
>
> **A moderate paddle on a scenic lake with mountain views and wild shorelines.**

EAGLE LAKE is the largest lake on the eastern side of Mount Desert Island and is a popular spot due to its close proximity to Bar Harbor. All of Eagle Lake is part of Acadia National Park, giving it a wild shoreline with none of the cottages and camps you find on most of the other lakes on the island. Its views of Cadillac and Pemetic Mountains, as well as the Bubbles, are breathtaking. It is four miles around the edge of the lake, making it possible to spend a leisurely day taking in the scenery and watching for loons, mergansers, and ospreys. Carriage roads circle the lake and connect with hiking trails, creating the opportunity to spend the whole day in the area, paddling, hiking, and biking. Swimming is prohibited, however, since the lake is the water supply for Bar Harbor.

Eagle Lake was saved from development before Acadia National Park existed. In 1908 a prominent Bar Harbor summer resident quietly made plans to build a summer home on the high ground to the west of Eagle Lake. When word of his plans became public and it was learned that outflow from the house had nowhere to drain but Eagle Lake, concerned citizens sprang into action. George Dorr, unquestionably the father of Acadia National Park and its first superintendent, rallied his wealthy and prominent friends to publicize the harmful sanitation effects of such a project on the pristine lake. His efforts convinced the state of Maine to pass legislation condemning the watersheds of Eagle Lake and Jordan Pond, effectively preserving the water quality of the two ponds and preventing development on either body water. Eagle Lake achieved federal protection with the creation of Sieur de Monts National Monument in 1916. Today, Eagle Lake is the largest body of water on the island without any buildings on its shoreline.

A paddling trip on Eagle Lake begins at the north end of the lake, at the Eagle Lake parking area on the south side of Maine Route 233. Motorboats are allowed on the lake, but there is a ten-horsepower limit on motors. If you see motorized vehicles on the lake, they will most likely be slow-moving boats of fishermen dropping their lines into the 110-foot-deep water trying to hook the salmon and trout that thrive in the lake's cold water. These fish make up the diet of the common mergansers and common loons that nest around the lake. The fish are also what draw ospreys to the wild southern end of the lake. Ospreys are impressive fishermen, diving into the water talons first and emerging with a fish more than 50 percent of the time. It is no wonder bald eagles often spend their time harassing ospreys in an attempt to get them to drop their prey.

Paddling Eagle Lake can take as much or as little time as you want. The shoreline is wooded and rocky, with just a few coves and inlets to explore. Either follow the shoreline for a 4-mile paddle or paddle straight across to the southern end of the lake, 1.75 miles away. As on all of the lakes on Mount Desert Island, a wind out of the north can create some large waves at the southern end of the pond. On a windy day, keep in mind the fact that you will have to paddle against these waves on the return trip. At the southern end of the pond, directly opposite the put-in, is a shallow gravel area, which makes it easy to land your boat and take a break on shore. The Eagle Lake Hiking Trail can be found here. Hiking the trail to the right makes for a flat 0.5-mile walk along the southwestern shore of the lake. Following the trail to your left can connect you to the Jordan Pond Carry Trail, which is a 1.1-mile footpath through northern hardwood forest that ends at the northeastern shore of Jordan Pond. These trails also connect with the extensive system of gravel carriage roads. For biking around Eagle Lake, see trip #23 in the biking chapter.

Whether you follow the shoreline back or paddle down the middle of the lake, see if your hearing is as keen as that of painter Thomas Cole, who first visited Eagle Lake in 1844. According to *Mount Desert Island and Acadia National Park: An Informal History* by Sargent Collier, Cole named the lake for the bald eagles that soared over his easel, and he once remarked that at Eagle Lake "one may fancy himself in the forests of the Alleghenies, but for the dull roar of the ocean breaking the stillness." The ocean is three miles away.

Directions

From the intersection of Route 3 and Route 233 in Bar Harbor, take Route 233 west toward Cadillac Mountain. The parking area for Eagle Lake is at 2.1 miles on the left.

Long Pond, North End

Distance: 7.5 miles round-trip

Estimated Time: 4 hours

A long and popular paddle which explores the wooded coves of Mount Desert Island's biggest lake.

IF YOU DO NOT have your own boat, this is the easiest place to paddle in Acadia, as National Park Canoe Rental is just across the street from the put-in at the north end of Long Pond (see appendix E for a complete list of canoe outfitters). With deep blue waters and scenic views of Beech, Bernard, and Mansell Mountains, Long Pond is a beautiful place to paddle. You will not have the pond to yourself on a busy summer weekend, but there are plenty of quiet coves where you can find solitude and study the shoreline. This trip explores the northern end of the pond and its secluded coves, which are hidden by two peninsulas, Northern Neck and Southern Neck.

You begin the paddle at the boat launch on Pretty Marsh Road. The first 1.25 miles are a straight paddle up the narrow north end of the pond. The western mountains fill your views to the south, while the shoreline is lined by summer cottages. Boat traffic can get busy in this part of the pond, so stay near the shore and be prepared to ride the wakes of motorboats. The spit of land on your right is Northern Neck. As you come to the end of Northern Neck, the pond opens up to the right. At this point, Southern Neck is the narrow peninsula directly across from Northern Neck. Paddle your boat south toward Southern Neck. The shoreline of Southern Neck and all of the coves to the right of it are part of Acadia National Park.

This is the wildest part of Long Pond, with an undeveloped shoreline of white cedar, white pine, and balsam fir. Horsetail and fragrant waterlilies add color to the pond in the shallows. Black ducks, mallards, and common mergansers are numerous throughout this area, and the forest is filled with the songs of thrushes and wood warblers. Twenty-three species of warblers and thrushes nest in Acadia, including the colorful yellow warbler and the ovenbird, with its unmistakable forest-filling song of *teacher, teacher, teacher, teacher, teacher*. In late fall, America's smallest duck, the bufflehead, arrives in small groups which entertain paddlers by popping up out of the water in all directions like black-and-white lobster buoys.

If you keep the shore on your left, eventually you will turn around and be heading north. As you enter the bay behind Northern Neck, the woods remain wild, though houses do begin to appear behind the trees. With a couple of islands and some marshy shoreline, this bay is worth exploring despite the summer cottages. From the westernmost part of the pond, you can even get a glimpse of Cadillac Mountain, eight miles to the east. You can also look for small boggy areas filled with sphagnum moss and northern New England's most common carnivorous plants, sundews and pitcher plants. These plants trap insects and digest them with enzymes, feeding the plant with much-needed nutrients not available in the acidic soil of bogs.

By keeping to the shoreline on your left, you will emerge from the western side of Northern Neck and find yourself back in the main part of Long Pond. From here, the put-in is 1.25 miles to the left (north).

Directions

The parking area for the Long Pond put-in is on Pretty Marsh Road, 1.5 miles west of Maine Route 102 in Somesville.

7

sea kayaking the waters of mount desert island

ACADIA NATIONAL PARK is as much about water as it is about mountains, with the cold waters of the Gulf of Maine creating rich food supplies for large numbers of seabirds and mammals. Sea kayaking in the bays and narrows around Mount Desert Island is like no other experience in the park, with dramatic scenery and wildlife sightings practically guaranteed. Taking a naturalist cruise or a whale watch is a great way to see Acadia from the water, but you get a much better look at the intricate details of the ocean ecosystem by sitting at the water level in a kayak. You also gain a lot more freedom to explore the myriad inlets and coves that make up the shoreline of Mount Desert Island and the other islands in Frenchman Bay, Blue Hill Bay, and Somes Sound. If you have never been in a sea kayak before, you can get a great introduction to the sport by taking a guided tour offered by one of the outfitters listed in the appendix to this book. (Taking a guided tour around the Porcupine Islands was our first experience in a sea kayak, and we have been hooked on ocean paddling ever since.) To get sufficient experience to paddle on your own, however, you should take a multiday sea-kayaking class.

Safety and Etiquette

Registered Maine Guides are excellent sources for kayaking information. The safety information in this chapter was compiled with the gracious help of Natalie Springel, lead kayaking guide at Coastal Kayaking Tours. Sea kayaking in the waters around Mount Desert Island can be safely enjoyed, but not without sufficient training and experience. At its warmest, the water temperature reaches the low fifties, and even at that temperature a submerged paddler can become hypothermic in minutes. The weather also can cause dangerous conditions, especially fog that can roll in off the ocean at any time, making strong navigation skills vital. Local outfitters will require you to prove your experience before renting you a kayak. In order to safely sea-kayak in Maine, you should have at least the following minimum level of experience:

- Previous paddling experience in a sea kayak

- Knowledge of the basic paddle strokes: forward, reverse, sweep, skull, brace, draw

- Knowledge of how to use a nautical chart and compass

- Previous practice of self-rescues and knowledge of how to use a paddle float

How do you get this experience? Some local outfitters in Bar Harbor and Camden, Maine, give multiday classes on sea kayaking. Your local recreation department may offer introductory pool sessions where you can practice self-rescues in a controlled environment. Ask at the outdoors shops in your hometown if they know of any classes you can take locally. Sometimes the stores themselves have classes because they sell sea kayaks. Of course, you can always ask an experienced paddler you know if he or she is willing to show you the ropes.

Before putting your boat in the water, you should always check the tide and weather forecasts. Tides are usually listed in local papers such as the *Bar Harbor Times,* the *Acadia Weekly*, and the National Park Service's *Beaver Log*. You can also buy official tide charts at local bookstores. Tides and weather forecasts can be heard on a NOAA weather radio. The NOAA weather forecasts are excellent for long-range forecasts, but for the best up-to-date Acadia weather information, call the weather phone for local radio station WDEA at 207-667-8910. In addition to listening to the weather forecast, use your common sense and take a look at the conditions when you put your boat in the water. If you see whitecaps on the water, it is probably too windy for a safe and pleasant paddle. Also, if it is foggy at your put-in, you should choose another trip. Besides causing navigational problems, fog can make you invisible to the many fishing and pleasure boats that travel through the area. What is convenient about kayaking around Mount Desert Island is that weather conditions, especially fog, can be very localized, and you can often drive to another part of the island and have a safe and sunny paddle. Even in sunny conditions, it is advisable to keep your group in a tightly knit formation, as this makes you much more visible to boats. Also, you should never paddle alone.

Everyone in your group should have the following essential gear with them:

- Life jacket (PFD)—Wear a life jacket while sea-kayaking in Maine. If you end up in the water, a life jacket can save the precious energy you will need to stave off hypothermia. The few minutes of time a life jacket saves you while you try to get back into your boat can save your life.

- Spare paddle

- Paddle float

- Sprayskirt

- Bilge pump

- Lunch, snacks, and emergency food

- Drinking water—at least a gallon if you are out for the entire day

- Sunglasses, sunscreen, and a hat

- Appropriate clothing—Dress for the water temperature, not the air temperature. A wet or dry suit is great, but at the least wear synthetic materials and dress in layers. Neoprene or Gore-Tex gloves and booties are also good to have. Do not wear cotton.

- Dry bag to keep all of the above dry

- Binoculars for wildlife viewing

You should also carry at least one set of each of the following for the entire group:

- Compass and charts
- First-aid kit
- Foghorn
- Flare gun
- VHF radio or cell phone, although cell phones do not work in all locations

In addition to paying close attention to safety, kayakers in the waters around Mount Desert Island need to follow certain guidelines to avoid having a negative impact on the environment and local residents. First, it is important to respect private property and never land your boat near a house or on land marked No Trespassing. You should land your boat only in the national park or on other public lands, except for the few locations where it is acceptable to land on private property, which are listed in the individual trip descriptions in this chapter. You may want to discuss your trip with an outfitter or Park Service employee before heading out, to find out about possible changes in land status. Also, the Park Service prohibits the landing of a kayak on an island with an active eagle, osprey, or seabird nest.

Second, give wildlife a wide berth. Seals in particular are easily stressed by kayaks, possibly because kayaks are shaped like seals' main predator, killer whales. It is also possible that they have an inherited memory of when seals were hunted by men in kayaks. In any event, never approach seals in a kayak, particularly if they have hauled themselves out onto rocks, where they feel especially vulnerable. Try to stay at least 0.5 mile from basking seals. You should also enjoy eagle and osprey nests from a distance, trying to stay at least 0.25 mile away from an active nest. If any animal changes its behavior as you approach, you are too close.

Third, practice no impact techniques both on and off the water. Pack out all of your trash, including toilet paper and solid human waste. Urinating below the high-tide line is the most effective way to ensure quick dispersal of urine. However, do not urinate in a tide pool, as this can have negative consequences on the delicate life there. Also, try to stay below the high-tide line at all times to minimize your impact on fragile island habitats. Please do not take rocks and shells home as souvenirs.

Finally, remember that fishermen are out there trying to make a living. Always let them have the right of way and try to stay out of their path. Do not go near lobster traps, and be as quick as possible while using local boat ramps. Theoretically, kayaks have the right of way when passing other boats. However, larger boats do not always see kayaks or are traveling too fast to change course quickly. Play it safe and move aside when possible.

This chapter highlights five possible trips that vary in length and difficulty. The islands in this part of Maine provide a great variety of scenery and wildlife habitat, and these trips explore many of them, from quiet, marshy coves to dramatic seaside cliffs and open ocean. The shorelines of Mount Desert Island and the surrounding smaller islands are a great place to study the intertidal zones of sea life present on rocky outcroppings. Students of geology will find the variety of rocks fascinating and will enjoy seeing evidence of volcanism, tectonics, and glaciation. Rocky ledges are interspersed with cobble and sand beaches, and in the shallows, low tide reveals mud flats that attract a variety of shorebirds and wading birds like sandpipers and great blue herons. Seals and porpoises frequent the spaces between islands, as do seabirds like loons, guillemots, and cormorants. Soaring overhead and nesting in island trees are ospreys and bald eagles, and watching it all are paddlers in their quiet kayaks.

Trip #36

Mount Desert Narrows

> Distance: **6.0 miles round-trip**
>
> Estimated Time: **3 hours**
>
> **A relatively sheltered paddle in shallow waters, with the chance to see seals, porpoises, and an eagle's nest.**

WEATHER AND TIDE CONSIDERATIONS: We recommend making this paddle during the hours around high tide. There are extensive mud flats near Thompson Island as well as in Thomas Bay and surrounding Thomas Island and the Twinnies. At low tide, these mud flats may be filled with feeding shorebirds, but they also drastically reduce the amount of paddling you can accomplish. The mud flats around Thompson Island make it quite difficult and unpleasant to land a boat there. Try to start your paddle at least two hours after low tide and plan to finish it at least two hours before low tide. The national park visitor center can give you tide information. Occasionally a strong southwest wind can cause some unpleasant paddling conditions, but in general this is a good trip in windy conditions, as it is relatively sheltered. If you do not see whitecaps from Hadley Point, you should be all set. If you have strong navigational skills, this trip is a good choice in foggy weather, as there is not much boat traffic.

Mount Desert Narrows is the body of water that separates Mount Desert Island from the mainland. This paddle, which explores the narrows east of Thompson Island, is a good choice in strong winds. It also makes a great sunset paddle. Wildlife such as harbor porpoises, great blue herons, and bald eagles can be found in this area of uninhabited islands, mud flats, and salt marshes. Beginning at Hadley Point, this trip follows the shoreline of Mount Desert Island

Taking a break from kayaking Mount Desert Narrows.

past Northeast Creek to Thompson Island before circling back around Thomas Island and the Twinnies. Please note that Thompson Island and Hadley Point are the only landing spots on this trip. The remainder of the shoreline on Mount Desert Island is private property, as are the islands in the narrows.

From the put-in at Hadley Point, follow the shoreline to your left (west). The first mile or so of shoreline is wooded and rocky, with eelgrass becoming more prominent as you make your way toward Thomas Bay. Approximately 1.3 miles from Hadley Point, the Twinnies will appear on your right. These two islands, named for their similar size and shape, are uninhabited and provide an important nesting site for bald eagles. Please remember that it is illegal to disturb nesting eagles. On the return portion of this trip, you can paddle near the Twinnies and take a look at the nest from a safe distance. For now, continue to follow the shoreline of Mount Desert Island on your left. Marshes and mud flats dominate your surroundings as you enter Thomas Bay, with the outlet of Northeast Creek providing a rare look on Mount Desert Island of an area where fresh water enters salt water. The marsh grasses and concentration of food in the form of mollusks, crustaceans, and small fish make this an area frequented by great blue herons, mallard and black ducks, and green-winged teals. To paddle up Northeast Creek, see trip #33.

Continuing through Thomas Bay, you will run into a peninsula of land known as Israel Point. Paddle around Israel Point, keeping the shoreline on your left, and head toward Thompson Island, where you can see the bridge that connects Mount Desert Island with the rest of Maine. Thompson Island and about 0.5 mile of the surrounding shoreline on Mount Desert Island are part of Acadia National Park, and therefore it is acceptable to land your boat here to rest before heading into the deeper waters of Mount Desert Narrows. To start your return to Hadley Point, paddle past Israel Point toward the left side of Thomas Island, which is about 1.0 mile from Thompson Island. Abenaki Indians apparently made use of Thomas Island, as there is evidence of a shell midden on the island. Shell middens are areas where Native Americans discarded huge amounts of mussel and clam shells, as well as other refuse, over hundreds of years.

As you paddle around the northern (left) end of Thomas Island, you will enter the deeper waters of Mount Desert Narrows, where you are most likely to see harbor porpoises surfacing to breathe. Harbor porpoises and seals use the narrows as feeding grounds when the tides are highest. Traveling in pods of two to five animals, porpoises may come quite close to your kayak, as they feel no threat from the small boats. If you hear a porpoise blow, which sounds like a loud sneeze, stay still and soak in the magnificent sight of these sleek animals passing nearby. In addition to seals and porpoises, seabirds such as black guillemots, double-crested cormorants, and common loons are also found in the narrows.

As you pass Thomas Island, follow its shoreline to the right. At this point, the Twinnies come back into view. Using binoculars, look for a gray mass of branches—a bald eagle's nest—at the top of a large spruce. The birds often can be seen perching in the area, but please do not approach them or their nest too closely, as they are very wary of people and will abandon a nest site if disturbed often. Stay at least a 0.25 mile away from the nest site. To complete this wildlife-rich trip, paddle to the left of the more northerly of the Twinnies and then follow the shoreline of Mount Desert Island on your right for the final 1.2 miles back to Hadley Point.

loon or cormorant?

In Acadia, common loons can be found both in coastal and inland water.

While common loons and double-crested cormorants have very different markings, it is difficult to distinguish between the two in bright light because of their similar shapes. With a little practice, however, it is easy to tell the two birds apart by looking at their bills. A loon's bill is much thicker than a cormorant's, and loons tend to hold their bills level with the water. Cormorants strike a somewhat "snooty" pose, with their bills pointed slightly upward.

Common loons, with their haunting call, are among the most popular birds in North America. They are easily seen in the waters surrounding Mount Desert Island, particularly from early fall through spring. Loons that are not old enough to breed will often stay in the area year-round. During the summer, mature loons nest on inland lakes and ponds, but during the rest of the year they feed in the ice-free waters of the Gulf of Maine. With their black heads, red eyes, black-and-white-striped neck, and black-and-white bodies, common loons are stunning birds. Occasionally red-throated loons, with their gray bodies and red throat patches, are also seen in the waters around Acadia.

Double-crested cormorants are very common in Acadia from spring through late fall. Except for their yellow bills and throat pouches, double-crested cormorants are black birds with an iridescent green or purple gloss. Like loons, cormorants are about the size of a goose and are excellent swimmers that are much more adept in the water than on the land. Cormorants lack the oils that other ducks and seabirds have to keep their feathers dry. Instead they perch on rocks, logs, and piers, and hold their wings up to dry. Great cormorants can also be seen in Acadia. They are larger than double-crested cormorants and have a white chin or throat patch.

Directions

From the Thompson Island Information Center, drive east on Maine Route 3 for 4.0 miles, where you should turn left on Hadley Point Road. It is 0.6 mile to the end of the road, where there is plenty of parking. One problem here is that during full-moon high tides, this parking area can flood.

Frenchman Bay and the Porcupine Islands

> Distance: **6.5 miles round-trip**
>
> Estimated Time: **3 hours**
>
> **An exciting paddle around the beautiful and wild Porcupine Islands.**

WEATHER AND TIDE CONSIDERATIONS: Tide is a concern only at the put-in on the Bar Island bar. Do not expect to land your boat on the southern side of the bar during low tide because of extensive mud flats. This trip is not recommended during foggy conditions, due to heavy boat traffic in the area. Even during sunny weather, larger boats may have trouble seeing kayaks. This paddle has a fair amount of exposure to the open ocean and can be difficult in winds stronger than 10–15 knots from any direction. West winds in particular can make it slow going on the return leg of the trip. On windy or foggy days, consider paddling trip #36 or trip #40 instead.

Our first kayak trip in Acadia was a drizzly August ride through 5-foot swells around the Porcupine Islands in Frenchman Bay. Despite the wet weather and menacing seas, we were instantly hooked on the beauty of this place of 100-foot cliffs, seals, seabirds, and bald eagles. This trip passes near Bar Island and Sheep, Burnt, and Bald Porcupine, with a view of Long Porcupine thrown in for good measure. The mountains of Acadia provide the backdrop for some of the most scenic paddling on the Maine coast. This trip definitely should be undertaken only by experienced paddlers, as there are several open-water passages up to a mile long, fog can creep in at any time, and large swells can roll in from the Atlantic. If you lack experience with open-ocean paddling, consider joining a guided trip for a safe group exploration of the Porcupines.

Begin this trip at the put-in on the Bar Harbor bar, a gravel spit that connects Bar Harbor with Bar Island at low tide. You can drive a car on the bar at low tide or even hike across the bar to a short trail on the island. Take note that the bar does disappear underwater as the tide comes in, so park your vehicle back at the end of West Street. Start paddling on the left side of the bar and head for the eastern end of Bar Island. Paddle around the end of the island, turning right and following the northern shore. Daniel Rodick, whose fashionable Rodick House in Bar Harbor could accommodate more than 600 guests, bought Bar Island in the late 1800s. Eventually the island was sold to the Rockefeller family, who in turn donated it to Acadia National Park. Except for one year-round resident, Bar Island is now populated only by spruce and birch, herons and hawks.

Once you are on the north side of the island, the hustle and bustle of Bar Harbor disappear and you are immersed in the intricacies of the intertidal zones that are so apparent on Bar Island's rocky shore. Barnacles, periwinkles, and limpets share the rocks with seaweeds such as bladder wrack and Irish moss, while crabs, starfish, and sea urchins forage on and around the rocks. The intertidal shorelines around Mount Desert Island can be as exciting a habitat to explore as the high subalpine meadows of Cadillac or Sargent Mountains. You will notice that different plants and animals inhabit different layers of the intertidal zones depending on their requirements for light, water, and air.

When you reach the end of Bar Island, you face the first of three open-water crossings on this trip. Sheep Porcupine is straight ahead, approximately 0.3 mile away. Aim for the left side of the island. Sheep Porcupine is home to nesting bald eagles, so you will want to keep your eyes open for flashes of white among the dark green of the spruce trees that cover the island. Only adult eagles have the distinctive white heads and tails, but you are likely to see immatures in the area as well. Bald eagles that are less than four or five years old are brown with a varying amount of mottled white feathers. You will recognize them as eagles, though, as they are just as big as adults, with wingspans up to eight feet. The Park Service has closed this island to foot traffic in order to give the eagles a better chance of successfully nesting. Stay at least 0.25 mile from the island.

During the crossing from Bar Island, you may also begin to see some of the other well-known wildlife that frequent Frenchman Bay, such as harbor seals and black guillemots. While not as popular as Atlantic puffins, which spend most of their time far off at sea, black guillemots are easily seen in Frenchman Bay and are just as fun to watch. Only about a foot long, these true seabirds are built like torpedoes, with their bright red feet trailing a black body with white wing patches. Also known as sea pigeons or pigeon guillemots, they are expert swimmers, feeding on small fish and crustaceans. Harbor seals seem more wary than guillemots, but you can occasionally look around and see them checking you out from behind. Other common animals in the bay are double-crested cormorants, common loons, harbor porpoises, gulls, and terns. Minke whales may also make an appearance in late summer.

Paddle around the north end of Sheep Porcupine, which was actually home to grazing sheep in the 1800s. The sheep are now gone and the forest has returned, as the island is now entirely a protected part of Acadia National Park. As you paddle around the northern end of the island, Burnt Porcupine comes into view. The crossing to Burnt Porcupine is about 0.5 mile in length, and it is fairly exposed to the seas coming in from the open Atlantic. A deep channel between the two islands is used extensively by boats, including the large catamaran the *Cat*, which travels between Bar Harbor and Halifax, Nova Scotia, at speeds up to fifty-five knots. Needless to say, steer clear of large vessels during this crossing, and if the fog is in, consider turning around and returning to Bar Harbor. Traveling in a compact group of kayaks can make you more visible to the larger boats and help reduce the possibility of an accident.

Burnt Porcupine is slightly larger than Sheep Porcupine, and its shoreline consists of a combination of cobble beaches, rocky shoreline, and high cliffs. Burnt Porcupine has been preserved by The Nature Conservancy, making it possible to enjoy the beauty of its thick spruce forest and dramatic coast from the seat of your kayak for years to come. Paddle around the north end of the island and you will eventually see a small island just off the western edge of Burnt Porcupine. This island is called Rum Key, and, though private, it is permissible to land on its cobble beach to take a break. Nonetheless, Rum Key is a fragile island environment, so try to remain on the rocks and below the high-tide line. From Rum Key you can see a

The Porcupine Islands in Frenchman Bay are a popular spot for sea-kayakers, nature cruises, and bald eagles.

receding set of islands to the southeast. The first two islands are Long Porcupine and Ironbound Island, the largest island in Frenchman Bay. The farthest island is not actually an island but the Schoodic Peninsula, the only portion of Acadia National Park on the mainland.

A longer day can be spent exploring Long Porcupine and Ironbound, but our trip heads back to Bar Harbor via Bald Porcupine. To the south of Rum Key, you will see Bald Porcupine across a mile of open ocean. Like the crossing between Sheep and Burnt Porcupine, this crossing can have heavy boat traffic as well as heavy seas, but it is also a good opportunity to paddle among seabirds and mammals.

Head for the east end of Bald Porcupine, which will be on your left. Like the rest of the Porcupine Islands, Bald Porcupine has a gently sloping northern end, with steep cliffs on its south side. This shape is a landscape feature created by glaciers known as *roches moutannées*, or whalebacks. The cliffs on the southern end of Bald Porcupine are impressive, rising 100 feet up out of the waters of Frenchman Bay. Stay well clear of the cliffs, especially if there are winds or swells out of the south, as rebounding surf can topple a kayak.

As you paddle around the southern end of Bald Porcupine, you eventually come to a breakwater that leads toward the shore in Bar Harbor. During most tides the breakwater is not passable, so paddle its length toward the shore. At the end of the breakwater you can continue to the shore and turn right, keeping Bar Harbor on your left as you get a good look at some of the largest houses in town. This part of town was spared during the 1947 fire, giving you a glimpse of the "cottage life" that existed before most of the large vacation homes were destroyed. As you follow the shoreline toward the harbor, you will need to maneuver around the sailboats, whale-watching boats, and lobster boats moored there. Once past the boats, you will be back at the Bar Island bar, with Bridge Street on your left.

Directions

From the intersection of Maine Route 3 and West Street in Bar Harbor, drive east on West Street for about 0.3 mile. Turn left at the first street, which is Bridge Street. Drop your boat off on the Bar Harbor bar, and then park your car back on West Street.

humpback whales

In *Moby Dick* Herman Melville wrote about the humpback whale, saying, "He is the most gamesome and light-hearted of all the whales, making more gay foam and whitewater than any other of them." Humpbacks are naturally curious about boats, sometimes sitting in the water within a few feet of a boat for several minutes, slapping and waving their flippers, swimming under the boat, and sticking their huge barnacle-laden heads out of the water in an apparent attempt to get a better look at the boat's occupants. Anyone who has seen one of these twenty-five ton behemoths breaching its entire body out of the water has definitely been impressed with its size and agility. For these reasons, humpbacks have become the darlings of the whale-watching industry, and Bar Harbor is a great place to take a whale-watching cruise. Several tour companies have two or more whale-watching trips a day during the summer, and most of them guarantee a sighting.

Humpbacks live in all of the world's oceans and tend to favor coastal waters or shallower shelf waters out at sea. They are huge animals, with adults reaching forty-six to fifty feet in length and weighing as much as thirty tons. They weigh two tons at birth. Now, that is a big kid! Humpbacks generally migrate up to 5,000 miles between summer feeding grounds and winter breeding grounds. The animals that live in the Gulf of Maine during the summer generally swim to the Caribbean Sea in winter to breed and give birth. Like most migratory whales, humpbacks bulk up in the food-rich waters of their summer feeding grounds in order to go the rest of the year without eating. In winter, mother humpbacks will leave their yearling calves off the coast of Virginia, where they can continue to feed in relatively warm waters without making the long trip south. The young whales regroup with the mature whales during the spring migration.

Humpbacks belong to the rorqual family of whales, which also includes minke, fin, blue, sei, and Bryde's whales, all relatively large baleen whales. Minke and fin, or finback, whales are also commonly seen during whale-watching excursions in the Gulf of Maine. Baleen whales feed by filling their mouths with tons of water and then filtering out trapped fish or krill through their baleen, a substitute for teeth which hangs down from the upper jaws of the whale in a comblike plate that includes stiff hairs to aid in trapping the smallest of prey. These huge animals rarely eat anything larger than shrimp.

Humpbacks are the most creative feeders in the rorqual family. They trap or confuse their prey by blowing huge "nets" and "clouds" of air bubbles before lunging into the trapped school of fish or shrimp with mouths agape. Bubble clouds seem to be unique to the North Atlantic population of humpbacks. To create a bubble cloud, the whale swims upward in a spiral, releasing bubbles as it goes, until the prey are concentrated in a confined area of space just as the whale makes its feeding lunge. A little Yankee ingenuity at sea. Humpbacks will feed and play together, and it is common to see two or three of them visiting a whale-watching boat while taking a break from feeding.

Humpbacks are unique among rorqual whales in that they have a fairly rotund appearance, as opposed to the long, sleek appearance of the other members of this family. They also have very long flippers (up to fifteen feet in length) with unique black and white markings that aid in the identification of individuals. Using tail and flipper markings, scientists are meticulously identifying individual North Atlantic humpbacks in an attempt to better understand their behavior, breeding success, and longevity. Naturalists on the local whale-watching boats are familiar with most of the whales by name and contribute a great deal of information

to the body of knowledge being used to determine the overall health of the humpback population.

While you will not see a humpback from shore, if you take a whale-watching excursion you are likely to see one or more of the following behaviors:

Breaching is perhaps the most exciting behavior to witness, as humpbacks propel their huge bulk out of the water. Humpbacks use their tails to shoot themselves out of the water sideways with their flippers outstretched. They then arch their backs, do a half-turn, and land on their backs in what looks like a huge explosion. Why they breach is not known for sure. It could be to stun prey or knock barnacles off their skin. It might also just be fun.

Lobtailing is when a whale repeatedly slaps the water

with its tail. The rest of the whale's body remains under water in a "head-down" position.

Fluking is when a whale lifts its tail high above its body as a prelude to making a deep dive. If you see humpbacks, you will most likely witness this behavior. After fluking, a whale may stay under water for as long as forty-five minutes.

Flipper slapping gives many whale watchers the impression that a whale is waving at them. Sometimes a humpback will lie at the surface of the water on its side and simply slap the water repeatedly with its huge flipper. Occasionally an individual will lie on its back and slap both flippers simultaneously.

Spyhopping is what whales do when they just want to take a look around. While spyhopping, they slowly lift their heads straight out of the water until their eyes are above the water's surface. Spyhopping is a common behavior for whales that voluntarily approach a whale-watching boat.

Humpbacks' natural inquisitiveness and the fact that they live in coastal waters made them an easy target for whalers during the last 200 years. While their oil and bones were considered inferior in quality to other whales such as sperm whales, they were hunted relentlessly nonetheless. It is estimated that several hundred thousand humpbacks were killed around the world during the whaling era, reducing their overall population by 95 percent. Now a protected species, humpback populations are making a dramatic comeback. It is estimated that there are now more than 10,000 humpbacks in the current North Atlantic population. The largest threats to humpbacks now are entanglement in fishing nets and depletion of their food sources by commercial overfishing. With thousands of people now enjoying humpbacks up close and personal every year, there is hope that we humans will do what is needed to ensure the survival of these magnificent animals.

See Appendix E for a list of the whale-watching companies at Acadia.

Sutton and Bear Islands

Distance: 6.0 miles round-trip

Estimated Time: 3 hours

A moderate paddle past a remote lighthouse and a sea arch providing a nice view of the mountains on Mount Desert Island.

WEATHER AND TIDE CONSIDERATIONS: Tide is not an issue on this trip. With heavy boat traffic in the area, it is advisable not to paddle here in foggy weather. Strong winds (above ten to fifteen knots) from the east or west can cause problems, and winds out of the north can funnel through the mountains, making the return part of the trip difficult. Winds from the southwest are the most favorable.

This six-mile loop explores the shoreline of Mount Desert Island near Seal Harbor, as well as Sutton and Bear Islands, which are part of the group of islands known as the Cranberry Islands. A lighthouse is perched atop a cliff on the western side of Bear Island, while Sutton Island boasts a fascinating sea arch and sweeping views of the mountains on the eastern side of Mount Desert Island. Like most of the waters surrounding Acadia, this area is rich in wildlife, giving any paddler a good chance to see guillemots, loons, seals, ospreys, and bald eagles.

The put-in for this trip is at the sand beach in Seal Harbor. While you may have a long walk across the beach at low tide, the sand is firm and you do not have to worry about sinking up to your knees in muck. Seal Harbor is a picturesque spot, with sailboats filling the harbor enclosed by a gently curving shoreline populated by spruce and summer homes. The Cranberry Islands are directly

The view from Sutton Island across the Eastern Way to Mount Desert Island.

across from the mouth of the harbor, inviting boaters of all types to escape the summer crowds of Mount Desert Island. Begin your trip by paddling toward the point of land on the southwest end of the harbor known as Crowninshield Point. The very large house near this point should make it apparent that the shoreline here is privately owned and landing your boat is discouraged. Stay well clear of red bell #6 in this area. In the right conditions, a large rock underwater here can cause a rogue wave to topple a kayak. After rounding Crowninshield Point, keep Mount Desert Island on your right and follow the shoreline for about 0.75 mile, at which point you will be in a protected cove known as Bracy Cove. Other than Seal Harbor, Bracy Cove is the only allowable landing spot on this trip. Directly across the road from Bracy Cove is Little Long Pond, a picturesque body of water described in trip #28.

Continue along the shoreline, which alternates between cobble beaches and rocky coast. Some of the larger summer homes on the island are in Seal and Northeast Harbors, and this stretch of coastline boasts a few. To the southwest of Bracy Cove is Bear Island, the smallest of the Cranberry Islands. When opposite Bear Island, turn away from the coast and make the 1,200-foot crossing to the north end of the island. Like many of the islands in the area, Bear Island was used as sheep pasture for many years. Islands were popular for this purpose because the sheep were easy to keep track of without building fences. As you paddle around the western end of the island, you will see a white lighthouse sitting among tall spruce 100 feet above cliffs, caves, and rocky rubble. Bear Island Light was built in 1839 and rebuilt in 1889, and was attended until 1982, when its flashing beacon was deactivated and replaced with lighted buoys.

From the lighthouse and the west end of Bear Island, paddle due south for a little more than 0.5 mile to reach the west end of Sutton Island. While making this crossing, watch for black guillemots and double-crested cormorants. Also keep an eye out for both harbor seals and their rare cousins, gray seals. While harbor seals are much more common on the Maine coast, gray seals do frequent this area. Much bigger than harbor seals, gray seals can grow to be 10 feet long and 650 pounds, while harbor seals reach 5 feet and 250 pounds. A gray seal's uniform black or gray color contrasts with the spotted fur of a harbor seal. Gray seals can dive to almost 500 feet while feeding on fish and cuttlefish.

On the northwestern corner of Sutton Island is an amazing osprey nest built on a rock outcropping separated from the island by a thin stretch of water. The nest may be as old as 100 years, and the sticks it is made of are piled several feet high. Keep at least 0.25 mile from the nest, as the birds experience a lot of disturbance from boats in this area. If the adults are forced to leave the nest too often, the chicks may not survive. Nonetheless, it is a wonderful experience to sit in your kayak with binoculars and watch an adult osprey bring fish to its young and eager chicks. Instead of paddling around the western end of Sutton Island, turn left before reaching the osprey nest and follow the northern shore, keeping the island on your right. There is a cobble beach at the western end of the northern shore, but steep granite cliffs wall much of this side of the island. A sea arch can also be found here. The arch, created by eroding waves, is about forty feet tall.

As you reach the eastern end of Sutton Island, Little Cranberry Island comes into view to the southeast. Great Cranberry Island is farther away to the southwest. Excellent views of Acadia's mountains can be found by looking north. Turn your boat to the north in order to return to Seal Harbor. Crowninshield Point at the entrance to Seal Harbor is about a mile due north of the eastern end of Sutton Island. This is a long crossing in an area with heavy boat traffic. If you are traveling in a group, stay close together so you are easier for boats to spot and avoid, and try not to make this crossing in foggy conditions. As you re-enter Seal Harbor, keep an eye out for bald eagles, which sometimes soar above the harbor's shoreline.

Directions

From downtown Bar Harbor, follow Maine Route 3 south for 8.1 miles. Seal Harbor will be on your left. A public parking area is on the right.

fog

The sun rises above thick fog over the Atlantic Ocean as seen from Cadillac Mountain.

Fog is a common weather phenomenon in Acadia National Park, particularly during summer. Fog is basically a cloud that forms just above land or water when wind blows warm, moist air over a cool surface. Since the water temperature in the Gulf of Maine is usually below fifty-five degrees, summer's warm southwesterly winds often create fog in the waters around Mount Desert Island. For this reason, a warm sunny day does not preclude the possibility that thick, menacing fog can roll in from the ocean at any time. The type of fog that forms in the Gulf of Maine is called advection fog and forms when warm, moist air passes over a cold body of water or ice. In contrast, the fog you may find in places like the Great Heath near Seawall or the ball field in Bar Harbor is called radiation fog. Radiation fog forms when the ground radiates its warmth outward on a clear night.

Fog obviously can cause dangers for boaters of all kinds. When sea-kayaking around Acadia, carry a foghorn in case you get stuck in an unexpected fog bank, because typically a kayak will not show up on a larger boat's radar screen. You also should be experienced at using a compass and nautical chart so that you can navigate yourself to safety. Often you can see a bank of fog offshore slowly making its way inland when there is a sea breeze. In this case, head back to shore and wait for better weather. The Hadley Point and Seal Cove trips in this chapter are generally the safest in fog due to the fact that they have less boat traffic than other areas around Mount Desert Island and there are no large open-water crossings, but kayak in the fog only if you have sufficient navigational experience.

Trip #39

Somes Sound

> Distance: **7.5 miles round–trip**
>
> Estimated Time: **4 hours**
>
> **A paddle in the only fiord in the eastern United States, with views of tall ocean–side cliffs and good wildlife–watching opportunities.**

WEATHER AND TIDE CONSIDERATIONS: When the wind and tide are moving in opposite directions, ominous standing waves can develop in the shallow and narrow mouth of the sound, known as the Narrows. Otherwise, the tides are not much of an issue in Somes Sound. The wind is another story. Running north to south, with mountains rising up on both its eastern and western shores, Somes Sound experiences a strong wind-tunnel effect when winds are out of the north or south. These winds can make it very difficult to paddle, and you are better off trying an alternate trip like Hadley Point (trip #36). Winds out of the east or west are usually not a problem.

Somes Sound is a narrow finger of water that almost cuts Mount Desert Island in two. A glacier created Somes Sound, scouring a deep U-shaped valley between Acadia and Norumbega Mountains. The glacier carved through Mount Desert Island all the way to the ocean, and now the valley is filled with sea water. This paddling trip starts near the mouth of the sound in the working harbor of Mansett, where you can explore the shoreline of Greening Island before making your way up the sound to Valley Cove, Eagle Cliff, and a waterfall at Man o' War Brook. Like all of the kayaking trips around Mount Desert Island, Somes Sound provides good opportunities for seeing wildlife such as seabirds, bald eagles, and seals.

From the boat ramp in Mansett, Southwest Harbor is to your left and Greening Island is across the water to the northeast. Straight ahead is a passage between Southwest Harbor and Greening Island that is the most direct route to Somes Sound. The water is shallow in this passage, which sometimes makes for a bumpy crossing. For this trip, head to the eastern tip of Greening Island and paddle around the northeastern side of the island before heading north into the sound. With Southwest Harbor to the west and Northeast Harbor to the east, the waters around Greening Island get a fair amount of boat traffic, so keep your group together and be aware of your surroundings. Abraham Somes purchased the island in 1775 from Abenaki Indians for a gallon of rum. Somes was one of the first permanent settlers on Mount Desert Island, having built a log cabin at Somes Point after sailing to Somes Sound from Gloucester, Massachusetts, in 1761. Still privately owned, Greening Island has stunning views of Somes Sound and the mountains of Mount Desert Island.

As you paddle north from Greening Island, you will make your way through the mouth of Somes Sound, known as the Narrows. Here the sound is only about 1,000 feet across and the water is very shallow—less than 10 feet deep in spots. If the wind is blowing against the tide here, there can be some fairly choppy water. Further north in Somes Sound, the water attains depths of up to 150 feet. The gently sloping field on the western shore of the Narrows is known as Jesuit Spring. This is the site of a French colony settled in 1613 which was quickly attacked and destroyed by the English in one of many skirmishes between the two naval powers in eastern Maine and Maritime Canada during the seventeenth and eighteenth centuries.

Just beyond Jesuit Spring, Flying Mountain rises 271 feet from the waters of Somes Sound. Follow the shoreline on your left around Flying Mountain and into Valley Cove, a sheltered inlet bordered by Flying Mountain on the south and the spectacular 400-foot cliffs of Eagle Cliff on the west. This is one of the most sheltered coves on the island, and it is still used as a place to anchor boats in extremely rough weather. The shoreline here is part of Acadia National Park and makes an excellent spot to stop and take a break. The Flying Mountain Trail is only a few yards from shore and can quickly take you to the summit of Flying Mountain or the top of Eagle Cliff, both of which have excellent views of Somes Sound. We

Somes Sound is the only fiord in the eastern United States.

have never seen bald eagles on Eagle Cliff, but they are common visitors to Somes Sound and can be seen at any point during this trip. To the north of Valley Cove is Acadia Mountain, and across the water to the northeast is Norumbega Mountain, which at 850 feet is the highest point above the sound.

From Valley Cove, continue north along the western shore of Somes Sound. Eagle Cliff and the northeastern shoulder of Saint Sauveur Mountain dominate the shoreline for much of the way to Man o' War Brook, which marks the low point between Saint Sauveur and Acadia Mountains. At Man o' War Brook, water rushes over steep rocks into the sound at a point where the water is deep enough for large boats. The deep water made it easy for schooners to sail into the sound, quickly collect fresh water, and head back out to sea. This historical easy access to fresh water in a hidden cove probably is responsible for the stories of pirate ships using this area. Today, Man o' War Brook is a scenic stop for boats, with its cool, cedar-lined shoreline flanked by the dramatic slopes of Acadia and Saint Sauveur Mountains providing beautiful visual relief.

From here you can return to Mansett by either following the western shore or paddling across the sound to the rugged shoreline under Norumbega Mountain. South of Norumbega, the shoreline becomes gentler as you pass some of the biggest summer homes on Mount Desert Island in the woods on the outskirts of the town of Northeast Harbor. On your return paddle to Mansett, keep your eyes open for guillemots, cormorants, and loons, as well as both harbor and gray seals. Looking south and east past Greening Island, you can see Sutton Island and the Cranberries and out to the open Atlantic.

Directions

Just south of downtown Southwest Harbor, turn left off Maine Route 102 onto Route 102A. After 1.0 mile, turn left onto Mansett Lane. At the end of the road, turn left onto Shore Road. The boat ramp is a short distance on the right.

what is a fiord?

Somes Sound is the only fiord (also spelled fjord) on the East Coast of the United States. Fjord is a Norwegian word used to describe the deep bays and inlets that line the coast of Norway on the Norwegian Sea. In addition to Norway, fiords are also common in British Columbia, Alaska, and New Zealand. Most fiords were carved by glaciers during the last ice age, between 15,000 and 25,000 years ago. They are typically deep fingers of sea water surrounded by tall cliffs or mountains. In the case of Somes Sound, the mountains rise 850 feet above the water, which attains depths of 150 feet. If you drained Somes Sound, it would look much like the U-shaped valleys between Dorr Mountain and Huguenot Head, and Cadillac and Pemetic Mountains. While a fiord is usually very deep for most of its length, it is often much more shallow at its mouth. In the case of Somes Sound, when the Wisconsin Glacier retreated about 13,000 years ago, it left a pile of debris, called a terminal moraine, at the mouth of the sound. The water here is only about 10 feet deep. The narrow and shallow mouth of Somes Sound makes it harder for water to leave and enter the sound during changes in tides; creating a unique mix of water and nutrients that supports a wide variety of wildlife including lobsters, loons, seals, great blue herons, and bald eagles.

Seal Cove to Pretty Marsh

> **Distance: 10.0 miles round-trip**
>
> **Estimated Time: 7 hours**
>
> **A paddle on the "quiet" side of Mount Desert Island filled with wooded shoreline, beautiful islands, and bountiful wildlife.**

WEATHER AND TIDE CONSIDERATIONS: Low tide will make it necessary to paddle on the west side of Moose Island, but this will not add additional time to your trip. A strong wind out of the southwest can cause a fair amount of choppiness at the southern ends of Moose and Hardwood Islands. Otherwise, the wind and tides should not cause too many problems. There is a small amount of boat traffic in this area, but much less than most other areas around Mount Desert Island.

Mount Desert Island is bordered on the west by a body of water known as Blue Hill Bay. From Seal Cove north to Pretty Marsh, views to the west of Blue Hill give way to the gentle shoreline of Bartlett Island as the bay funnels though the Bartlett Narrows. Here seals and porpoises regularly come to feed on the fish that become concentrated between the islands. There is much to explore here: the rocky intertidal zones of Mount Desert Island, the beautiful shoreline of Moose Island, and the pastoral views of the historically preserved farms of Bartlett Island. Trips of almost any length are possible in this area, but this trip highlights the five miles between Seal Cove and Pretty Marsh Harbor. While there is a boat ramp in Pretty Marsh, parking is restricted to residents of the town of Mount Desert, so you must begin your trip in Seal Cove.

    This trip can take most of the day, so be sure to carry plenty of food, water, and extra clothing. Also note that all of the islands in

The Bartlett Narrows is a great place to watch for such wildlife as harbor seals and porpoises.

Blue Hill Bay are privately owned and landing on them for any reason is discouraged. The one exception to this is on Bartlett Island, which is owned by the Rockefeller family. If you land on Bartlett Island, try to remain below the high-tide line in order to minimize impact on the island. There is also a small picnic area in the national park on the eastern side of Pretty Marsh Harbor where it is allowable to land. The rest of Mount Desert Island in this area is private property. In addition to respecting private property, be sure to give a wide berth to seals hauled out on the ledges of Bartlett Island and north of Pretty Marsh. They are very skittish of kayaks and lose a lot of valuable energy going in and out of the water. Stay at least 0.5 mile away from any seals hauled out on land.

With those logistical concerns out of the way, be prepared to enjoy a wonderful paddle. From the put-in at Seal Cove, paddle west to leave the cove and then turn right around Reed Point. From here you can see Moose, Hardwood, and Bartlett Islands to the north and west. Moose Island is particularly beautiful, with its gravel beaches giving way to heath and blueberry bushes before a forest of tall spruce takes over. Like many of the islands in Maine, Moose Island was used to graze livestock for much of the nineteenth century. Moose Island was particularly useful for this because a gravel bar connects it with Mount Desert Island at low tide. As a kayaker, you will need to pay attention to the tide in order to avoid having to carry your boat over the bar. The bar is usually above water during the two hours on either side of low tide. Of course, you can paddle around the western side of the island during any tide.

From Moose Island, paddle to the northwest toward Hardwood Island. Hardwood Island is indeed named for its forest of hardwoods, in this case birch, maple, and beech. Hardwood Island has a shoreline of gravel beaches with good views to the east of Mount Desert Island's western mountains. Paddle along the eastern shore of this island until you reach its northern tip. From here it is a 0.75-mile paddle to the southern end of Bartlett Island. Feel free to take a break on Bartlett Island, but please stay below the high-tide mark, pack out all of your trash, and refrain from building fires. Bartlett Island was first settled in the 1760s and its fertile soil made it an excellent place to farm. However, by the early 1900s most families had moved to the mainland or Mount Desert Island where access to services was much more convenient. The Rockefeller family bought the island in the early 1970s in order to prevent it from being developed into a resort community. They now run the farm on the eastern side of the island that can be seen from the town landing in Pretty Marsh.

Follow the eastern shore of Bartlett Island by keeping the island on your left. You will see Folly Island to the east and the diminutive John Island to the northeast as you enter Bartlett Narrows. The waters and fish of Blue Hill Bay are funneled through this narrow passage between islands, creating an excellent feeding opportunity for harbor seals and harbor porpoises. This is one of the best areas around Acadia for spotting these marine mammals. Keep your eyes open for the periscoping, doglike heads of seals, and listen for the sounds of exhaling porpoises, which will sometimes approach quite close to a kayak. Ospreys nest in the area and can often be seen soaring above the water in search of fish. Double-crested cormorants and black guillemots are also frequent visitors to Bartlett Narrows.

Once you are past John Island, paddle east across Bartlett Narrows to the western shore of Mount Desert Island. Due east of John

Island is the Pretty Marsh picnic area in Acadia National Park. While it is a steep climb to the picnic tables from the shore, you can stop here in all but the highest tides and take a break before heading back to Seal Cove. However, the shoreline on Bartlett Island is more amenable to stopping and has good views of Acadia's mountains. No matter where you stop, to return to Seal Cove keep the shoreline of Mount Desert Island on your left. This stretch of shoreline has small cobble beaches, interesting rocky outcrops with veins of quartz, and good opportunities to observe the different layers of the intertidal zones. After returning to Seal Cove, you may want to drive to the town landing at Pretty Marsh to take in the sunset over Bartlett Island.

Directions

From the intersection of Seal Cove Road and Maine Route 102 in Seal Cove, follow Route 102 north for 0.3 mile. Turn left onto Cape Road. Drive past the boat ramp in Seal Cove to a small turnout, which is about 0.5 mile on the left. There is parking on the right.

harbor seals and porpoises

While you need to take a whale-watching excursion to see dolphins and whales near Acadia, it is quite common to enjoy visits from harbor seals and harbor porpoises while kayaking the waters around Mount Desert Island. Of course, both seals and porpoises are mammals and need to breathe air, which means they have to show themselves at the surface every now and then. If you are lucky, they will do this near your boat. Never approach seals, especially when they are hauled out onto rocks or a beach, where they rest in relative safety. They are easily startled and waste precious energy swimming back and forth between the rocks and the water when disturbed by careless paddlers. Give them 0.5 mile of breathing room.

Seals are much more comfortable in the water than on land and may sometimes come near a kayak to check it out. However, whether you see seals in the water or not is very much up to them. The same can be said of harbor porpoises, which seem to go about their business with no regard to kayaks. If they need to swim near your boat to get where they are going, they will do so, but they will not hang around or display any curiosity whatsoever. Nonetheless, seeing the sleek black bodies and dorsal fins of a pod of porpoises within a few yards of your kayak is an exciting experience. Harbor seals appear in all of the waters around Acadia, including Somes Sound. Harbor porpoises are similarly distributed, although you are most likely to see them during a paddle in Mount Desert Narrows, in Bartlett Narrows, or in Frenchman Bay around the Porcupine Islands.

While kayaking, you will usually hear harbor porpoises before you see them. Their exhalation blow is a sharp, puffing sound that sounds almost like a sneeze and is probably responsible for the nickname "puffing pig." Usually in groups of two to five animals, harbor porpoises generally come up to breathe

Harbor seals are common in the water around Acadia.

together, slowly arching their backs out of the water. While their undersides are white, you most likely will see only their black or dark gray backs. They are small for whales and porpoises, rarely exceeding six feet in length and weighing around 130 pounds. Harbor porpoises are found throughout the Northern Hemisphere in cold and subarctic coastal waters.

Like harbor porpoises, harbor seals are found throughout the Northern Hemisphere in cold coastal waters. They are year-round residents in the Gulf of Maine, where they feed on fish, crustaceans, and squid. Harbor seals have heads shaped much like a dog's, and they often poke their heads up out of the water to look around. Their five-foot-long bodies pack on as much as 250 pounds, much of which is a fatty blubber that allows them to stay warm in the chilly waters off the Maine coast. On rare occasions, you may see gray seals, which are much bigger than harbor seals and have heads shaped like that of a horse. Harbor seals come in a variety of colors including iron gray, brown, silver gray, and brownish black. They usually have spots of some kind.

intertidal zones

The tides around Mount Desert Island rise and fall between eight and ten feet. This twice-daily gradual change in water levels creates unique habitats on the rocky ledges that surround the island. These habitats vary drastically in the amount of sunlight they receive and in the amount of exposure they have to the air. In ten feet of rock at the water's edge, there are several different zones of life. Each zone supports a different group of organisms that have evolved to exploit these varying amounts of sunlight, surf, air, and water. The intertidal zones can be studied all around Mount Desert Island and the surrounding islands, most easily from a kayak. If you prefer to visit them on foot, however, look along the shore below Ocean Drive, at the end of the Ship Harbor Nature Trail, or below Bass Harbor Head Light.

Intertidal zones generally are broken down into five distinct sections, which support a variety of life from blue-green algae and periwinkles to kelp and sea urchins.

The spray zone: Just above the high-tide line, this zone is never submerged in sea water but receives a constant spray of salt water from crashing surf. Sometimes called the black zone, this zone is characterized by the presence of primitive blue-green algae (*Calothrix*) and black lichen (*Verrucaria*). The algae or lichen create a thin, black, very slippery covering over the rocks. A rough-shelled variety of periwinkle feeds on the algae in this zone and seeks shelter in crevices of rocks in both this zone and the barnacle zone.

The barnacle zone: Contrasting with the black spray zone is the barnacle zone, made up of masses of white acorn barnacles (*Balanus balanoides*). The barnacle zone is below the water only at high tide, so the barnacles must be able to withstand long periods of exposure to the air as well as Maine's pounding surf. Barnacles are crustaceans, and they attach themselves to rocks with a cementlike substance they also use to build a conical shell around themselves. At the top of these shells is a small valve they can close during low tide to protect themselves from the drying effects of the air. At high tide, they open this valve to feed, extending feathery comb-shaped arms to catch microscopic organisms.

The rockweed zone: This zone is out of the water about the same amount of time it is under the water. It is characterized by a covering of stringy, rubbery, brown algae known as rockweed. There are two dominant species of rockweed around Acadia: Bladder wrack is common in the upper level of the rockweed zone, while knotted wrack proliferates in the lower level of the zone. Both types of seaweed use gas bladders filled with air to keep them suspended near the light during high tide so they can

Intertidal creatures, periwinkles are most common in the rockweed zone.

continue to photosynthesize. During low tide they form a thick, protective covering that is inhabited by a wide variety of wildlife such as common periwinkles, blue mussels, and dog whelks, which prey on both mussels and barnacles.

The Irish moss zone: Exposed to the air only during low tide, the Irish moss zone is characterized by red algae such as Irish moss and dulse. Irish moss is a maroon-colored seaweed that has an iridescent sheen in bright sunlight. Dulse is a six-inch-long red seaweed with broad, flat fronds. Irish moss is harvested around the world to make carrageenin, a thickener used in food and cosmetic products. The Irish moss zone also provides habitat for a number of shellfish and crustaceans.

The kelp zone: This zone is above water only during extreme low tides in the spring and fall. This is a diverse underwater community that centers around kelp, a brown seaweed usually characterized by long, leathery blades. The kelp provides the ideal environment for aquatic animals such as starfish and sea urchins. Starfish feed on mussels, clams, and other shellfish by wrapping their arms around their prey, prying open the shell, inserting their stomachs and digesting the animal. Sea urchins are vegetarian, feeding mainly on kelp. Brittle stars, sea cucumbers, sea anemones, and crabs also inhabit the kelp zone.

8

the other acadia:
the schoodic peninsula and isle au haut

WHILE MOUNT DESERT ISLAND may be the physical and social heart of Acadia National Park, the Schoodic Peninsula and Isle au Haut sections of the park are just as compelling. The Schoodic Peninsula is the only part of Acadia on the mainland, its 2,100 acres of headland jutting out into the open Atlantic. Isle au Haut, perhaps the wildest part of Acadia, lies ten miles off the Maine coast and features spruce-covered highlands and dramatic seashore cliffs. Both sections of the park receive considerably less visitation than Mount Desert Island due to their distance from the main section of Acadia.

Schoodic Peninsula

The Schoodic Peninsula is a secluded section of the Maine coast approximately a one-hour drive east from Bar Harbor. It is the point of land that sits across Frenchman Bay from Mount Desert Island. Schoodic is a thickly forested headland, with a coastline that receives no protection from the relentless pounding of the Atlantic Ocean. Pink-granite ledges scoured of vegetation line the peninsula. These ledges are good places to soak in ocean views and get away from the crowds of Mount Desert Island. A visit to the Schoodic Peninsula should start with a drive on the Park Road.

Lighthouse as seen from the Schoodic Peninsula.

The Park Road follows the coast, providing ocean views at every turn. Across Frenchman Bay, you can see the full expanse of Cadillac Mountain. About three miles from the park boundary, a rough gravel road on the left leads to the summit of Schoodic Head. This road makes a good hiking or mountain-biking trail for those without a four-wheel-drive vehicle. The views from the 440-foot summit are excellent.

Farther down the Park Road is Schoodic Point. Its massive granite ledges are a must visit. The rocks here show intense wear from glaciers in the past as well as from pounding surf in the present. Look for grooves in the rock caused by the grinding action of rocks stuck in glacier ice as it moved over the peninsula thousands of years ago. Today Schoodic Point is at the mercy of the Atlantic Ocean, as there are no islands or reefs offshore to break up the waves, which can reach heights of thirty feet during storms. While Thunder Hole on Mount Desert Island is a popular spot for watching towering, geyserlike wave crashes, Schoodic Point may be the most reliable place in the park to see large waves making huge splashes.

The remainder of the peninsula continues to provide breathtaking scenery. Although there is not much hiking in the area, short trails leave from the Blueberry Hill parking area and ascend Schoodic Head as well as a small, rocky hill called the Anvil. Biking options are limited to the dirt road up Schoodic Head and the twelve-mile loop around the Park Road and Route 186. Sea-kayaking in this area can be dangerous due to the exposure to the open Atlantic.

Logistics

To get to the peninsula from Mount Desert Island, you need to drive back to Ellsworth, where you should turn right and head east on Route 1. Follow Maine 186 south in West Gouldsboro until you reach the Park Road, just beyond Winter Harbor. Overnight camping is not permitted in the Schoodic section of the park, although there are several private campgrounds near the park (see Other Activities, chapter 9).

Isle au Haut

The island of Isle au Haut has a unique wilderness character that can not be found anywhere else in Acadia National Park. Dramatic 100-foot cliffs drop down to the Atlantic Ocean on the southern end of the island. Beautiful cobblestone beaches fill the spaces between the cliffs. Seals, eagles, loons, and guillemots are common along the shore, while deer, coyote, and numerous songbirds fill the interior boreal forest. Ten miles out to sea, Isle au Haut sees fewer than 10,000 visitors a year, considerably fewer than the 3 million who visit Mount Desert Island. The one road that circles the island does not intrude on the coastline in the national park. All these factors contribute to make this an ideal place to find quiet solitude.

Evidence of Native Americans can be found all around the island in the form of shell middens and stone tools. Shell middens were basically garbage dumps where the Indians threw their used clamshells and other refuse. (If you happen to find a stone arrowhead or cutting blade, please leave it as you found it. It is illegal to disturb archaeological artifacts in a national park.) The first European to "discover" Isle au Haut was Samuel de Champlain, who first made note of the island during a voyage in 1603. He named the island Isle Haut, or High Island.

Like many of New England's outer islands, Isle au Haut was settled by fishermen who liked its close proximity to fertile fishing grounds. At one point, the island had a community of around 300 permanent residents, but during the last century that number has dwindled to around 70. The introduction of the gas-powered engine made it less of an advantage for fishermen to live on the island. However, fishing is still alive and well on Isle au Haut, accounting for the major percentage of the island's economy.

In the 1880s, residents of the big East Coast cities discovered Isle au Haut as a summer getaway. Unlike Mount Desert Island, with its proliferation of hotels, restaurants, and hectic social life, Isle au Haut was a quiet home away from home, with private summer cottages blending into the community. In 1945, descendants of one of these early summer visitors, Ernest Bowditch of Boston, donated almost half of the island to Acadia National Park. Today, 2,728 acres of Isle au Haut are part of the park.

Soaking up the views of Penobscot Bay from Ebens Head on Isle au Haut.

Logistics

Getting to Isle au Haut involves taking the mail boat from Stonington, which is at the southern tip of Deer Isle. It is a long day trip from Bar Harbor, as the drive takes about 1.5 hours and the boat ride is another 35 minutes. The mail boat makes two trips a day, three in the summer. For more information, contact the Isle au Haut Company at 207-367-5193. While day trips make a good introduction to the island, the best way to experience Isle au Haut is to spend two or three nights in the Duck Harbor Campground, open from May 15 through October 15. Run by the national park, the campground has only five lean-tos and no tent sites. This limited space is highly coveted, so you will want to make reservations early. Call the Park Service for the rules regarding reservations. Currently, reservations are taken beginning April 1 for the following summer.

From the campground, you have access to eighteen miles of hiking trails that explore both the dramatic seaside cliffs and the island's forested highlands. While the island's high point, Mount Champlain, reaches the lofty height of 556 feet, it is completely forested and has no views. The best views on the island are from Duck Harbor Mountain, which is a short hike from the campground. From the ledges of this modest 314-foot peak, there are spectacular views of Penobscot Bay, with its deep blue waters surrounding scores of islands. The Western Head, Cliff, and Goat Trails all provide excellent coastal hiking. Each of the three trails alternates between ascending rocky cliffs and traversing secluded cobble beaches. Harbor seals and gray seals can be seen feeding offshore, as well as black guillemots, loons, cormorants, common eiders, and harlequin ducks. (A complete list of hiking trails can be found in appendix A.)

Experienced paddlers will find that Isle au Haut is also a great place to sea-kayak. The Isle au Haut Company can transport your kayak to the island, or you can paddle the six miles from Stonington. Contact the Maine Island Trail Association (see appendix) to learn about paddling opportunities around the other islands in Penobscot Bay.

Biking on Isle au Haut is discouraged by the Park Service due to the rough nature of the roads and the fact that bikes are not allowed on hiking trails. Experienced mountain-bikers will find that the dirt roads are not a difficult ride, but those who prefer pavement or the carriage roads will find biking Isle au Haut unpleasant. In any event, there are only a few miles of road on the island, so it is not really worth the extra effort of transporting a bike on the mail boat.

Like the rest of Acadia, Isle au Haut is busiest during July and August. During these months, the mail boat drops park visitors off at the campground in Duck Harbor. During the rest of the year, visitors are taken to the town of Isle au Haut, which is about a five-mile hike from the campground. Therefore, park visits in May and early June, as well as in the fall, take a little extra effort, but the rewards are empty trails, fewer bugs, and peaceful solitude. Whenever you visit, you are sure to be charmed by the island's slow pace, relatively empty trails, and dramatic shoreline.

9
other activities

ACADIA OFFERS so much to do you could spend years there and never run out of ideas. This chapter lists things you can do to fill in the spaces between your hiking, bicycling, and paddling trips.

Airplane/Glider Rides

Nothing helps you get the big picture of Acadia better than seeing it from above. There are two options for getting airborne:

Acadia Air—Bar Harbor Airport, Trenton, ME; 207-667-5534. Many different trips are available, including Somes Sound, Mount Desert Island, Bar Harbor, or lighthouses.

Island Soaring Glider Rides—Bar Harbor Airport, Trenton, ME; 207-667-SOAR. A peaceful and quiet way to enjoy soaring above Acadia. Experience it as the bald eagles do.

Boats and Ferries

Seeing the beauty of Acadia from the water provides you with a unique perspective of the park. Boat rides are a great way to see seabirds and marine mammals up close. Ferries can take you to some of the outer islands in the area, which have their own culture and scenery separate from Mount Desert Island. See the appendix for a complete listing of ferries and tour companies.

Bus and Trolley Tours

Let someone else do the driving—sit back and enjoy the scenery while you listen to the story of the land. If you have never visited the park before, these tours are a good introduction to Acadia and Mount Desert Island.

Oli's Trolley—62 Main Street, Bar Harbor, ME; 207-288-9899. Go on a historical tour and hear tales of a lost era, the cottage days of Bar Harbor. Also find out about the park's flora and fauna.

Acadia National Park Tours—Testa's Restaurant, 53 Main Street, Bar Harbor, ME; 207-288-3327. Learn about the island's history, flora and fauna, geology, and mansions, and see the major sights. Handicapped accessible.

Gardens

Enjoy a peaceful stroll through a lovely garden.

Asticou Azalea Garden—Asticou Way, Maine Highway 3 and 198, Northeast Harbor, ME (no phone). This garden has an Oriental style. Enjoy some peace and quiet away from the summer crowds. June is the best time to find the azaleas in bloom.

Thuya Garden—Route 3, Northeast Harbor, ME; 207-276-5130. This garden is open seven days a week, all year long. It is an English-style garden, featuring 80 percent perennials and 20 percent annuals. The best time to catch everything in bloom is August. They also have hiking trails on their 260 acres of land.

Wild Gardens of Acadia—Sieur de Monts, Acadia National Park, ME; 207-288-3519. These gardens are perfect for those of you who want to study the local flora of Acadia. They have a wide variety of the flowers and foliage typically found in the park, and everything is labeled with common and scientific names.

Horse-Drawn-Carriage Rides

Experience the carriage roads as they were originally intended.

Wildwood Stables—Park Loop Road, Acadia National Park, ME; 207-276-3622. Handicapped-accessible carriage is available.

Jordan Pond Teahouse

On the Park Loop Road, Acadia National Park, ME; 207-276-3610. One of our favorite things to do is stop in at the Jordan Pond Teahouse for tea and popovers. The food is delicious and the scenery is spectacular.

Museums

A great way to learn about the island (especially on a rainy day). Most museums are seasonal, so be sure to call ahead for hours.

Abbe Museum—Sieur de Monts Spring, Acadia National Park, ME; 207-288-3519. This museum celebrates Maine's Native American heritage through exhibits, craft workshops with native people, and ongoing archaeological research.

Bar Harbor Historical Society—33 Ledgelawn Avenue, Bar Harbor, ME; 207-288-0000. Experience the "lost" Bar Harbor and its famous summer colony through this fine collection of early drawings, hotel memorabilia, photographs, sketches, and pictures of the devastating fire of 1947.

Islesford Museum—Little Cranberry Island, ME; 207-244-9224. This historic maritime museum is part of Acadia National Park. The exhibits portray the lives of the hardy seafaring people of the Cranberry Islands. You need to take a ferry to get there (see appendix). Call Acadia National Park for information: 207-288-3338.

Mount Desert Island Historical Society—1119 Main St., Somesville, ME; 207-244-5043 (moving to Route 198 Old Sound School House in June 2000). Explore Mount Desert Island's history with their rotating exhibits, genealogy collection, photo archive, business records, and settlement artifacts (furniture, household items). Be sure to visit the first town office by walking over the scenic (and highly photographed) decorative bridge.

Mount Desert Oceanarium—Two locations: Route 3, Bar Harbor, ME; 207-288-5005; and Clark Point Road, Southwest Harbor, ME; 207-244-7330. These museums offer a great way for kids to explore the ocean life of Acadia. The Southwest Harbor location has twenty-six tanks filled with local sea life, as well as informal staff talks and hands-on and interactive exhibits. The Bar Harbor location offers a lobster museum; staff walks out on a salt marsh; and programs about lobsters, lobster fishing, and harbor seals; a lobster hatchery (opens in June of each year).

Wendell Gilley Museum—Corner of Main and Herrick, Southeast Harbor, ME; 207-244-7555. This museum features wood bird carvings made by Wendell Gilley, a famous native Maine carver. It also has wildlife art exhibits and natural-history video programs.

Nature Tours

Down East Nature Tours—P.O. Box 521, Bar Harbor, ME; 207-288-8128. Explore the natural beauty of the park with qualified naturalists and biologists. Get a personalized tour, one-on-one with a guide. Their specialty is native birds. Please call in advance to make reservations.

Photography

Of course you can aim your camera practically anywhere and get a nice photo, but for some special tips and free advice, contact the Park Service and hook up with the Kodak representative, who gives talks on techniques and the best places to shoot; 207-288-3338.

Picnics

The places to picnic are limited only by your imagination. If you like official picnic sites complete with tables and restrooms, try these:

Bear Brook—Park Loop Road between the visitor center and Champlain Mountain (handicapped accessible).

Fabbri—Park Loop Road just after Otter Cliffs (handicapped accessible).

Frazer Point—Schoodic Peninsula.

Pretty Marsh—on Route 102 between Pretty Marsh and Seal Cove.

Seawall—across Route 102A from the Seawall Campground (handicapped accessible).

Thompson Island—Route 3 just before Mount Desert Island (handicapped accessible).

Ranger Programs

The Park Service has programs on just about everything. There are ranger programs while hiking, on sea cruises, on bus tours, and in the campground amphitheaters and other special areas like the base of Champlain Mountain for peregrine watching. Ask at the visitor center for a complete listing of programs available during your stay, read up on the different programs in the *Beaver Log* or *Acadia Weekly* (provided free and found in many restaurants, shops, and at the visitor centers), or call 207-288-3338.

Rock-Climbing

While Acadia is not one of the premier climbing areas in the East, the glaciers did leave behind some wonderful rock-climbing in places such as Otter Cliffs, Champlain Mountain, and South Bubble. For information about climbing routes or to explore these climbs safely by hiring a guide, contact:

Acadia Mountain Guides Climbing School—198 Main Street, Bar Harbor, ME; 207-288-8186.

Atlantic Climbing School—24 Cottage Street, Bar Harbor, ME; 207-288-2521.

Snowshoeing or Cross-Country Skiing

On those rare occasions when the coast gets hit with a big snow, the carriage roads are a fantastic place to get into the backcountry. Use this book's biking chapter as a guide for skiing. Most hiking trails should be attempted only by experienced winter hikers, since the steep trails often require crampon use. When planning a hike, you should realize that the Park Loop Road is closed in winter, except for the Ocean Drive portion of the road and the access to Jordan Pond from Seal Harbor.

Swimming

On a hot summer day, nothing will cool you off faster than jumping into refreshing Maine waters. There are only two places to swim in Acadia: Echo Lake Beach and Sand Beach. By July the water at Echo Lake Beach, at the south end of Echo Lake, is considerably warmer than the cold waters of the Atlantic, which rarely get warmer than fifty-five degrees. Most of the lakes and ponds on Mount Desert Island are used as public water supplies, so please respect the no-swimming rules.

Theaters

Acadia Repertory Theatre—Route 102, Mount Desert, ME; 207-244-7260. Enjoy live, professional theater.

Reel Pizza—Top of Rodick Street, Bar Harbor, ME; 207-288-3811. Enjoy a pizza while you watch the movie.

Criterion Theatre—35 Cottage Street, Bar Harbor, ME; 207-288-3441. Good to know: this theater will have matinees in the summer if it's raining at noon.

Trail Maintenance

It takes a huge amount of work to keep hiking trails and carriage roads in good condition. Volunteering to help out with trail maintenance is a great way to give back to the park. Friends of Acadia runs a volunteer trail-maintenance program in conjunction with the national park. Currently, maintenance is scheduled on Tuesdays, Thursdays, and Saturdays. For more information, call Friends of

Acadia at 207-288-3340 or the Park Service at 207-288-3338. The AMC's Echo Lake Camp also leads trail-maintenance trips twice a week. Echo Lake Camp can be reached at 207-244-3747.

Whale Watch

If you have never gone on a whale watch before, this is a fantastic place to do it. Sighting whales is so common that all of the tour operators guarantee that you will see at least one whale (or your money back or a free ride on another trip). See the appendix for a complete listing of whale-watch boats.

appendix a
hiking trails

THE FOLLOWING BRIEF TRAIL DESCRIPTIONS do not cover all the trails in the park. Those selected for detailed treatment here are well marked, offically recognized and maintained paths that give access to all of the preferred summits on Mount Desert Island and Isle au Haut (the Schoodic Peninsula, with five short, forested trails, is excluded). For the most part, you can reach the individual summits in comfortable half-day walks. To simplify reference and to conform with Acadia National Park nomenclature, the island is divided into an eastern district and a western district. The NPS maintains all trails described, and markings include signs, cairns, blue painted blazes, and metal markers. In addition to the map in this guide, refer to the AMC Acadia/Mt. Desert map in this book.

The National Park Service has rated each trail based on the following criteria:

Easy: Fairly level ground.

Moderate: Uneven ground with some steep grades and/or gradual climbing. Footing may be difficult in places.

Strenuous: Steep and/or long grades; steady climbing or descending. Sometimes difficult footing, difficult maneuvering.

Ladder: Iron-rung ladders and handrails placed on steep grades or difficult terrain. These trails are very difficult.

Eastern District
(East of Somes Sound)
Champlain Mountain (1,058 ft./322 m.)
Area

Precipice Trail

NPS rating: **Ladder**

This trail starts from the Precipice Trail parking area, located 1.75 mi. beyond the Sieur de Monts Spring entrance on Park Loop Rd. at the foot of Champlain Mountain. The trailhead is located just before the entrance-fee station on Park Loop Road.

Following a rugged talus slope full of big boulders, the trail ascends northwest about 0.4 mi. Here, the right fork runs under the east face of the mountain to connect with the Bear Brook Trail 0.5 mi. from the summit on the north ridge. From the fork, the Precipice climbs southwest, rising steeply to a point directly west of the parking area. The direction is now west-northwest. Along this section of the trail, ladders and iron rungs help hikers negotiate precipitous vertical drop-offs. The final 500 ft. to the summit follow gentle slopes and ledges. People afraid of heights should not climb the Precipice Trail. In addition, hikers under 5 ft. tall may have difficulty reaching some handholds. Caution: It is most important that Precipice Trail hikers remain on the designated trail. Wandering off the trail can quickly lead hikers onto cliffs that require technical mountain-climbing skills and equipment.

Note: The Precipice Trail can be closed for an undetermined amount of time each spring and summer because of the reintroduction of peregrine falcons to the park. Violators of the closure are subject to a $10,000 fine. Those wishing the experience of a ladder trail should consider the nearby Beehive Trail, the Dorr Mountain Ladder Trail, the Jordan Cliffs Trail, Giant Slide Trail, or the Beech Cliffs Trail.

Distances from Park Loop Rd.

to right fork to Bear Brook Trail: 0.4 mi., 15 min.

to Champlain summit: 0.8 mi. (1.3 km.), 1 hr.

Bear Brook Trail

NPS rating: Moderate

This trail begins on the Park Loop Rd., 0.2 mi. east of the entrance to the Bear Brook picnic area. The trail ends at the northern terminus of the Gorham Mountain Trail, located at the south end of the Bowl.

This trail climbs gradually from the parking area through a mixed forest of birch, pine, and spruce to a junction on the north slope of Champlain with the Champlain East Face Trail entering left at 0.5 miles. Continuing left, the Bear Brook Trail steadily emerges from the forest canopy giving outstanding views of Frenchman Bay and Schoodic Peninsula on the mainland to the east. At 1 mi. the trail reaches the open, rocky summit of Champlain. Descending, it meets the Precipice Trail, entering left at 1.1 mi., then descends into the Bowl and terminates at the Gorham Mountain Trail.

Distances from Park Loop Rd.

to junction with the Champlain East Face Trail: 0.5 mi., 30 min.
to Champlain summit: 1.0 mi., 55 min.
to junction with the Precipice Trail: 1.1 mi., 1 hr.
to Gorham Mt. Trail: 2.6 mi. (4.2 km.), 1 hr. 45 min.

Beachcroft Trail

NPS rating: Moderate

A convenient route between Champlain Mountain and the area to the west. For the most part, the trail is entirely open. While the ascent to Hugenot Head from ME 3 is gradual and easily traveled, the character of the trail becomes more difficult on the actual ascent of Champlain.

The trail leaves ME 3 close to the north end of the Tarn and begins with a flight of granite steps on the east side of the highway. (There is parking above the north end of the Tarn off the west side of the highway.) It then runs southeast, often on carefully placed stone stairs. Following switchbacks and stone steps, it rises up and across the west face of Huguenot Head. The trail passes to the south of (not over) the summit of Huguenot Head at about 0.4 mi. A brief, gradual descent into the gully between Huguenot Head and Champlain Mountain is followed by a sharp, difficult ascent over rocks up the northwest slope of Champlain Mountain to the summit at 0.8 mi.

Distances from ME 3

to shoulder of Huguenot Head: 0.4 mi., 25 min.
to Champlain summit: 0.8 mi. (1.3 km.), 55 min.

Bowl Trail

NPS rating: Moderate

This trail leaves from opposite the Sand Beach parking area, located 3.25 miles beyond Sieur de Monts Spring on the Park Loop Rd. Using this trailhead means paying an entrance fee on the Park Loop Road.

The Bowl Trail is a gently sloping path that offers access to the Beehive Trail and the Gorham Mountain Trail. It connects Sand Beach to the Bowl, a lovely lake at the base of Halfway Mountain. At the Bowl a connector trail to the Beehive bears right.

Distances from Sand Beach parking area

to junction with the Beehive Trail: 0.2 mi., 5 min.
to the Bowl and junction with the Beehive and Gorham Mt.
trails: 0.6 mi. (1 km.), 25 min.

Beehive Trail

NPS rating: Ladder

This trail begins 0.2 mi. up the Bowl Trail from the Sand Beach parking area. Take a sharp right at the sign marked Beehive. For 0.3 mi., the trail rises abruptly via switchbacks and iron ladders over steep ledges to the summit of the Beehive. This trail is challenging and not for those who are uneasy on precipitous heights. The views of Frenchman Bay, Sand Beach, and Otter Cliff area are magnificent.

The trail continues down the northwest slope of the Beehive and dips steeply to the south for 0.2 mi. to a junction with the Gorham Mountain and Bowl trails. Take the left fork for 0.6 mi. to return to Park Loop Road.

Distances from Park Loop Rd.

to the Beehive: 0.5 mi., 25 min.
to complete loop back to the Sand Beach area (via Bowl Trail):
est. 1.3 mi. (2.1 km.), 50 min.

Gorham Mountain Trail

NPS rating: Moderate (Cadillac Cliffs: Strenuous)

The trail starts at the Gorham Mountain Trail parking area (also known as the Monument Cove parking area) on Park Loop Rd. (fee) 1 mi. past Sand

Beach. It rises gently over open ledges 0.3 mi. to a junction with the Cadillac Cliffs Trail [(NPS rating: Strenuous). The Cadillac Cliffs Trail is a loop that leads right and rejoins the Gorham Mountain Trail 0.5 mi. later, after passing under ancient sea cliffs and by an ancient sea cave. The Gorham Mountain Trail continues 0.3 mi. over easy open granite ledges to where the Cadillac Cliffs loop rejoins the main trail.

The main trail continues north over the Gorham Mountain summit, which is open and bare, with some of the finest panoramas on Mount Desert Island. Descending, the trail reaches a junction with the Bowl Trail in another 0.7 mi. For the Bowl, go left 0.2 mi. To reach the Beehive, turn right, then left at the next junction, about 0.1 mi. farther. (Continuing straight ahead at this junction will bring you to Park Loop Rd. at Sand Beach.)

Distances from trailhead parking area

to summit of Gorham Mt.: 1.0 mi., 45 min.
to the Bowl: 1.7 mi., 1 hr. 5 min.
to Park Loop Rd. in Sand Beach area: est. 2.3 mi. (3.7 km.), 1 hr. 30 min.

Great Head Trail

NPS rating: Moderate

A scenic, short walk that passes largely along cliffs directly above the sea. From the Sand Beach parking area on Park Loop Rd. (fee), cross Sand Beach to the east end. Near the seaward end of the interior lagoon, look for a trailhead post and a series of granite steps with a hand rail ascending a high bank. The trail quickly reaches a huge millstone, where the trail turns sharply right (south) switchbacking up the cliff. The path continues to the extremity of the peninsula, then turns northeast along the cliff to the high point, Great Head (145 ft.), where there are ruins of a stone teahouse. The trail descends northwest to a junction at which the right path returns more quickly to the east end of Sand Beach. The path that leads north reaches an abandoned service road in about 0.3 mi. Turn left on the road, and follow it south for about 0.3 mi. to the east side of Sand Beach.

Distances from east side of Sand Beach

to south end of peninsula (via millstone): 0.5 mi., 15 min.
to teahouse ruins: 0.8 mi., 20 min.
to junction with Schooner Head Rd./Sand Beach paths: 1.3 mi., 35 min.
to start (via service road): 1.6 mi. (2.6 km.), 55 min.

Ocean Trail (also called Shore Path)

NPS rating: Easy

Park at the large, lower Sand Beach parking area on the Park Loop Rd. (fee). From the parking area, follow the asphalt trail about 50 ft. toward the beach. Where the staircase descends to the left, turn right to begin the Ocean Trail. The trail leads uphill several hundred yards, crosses through a small, paved upper parking area, and continues south to Otter Point, paralleling Park Loop Rd. for 1.8 mi. The Ocean Trail offers spectacular shoreline scenery and follows a level grade. Of interest en route are Thunder Hole, Monument Cove, and Otter Cliffs.

Distance from Sand Beach

to Otter Point: 1.8 mi. (2.9 km.), 55 min.

DORR MOUNTAIN

DORR MOUNTAIN lies immediately west of Sieur de Monts Spring. Two routes up the mountain are possible from Sieur de Monts Spring. Trails also ascend from the north and south over long ridges. The east and west slopes are steep. With properly placed cars, a party can have a good climb leaving from Sieur de Monts Spring, traversing Dorr, and continuing west to the summit of Cadillac Mountain (1,530 ft.). The route descends to about 1,000 ft. between the two summits. There is parking both at the nearby Tarn and on Cadillac's summit. (Hikers are encouraged not to park at the very congested Sieur de Monts Spring parking area. There is a connecting path between the Tarn and the spring parking areas for hikers wishing to visit or begin a hike at the spring.)

Dorr Mountain Trail

NPS rating: Moderate (East Face Trail: Strenuous)

Follow the paved walkway from the Nature Center Parking Area at Sieur de Monts Spring toward the Springhouse. At the rock inscribed Sweet Waters of Acadia, turn right on a walkway that remains paved for a few feet. The trail continues, following a series of switchbacks up the northeast shoulder of Dorr Mountain. The first half has many stone steps. At 0.5 mi., the trail is joined by the Dorr Mountain East Face Trail, entering left, which comes directly up from the north end of the Tarn, a lovely mountain lake. At 1.1 mi. is a junction on the left with a short trail leading to the Dorr Mountain

Ladder Trail, which comes directly up from the south end of the Tarn. Much of the next 0.4 mi. to the summit is steep and exposed.

Distances from Sieur de Monts Spring

to Dorr Mountain East Face Trail junction: 0.5 mi., 30 min.
to link to Dorr Mountain Ladder Trail: 1.1 mi., 1 hr.
to Dorr summit: 1.5 mi. (2.4 km.), 1 hr. 20 min.

Dorr Mountain Ladder Trail

NPS rating: Ladder

This trail climbs from the south end of the Tarn up the eastern side of Dorr Mountain. The first half is steep, climbing many stone steps and over iron rungs. At 0.3 mi. the trail bears right to join with the Dorr Mountain Trail. Much of the next 0.4 mi. to the summit is steep and exposed.

Distance from south end of the Tarn

to Dorr Summit: 0.6 mi. (1 km.), 50 min.

Dorr Mountain North Ridge Trail

NPS rating: Moderate

This trail begins on the south side of Park Loop Rd. about 1 mi. after the road becomes one-way. It climbs south over the summit of Kebo Mountain (407 ft.), traverses a second hump, and ascends the burned-over ledges of the north ridge to reach the summit of Dorr Mountain.

Distance from Park Loop Rd.

to Dorr summit: 1.9 mi. (3.1 km.), 1 hr. 25 min.

Dorr Mountain South Ridge Trail

NPS rating: Moderate

This trail diverges right from the Canon Brook Trail 0.6 mi. from ME 3 at the southern extremity of Dorr Mountain. It rises with moderate grade over rocky ledges and through evergreen forest. Views of Champlain, Cadillac, and the ocean are frequent during the ascent of the south ridge to the summit.

Distances from ME 3

to start (via Canon Brook Trail): 0.6 mi., 20 min.
to Dorr summit: 1.9 mi. (3.1 km.), 1 hr. 25 min.

Dorr Mountain Notch Trail

NPS rating: **Strenuous**

This short trail links the summits of Dorr and Cadillac Mountains. From the summit of Dorr Mountain, go north on the North Ridge Trail about 0.1 mi. Then turn left (west) on the Dorr Mountain Notch Trail, which drops quickly and in another 0.3 mi. reaches junctions with the Gorge Path and the A. Murray Young Path in the valley between the two mountains. Cross these and continue southwest, ascending to reach the summit of Cadillac.

The start of the trail at the summit of Cadillac may be difficult to see. Walk counterclockwise along the paved trail on the summit to the interpretive sign about Bar Harbor. Look for cairns and paint marks on the granite indicating the beginning of the trail leading to the notch. About 0.3 mi. south of the Park Loop Rd., the trail turns left to cross a brook; be careful to avoid an old wood road that goes straight ahead.

Distances from Dorr Summit

to junction with the Gorge and A. Murray Young paths: 0.4 mi., 15 min.
to Cadillac summit: 0.9 mi. (1.4 km.), 40 min.

A. Murray Young Path

NPS rating: **Moderate**

Ascending the narrow valley between Dorr and Cadillac Mountains from the south, this trail leaves the Canon Brook Trail 0.7 mi. west of ME 3. It climbs gradually to the Gorge Path near its junction with the Dorr Mountain Notch Trail. This point affords relatively quick (if strenuous) access to the summit of either mountain.

Distances from ME 3

to start (via Canon Brook Trail): 0.7 mi., 25 min.
to Dorr Mountain Notch Trail: 1.9 mi., 1 hr.
to Dorr summit (via the Dorr Mt. Notch Trail): 2.3 mi., 1 hr. 20 min.

to Cadillac summit (via the Dorr Mt. Notch Trail): 2.4 mi.
(3.9 km.), 1 hr. 25 min.

Jessup Path

NPS rating: Easy

A pleasant, level woodland walk, this path begins on Park Loop Rd. opposite the first road on the left after the beginning of the one-way section of Park Loop Rd. It follows the west margin of Great Meadow, where it may be flooded as a result of beaver activity. The path passes through a mixed forest of hemlock and hardwood to Sieur de Monts Spring at 0.6 mi. Located here are the Abbe Museum, which has displays of ancient Indian culture; the Wild Gardens of Acadia, a formal garden of native plants; and the Nature Center, with a book-sales area and natural history exhibits. The trail terminates 0.3 mi. farther at the north end of the Tarn.

Distances from Park Loop Rd.

to Sieur de Monts Spring: 0.6 mi., 20 min.
to north end of the Tarn: 0.9 mi. (1.4 km.), 30 min.

The Tarn Trail (Kane Path)

NPS rating: Moderate

This path leads from the north end of the Tarn south to the Canon Brook Trail, and links the Sieur de Monts Spring area to the southern trails of Dorr and Cadillac Mountains, while avoiding ME 3. At its start the path runs south, over a rocky talus slope directly along the west side of the Tarn. After reaching the south end of the Tarn, the trail continues south past a beaver pond at 0.5 mi., then gently climbs until its junction with the Canon Brook Trail.

Distance from north end of the Tarn

to Canon Brook Trail: 1.4 mi. (2.3 km.), 45 min.

Canon Brook Trail

NPS rating: Strenuous

From a pullout on ME 3 about 0.5 mi. south of the south end of the Tarn and about 2 mi. north of Otter Creek Village, the Canon Brook Trail runs west to join the Pond Trail in the valley south of Bubble Pond. It gives access (via the Pond Trail) to the Jordan Pond area, as well as to the trails running north to Dorr and Cadillac Mountains.

From the highway, the trail descends west to Otter Creek and intersects the Tarn Trail at 0.3 mi. Turn left (south) at the intersection and follow the Tarn Trail in the valley of Otter Creek. After a brief, sharp rise from the valley, the trail reaches a junction with the Dorr Mountain South Ridge Trail, which diverges right at 0.6 mi. The trail descends to a junction with the A. Murray Young Path, which goes right at 0.7 mi. Then the trail runs steeply westward up the south bank of Canon Brook for about 0.5 mi. At this point, the trail swings away from the brook, passes a beaver pond at 1.3 mi., and ascends to a small pond known as the Featherbed, where it joins the Cadillac Mountain South Ridge Trail and the Pond Trail.

Distances from ME 3

to the Tarn Trail junction: 0.3 mi., 10 min.
to Dorr Mountain South Ridge Trail junction: 0.6 mi., 25 min.
to A. Murray Young Path junction: 0.7 mi., 30 min.
to junction with the Cadillac Mountain South Ridge Trail and
    the Pond Trail: 1.5 mi. (2.4 km.), 1 hr. 5 min.

CADILLAC MOUNTAIN

THIS PEAK is the highest point on the island. There is an automobile road to the summit, which has parking, a small gift shop, and bathrooms. Accessibility by car makes this summit the busiest in the park. Its height offers commanding views.

The North Ridge Trail, beginning on Park Loop Rd., can be connected with the Gorge Trail by the Dorr Mountain Notch Trail, which ends on Park Loop Rd. about 0.5 mi. east of the North Ridge trailhead, creating a pleasant loop up and down Cadillac.

Cadillac South Ridge Trail

NPS rating: Moderate

A relatively long hike for Mount Desert Island, this trail starts on the north side of ME 3, about 50 yd. west of the entrance to the NPS Blackwoods Campground (a flat, 0.7-mi. connector links the campground to the trailhead). It climbs generally north. At 1.0 mi. a short loop trail on the right leads to Eagle Crag, which has good views to the east and southeast. The loop trail rejoins the main trail in 0.2 mi. After leaving the woods, the South Ridge Trail rises gently over open ledges. It crosses the Canon Brook Trail about 2.3 mi. from ME 3, in a slight col at the Featherbed. Continuing in the open, it passes close to a switchback in the Summit Rd. and ends at the summit parking area.

Distances from ME 3

to junction with the Eagle Crag Spur: 1.0 mi., 40 min.
to Cadillac summit: 3.5 mi. (5.6 km.), 2 hrs. 30 min.
(descending Cadillac summit to ME 3, subtract 45 min.)

Cadillac West Face Trail

NPS rating: **Strenuous**

This steep trail, which starts at the north end of Bubble Pond, is the shortest route to the summit. Begin where Park Loop Rd. passes north of Bubble Pond, using the short spur road off Park Loop Rd. to reach the pond and trailhead. The trail rises steeply through woods and over open ledges to a junction with the Cadillac Mountain South Ridge Trail 0.5 mi. from the summit. For the summit turn left (north).

Distances from north end of Bubble Pond

to Cadillac South Ridge Trail junction: 0.9 mi., 1 hr. 5 min.
to Cadillac summit: 1.4 mi. (2.3 km.), 1 hr. 25 min.

Cadillac North Ridge Trail

NPS rating: **Moderate**

This trail follows the north ridge of Cadillac, quickly rising through the stunted evergreens onto open ledges. In winter, the North Ridge Trail is often clear of snow when Summit Rd. and trails on the other parts of the mountain are blocked. To reach the trailhead follow Park Loop Rd. south from the Visitor Center. Take the third left turn (about 3 mi.), following the sign for Sand Beach and Park Loop Rd. Park at a paved pulloff on the north side of the road 0.6 mi. beyond the intersection. The trail starts on the south side of the road. It climbs steadily, always keeping to the east of the automobile road, although it closely approaches road switchbacks on two occasions. For much of the distance both sides of the ridge are visible. The views of Bar Harbor, Eagle Lake, Egg Rock, and Dorr Mt. are excellent.

Distance from Park Loop Rd.

to Cadillac summit: est. 1.8 mi. (2.9 km.), 1 hr. 30 min.

Gorge Path

NPS rating: **Moderate**

Follow Park Loop Rd. south from the Visitor Center. Take the third left turn (about 3 mi.), following the sign for Sand Beach and Park Loop Rd. The Gorge Path starts from a gravel pullout on the south side of Park Loop Rd. 0.8 mi. beyond the intersection. The trail rises south up the gorge between Cadillac and Dorr Mountains for 1.3 mi. to the narrow notch between the two mountains. The trail ends at this notch at junctions with the Dorr Mountain Notch Trail and the A. Murray Young Path.

Distances from Park Loop Rd.

to Dorr-Cadillac notch: 1.3 mi., 1 hr. 5 min.
to Cadillac summit (via Dorr Mt. Notch Trail): 1.8 mi. (2.9 km.), 1 hr. 35 min. (in reverse direction, Cadillac summit to Park Loop Rd., subtract about 40 min.)

Bar Island Trail

NPS rating: **Easy**

A short trail that leads from the Bar Island Bar to the summit of Bar Island. The trail must be hiked during low tide, as the Bar Island Bar connecting Bar Island to Bar Harbor is completely underwater at high tide. Return to Bar Harbor no later than two hours after low tide. Trail begins at the end of Bridge Street in Bar Harbor. Walk 0.25 mi. across the bar to the island, then follow a dirt road through the forest. After about 300 yds, the Bar Island Trail leads to the left. At 0.2 mi. from the road it reaches the summit, offering good views of the harbor and the mountains of Acadia.

Distance from Bridge St., via Bar Island Bar and Bar Island dirt road.

to Bar Island Summit: 0.6 mi., 20 min.

JORDAN POND
AND SOUTHERN TRAILS AREA

JORDAN POND (274 ft.) is a central trailhead to the eastern side of Mount Desert Island. The view from the Jordan Pond House across the pond to the Bubbles is justifiably famous.

Jordan Pond Shore Trail

NPS rating: Moderate

This circuit around Jordan Pond is level most of the way, but crosses a rocky slope with occasional loose boulders at the pond's northeastern shore. It is 3.3 mi. long; directions here are for traveling the east shore first. Park at the Jordan Pond parking area, located off the west side of Park Loop Rd., about 0.1 mi. north of the Jordan Pond House. Follow the boat-launch road to the south shore of the pond.

When you reach the pond, turn right to start the circuit. The trails listed below all diverge to the right, because the route described is counterclockwise around the lake.

Along the west side of the pond, the trail runs under the sharp Jordan Cliffs and loses the sun early in the day. The trail along the west shore also has many wet spots and exposed tree trunks. An alternative route is a carriage road that runs along the pond uphill from the trail. Use the Deer Brook Trail to reach the carriage road. The circuit is completed at the south end of Jordan Pond.

Distances from Jordan Pond parking area

to Pond Trail (to Canon Brook Trail): 0.1 mi., 5 min.
to Jordan Pond Carry Trail (to Eagle Lake): 1.0 mi., 30 min.
to South Bubble Mountain Trail (to gap between North and
   South Bubble): 1.1 mi., 35 min.
to Bubble Gap Trail (to Bubble Gap): 1.5 mi., 45 min.
to Deer Brook Trail (to Penobscot Mountain): 1.6 mi., 50 min.
to Jordan Pond parking area: 3.3 mi. (5.3 km.), 1 hr. 40 min.

Jordan Stream Trail

NPS rating: Moderate

This walk along the outlet of Jordan Pond passes through pleasant cedar, maple, and spruce woods. The trailhead is reached by a short connecting path from the Jordan Pond House. The path essentially parallels a carriage road, which can be hiked for a return trip.

At 0.7 mi., the trail passes under a cobblestone bridge and continues descending along the stream. The trail takes a sharp left from the stream at 1.3 miles and rises to end at a carriage road at the base of Lookout Ledge, close to Little Long Pond.

Distances from the Jordan Pond House

to trailhead: 0.1 mi., 5 min.
to cobblestone bridge: 0.7 mi., 20 min.
to carriage road: 1.4 mi. (2.3 km.), 45 min.

Jordan Pond Seaside Trail

NPS rating: Easy

The Jordan Pond Seaside Trail offers an easy, level walk between the Jordan Pond House and Seal Harbor. Starting from the south side of the Jordan Pond House, the trail passes through an evergreen forest. After crossing a carriage road at 0.2 mi., the trail continues on a level course to a private driveway just west of Seal Harbor. Follow the driveway south to ME 3 and Seal Harbor. Parking on the southern terminus of the trail is best found at the entrance to the Park Loop Rd. at Seal Harbor.

Distance from the Jordan Pond House

to Seal Harbor: est. 2.0 mi. (3.2 km.), 1 hr.

Asticou Trail

NPS rating: Easy

The Asticou Trail is reached by the short connecting path from the west side of the Jordan Pond House. This trail follows a level course for most of its distance, yet gains some elevation to reach the Asticou Ridge Trail. It provides an important link to Eliot Mountain as well as a potential leg of a loop over Sargent and Penobscot Mountains.

Leaving from the trailhead, the trail goes through a mixed forest of birch, maple, white pine, and spruce. At 0.8 mi., the trail crosses a carriage road. At 0.9 mi., it crosses another carriage road. Access to the Amphitheater Trail leaves right from this second carriage road. Gradually descending from this point, the trail crosses Harbor Brook at 1.1 mi. The Harbor Brook Trail leaves left at this point. The trail then begins to climb up the Asticou Ridge. At 1.5 mi., the Asticou Ridge Trail leaves left, and the trail levels once again. The Asticou Trail follows straight ahead to a junction with the Sargent Mountain South Ridge Trail at 1.8 mi. At 2.0 mi., the trail ends at a private drive. Note: the private drive is not open to the public. It is recommended that hikers turn back or take other trails leading from the Asticou Trail to reach public areas.

Distances from the Jordan Pond House

to start of the Asticou Trail: 0.1 mi., 5 min.
to junction with the Amphitheater Trail: 0.9 mi., 30 min.
to junction with the Harbor Brook Trail: 1.1 mi., 35 min.
to junction with the Asticou Ridge Trail: 1.5 mi., 50 min.
to junction with the Sargent Mountain South Ridge Trail: 1.8 mi. (2.9 km.), 1 hr.

Asticou Ridge Trail

NPS rating: Moderate

This trail is reached by following the Asticou Trail for 1.5 mi. Traversing a ledgy ridge, this trail climbs over Eliot Mt., offering views to the south and east of the ocean, Day Mt., and The Triad. Gradually descending from the summit, the trail reaches a monument to Charles William Eliot, one of the founders of the park, at 0.9 mi. Descending into the woods, the trail reaches a junction with a side trail to ME 3 (0.4 mi. in length). Keeping right, the trail descends into the beautiful Thusa Gardens.

Distances from junction with the Asticou Trail

to summit of Eliot Mt.: 0.8 mi., 25 min.
to monument: 0.9 mi., 30 min.
to junction with ME 3 spur trail: 1.1 mi., 35 min.
to Thusa Gardens: 1.4 mi. (2.3 km.), 45 min.

Amphitheater Trail

NPS rating: Moderate

The Amphitheater Trail is a spur trail into the basin of Penobscot Mountain. It leaves right from the Asticou Trail and follows a carriage path for 0.5 mi., where it cuts right (north) off the carriage path to follow Little Harbor Brook to the Amphitheater. The Amphitheater is an impressive rim with the longest carriage-path bridge in Acadia National Park.

Distances from the Jordan Pond House (via Asticou Trail)

to beginning of trail: 0.9 mi., 30 min.
to Little Harbor Brook: est. 1.4 mi., 45 min.
to Amphitheater Bridge: est. 2.0 mi. (3.2 km.), 1 hr. 5 min.

Harbor Brook Trail

NPS rating: Moderate

The Harbor Brook Trail connects the Asticou Trail with a point on ME 3 between Bracy Cove and Northeast Harbor. Following the brook for its entire length, the trail passes through beautiful cedar groves, as well as mixed forest. At 1.1 mi., a connector to Eliot Mountain and the Asticou Ridge Trail leaves west. The trail ends on ME 3 at 2.0 mi.

Distance from the Asticou Trail

to ME 3: 2.0 mi. (3.2 km.), 1 hr.

THE BUBBLES (North Bubble 872 ft./266 m. and SOUTH BUBBLE 766 ft./ 233 m.)

THESE TWO finely shaped, almost symmetrical hills rise above the north end of Jordan Pond. Formerly covered with heavy evergreen growth, they were swept by fire in 1947, leaving many open views. The best access is from the Bubble Rock parking area about 1.1 mi. south of Bubble Pond on the west side of Park Loop Rd.

North Bubble Trail

NPS rating: **Strenuous**

Following the Bubble-Pemetic Trail west from the Bubble Rock parking area, this trail rises sharply for 0.2 mi. to a junction with the South Bubble Mountain Trail and Bubble Gap Trail. From the Bubble-Pemetic Trail, the North Bubble Trail leaves to the right and continues over the North Bubble summit at 0.4 mi. Beyond the summit, the trail descends to reach Eagle Lake at 1.9 mi. (To complete an excellent loop, go right on the Eagle Lake Trail, following the southwest shore to the junction with the Jordan Pond Carry Trail, entering right, which you can follow south back to the start of the North Bubble Trail.)

Distances from the Bubble Rock parking area

to beginning of the North Bubble Trail (via the Bubble-Pemetic Trail): 0.2 mi., 10 min.
to summit of North Bubble Mountain: 0.6 mi., 20 min.
to Eagle Lake: 1.9 mi., 1 hr.
to complete loop (via the Eagle Lake Trail): est. 3.7 mi (6.0 km.), 1 hr. 55 min.

South Bubble Trail

NPS rating: **Moderate**

From the junction of the Jordan Pond Carry and North Bubble trails, follow the Jordan Pond Carry Trail south for 0.4 mi. to the Jordan Pond Shore Trail. Turn right (north) and follow the Jordan Pond Shore Trail for less than 0.1 mi. to the start of the South Bubble Trail. The South Bubble Trail traverses South Bubble to the gap between South and North Bubble. There, 0.3 mi. from the Jordan Pond Shore Trail, it meets the Bubble Gap Trail in the gap between the two summits.

Distances from the Bubble Rock parking area

to beginning of the South Bubble Trail: 0.5 mi., 15 min.
to summit of the South Bubble Mountain: 0.7 mi., 30 min.
to junction with the Bubble Gap Trail: 0.8 mi. (1.3 km.), 35 min.

Bubble Gap Trail

NPS Rating: Moderate

This trail diverges from the Jordan Pond Shore Trail, about 0.4 mi. north of the South Bubble Trail, near the northern edge of Jordan Pond. The Bubble Gap Trail rises through the gap between North and South Bubble Mountains, offering a link between these mountains and the Jordan Pond Shore Trail. Rising through mixed forest, it meets a junction with the South Bubble and North Bubble trails at 0.2 mi.

Distance from Jordan Pond Shore Trail:

> to junction with the North and South Bubble Trails: 0.2 mi. (0.3 km.), 10 min.

PEMETIC MOUNTAIN (1,248 FT./380 M.) AREA

PEMETIC MOUNTAIN is located roughly in the center of the eastern district of the island and offers some of Mount Desert Island's best views. Trails up the west side are short and relatively steep, while routes from the north and south are more gradual and wooded. For the trails from the south, park at the Jordan Pond parking area. From the north, there is parking at Bubble Pond. From the west, parking is located at Bubble Rock.

Pemetic Mountain Trail

NPS rating: Strenuous

This trail traverses the length of the mountain north to south. The views of Jordan Pond, the Bubbles, Sargent Mountain, and Eagle Lake are outstanding.

From the north, the trail leaves from the Bubble Pond parking area at the north end of Bubble Pond. It quickly climbs through spruce-fir forest to a junction with the Bubbles-Pemetic Trail at 1.1 mi. The trail reaches the summit of Pemetic Mountain at 1.3 mi. There are excellent views of The Triad, Cadillac Mountain, and Jordan Pond from the summit. The trail then descends gradually to a junction with the West Cliff Trail. Go left to continue on the Pemetic Mountain Trail.

Steeply descending after the junction with the West Cliff Trail through delightful mixed forest, the trail meets the Pond Trail at the notch between Pemetic and The Triad. After crossing the Pond Trail, the trail climbs for 0.6 mi. to the summit of The Triad (698 ft.), giving views to the south and west.

The trail then descends over ledges to a carriage path at the base of Day Mountain.

Distances from Bubble Pond parking area

to Bubble-Pemetic Trail junction: 1.1 mi., 55 min.
to Pemetic summit: 1.3 mi., 1 hr. 5 min.
to West Cliff Trail junction: 1.9 mi., 1 hr. 20 min.
to Pond Trail: 2.2 mi., 1 hr. 30 min.
to summit of The Triad: 2.8 mi., 2 hrs.
to carriage road: 3.1 mi. (5 km.), 2 hrs. 10 min.

Bubble–Pemetic Trail

NPS rating: **Strenuous**

This trail begins at the Bubble Rock parking area, on the west side of Park Loop Rd. about 1.1 mi. south of Bubble Pond.

The path enters the woods east of Park Loop Rd. and climbs in almost constant cover. Sometimes following a rocky stream bed, the trail ends at a junction with the Pemetic Mountain Trail about 0.1 mi. north of the summit.

Distances from Bubble Rock parking area

to Pemetic Mountain Trail junction: 0.4 mi., 35 min.
to Pemetic summit (via Pemetic Mountain Trail): 0.5 mi. (0.8 km.), 40 min.

Pond Trail

NPS rating: **Moderate**

This slightly graded path leaves from the southeast shore of Jordan Pond to the valley south of Bubble Pond, where the Pond Trail meets the west end of the Canon Brook Trail.

The Pond Trail leaves the shore of Jordan Pond, traveling east, and crosses Park Loop Rd. at 0.1 mi. There is a small parking area at this crossing. Continuing through heavy woods and by easy grades, the path swings in the valley between The Triad and Pemetic Mountain. It crosses the Pemetic Mountain Trail at 0.8 mi., continues northeast to cross a carriage road at 1.1 mi. Continuing to climb, the trail joins the Canon Brook Trail and Cadillac South Ridge Trail at the Featherbed, a pond in the col on the south shoulder of Cadillac.

Distances from Jordan Pond

to Pemetic Mountain Trail: 0.8 mi., 25 min.
to carriage road: 1.1 mi., 40 min.
to the Featherbed: 2.3 mi. (3.7 km.), 1 hr. 35 min.

Pemetic West Cliff Trail

NPS rating: Strenuous

This very steep trail directly links the Pond Trail to the Pemetic Trail just south of the summit of Pemetic Mountain. Leaving from the Pond Trail, the trail quickly ascends through the forest onto a rocky slope. Occasionally, there are views of Jordan Pond from the cliffs. The climb to the summit of Pemetic Mountain along the Pemetic Mountain Trail is gradual.

Distances from Pond Trail parking area on Park Loop Rd.

to beginning of West Cliff Trail: 0.4 mi., 15 min.
to junction with the Pemetic Mountain Trail: 1.0 mi. (1.6 km.), 45 min.

Day Mountain Trail

NPS rating: Moderate

The Day Mountain Trail starts on the north side of ME 3 approximately 1.5 mi. south of the Blackwoods Campground. The parking area is located on the south side of the highway.

The Day Mountain Trail climbs moderately through the forest for its entire length. Periodically crossing carriage roads, the trail offers beautiful views of Hunter's Beach and Seal Harbor from ledges 0.6 mi. from the trailhead. At 0.9 mi., the summit of Day Mountain is reached. (There is a carriage road which also rises to the summit of Day.) Then descending into the forest quickly, the trail reaches another carriage road at 1.4 mi., across from the Pemetic Mountain Trail. (Cross a cobblestone carriage path bridge to reach the trailhead for the Pemetic Mountain Trail.)

Distances from ME 3

to summit of Day Mountain: 0.9 mi., 35 min.
to carriage road: 1.4 mi. (2.3 km.), 50 min.

Triad–Hunter's Brook Trail

NPS rating: Strenuous

This trail begins on the Park Loop Rd. near the southern overpass of ME 3. It follows along Hunter's Brook, passing through a canopy of cedar, maple, and spruce. At 1.25 mi. the trail bears west from the brook and climbs to a carriage road at 1.5 mi. Crossing the carriage path, the trail continues to climb to a junction with the Pemetic Mt. Trail near The Triad. Then the trail descends for 0.3 mi. to end at The Triad Pass Trail.

Distances from Park Loop Rd.

to carriage path: 1.5 mi., 45 min.
to junction with the Pemetic Trail: est. 2.2 mi., 1 hr. 15 min.
to Triad Pass Trail: est. 2.5 mi. (4.0 km.), 1 hr. 25 min.

SARGENT MOUNTAIN (1,373 ft./418 m.)
PENOBSCOT MOUNTAIN (1,194 ft./364 m.)

PENOBSCOT MOUNTAIN and Sargent Mountain are open summits about 1 mi. apart. Sargent Pond, a pleasant mountain pond, lies between the two summits. From the south, the preferred starting point is Jordan Pond parking area. The outlying territory to the southwest contains an interesting maze of trails and carriage roads around Bald Peak (974 ft.) and Parkman Mountain (941 ft.). Ample parking is available at two areas: One is on the west side of ME 3/198 and about 0.3 mi. north of Upper Hadlock Pond (reservoir, no swimming); and the other, Parkman Mountain parking area, is on the east side of ME 3/198, about 0.5 mi. north of Upper Hadlock Pond. Upper Hadlock Pond is approximately 2.5 mi. south of where ME 3/198 splits from ME 233.

Penobscot Mountain Trail

NPS rating: Strenuous

This trail starts from the west side of Jordan Stream (outlet of Jordan Pond) about 0.1 mi. west of the Jordan Pond House and is reached by a short connecting path starting from the house.

The trail runs west and, after crossing a carriage road, rises abruptly to the south end of Jordan Ridge, about 0.5 mi. from Jordan Pond House. The trail then swings north, climbing gradually over open granite ledges to the summit of Penobscot Mountain, where it terminates at the Sargent Pond Trail.

For Sargent Pond and the summit of Sargent Mountain, go left on the Sargent Pond Trail 0.2 mi. Sargent Pond (at about 1,060 ft.) is a delightful spot nestled between Penobscot and Sargent Mountains. From the pond, the Sargent Mountain South Ridge Trail offers easy access to the summit.

Distances from Jordan Pond House

to Penobscot summit: est. 1.5 mi., 1 hr. 10 min.

to Sargent Pond (via Sargent Pond Trail): est. 1.7 mi., 1 hr. 15 min.

to Sargent Mountain summit (via Sargent Pond and Sargent Mountain South Ridge trails): est. 2.5 mi. (4 km.), 1hr. 50 min.

Jordan Cliffs Trail

NPS rating: Ladder

Take the Penobscot Mountain Trail to reach the Jordan Cliffs Trail. This challenging yet scenic trail leaves the Penobscot Mountain Trail 0.4 mi. west of the Jordan Pond House, just northeast of the junction of the Penobscot Trail and a carriage road. Bearing right soon after crossing the carriage road, the trail to Jordan Cliffs heads north and rises up the east shoulder of Penobscot Mountain in gradual pitches to the cliffs at 0.8 mi. The trail traverses the Jordan Cliffs, via ladders and handrails, to a junction with the Penobscot East Trail. Turn left on the Penobscot East Trail to reach the summit of Penobscot Mountain. While very steep, the trail is spectacular, with views of the Bubbles, Pemetic, and Jordan Pond.

Continuing straight past the East Face Trail, the Jordan Cliffs Trail traverses the cliffs above Jordan Pond to cross the Deer Brook Trail. It ends on the summit of Sargent Mountain.

Distances from Jordan Pond House

to Jordan Cliffs Trail (via Penobscot Mountain Trail): 0.4 mi., 15 min.

to Jordan Cliffs: 1.2 mi., 55 min.

to Penobscot summit (via Penobscot East Trail): 1.7 mi., 1 hr. 20 min.

to junction with the Deer Brook Trail: est. 1.6 mi., 1 hr. 15 min.

to summit of Sargent Mountain: est. 2.0 mi. (3.2 km.), 1 hr. 30 min.

Deer Brook Trail

NPS rating: Strenuous

This is a steep, quick ascent of 0.8 mi. to Sargent Pond from the Jordan Pond Shore Trail at the north end of Jordan Pond. The route is entirely wooded and follows the course of Deer Brook. This trail joins the Sargent Pond Trail in the valley between Sargent and Penobscot.

Distance from Jordan Pond Shore Trail

to Sargent Pond Trail junction: 0.8 mi. (1.3 km.), 45 min.

Sargent Mountain South Ridge Trail

NPS rating: Moderate

This trail starts from a carriage path leaving from a mansion known as the Gate House. The trailhead is located about 1 mi. south of Upper Hadlock Pond, on the east side of ME 3/198. Follow the carriage path east, always bearing right at junctions for about 0.7 mi. There, the trail begins on the north side of the carriage path.

The Sargent Mountain South Ridge Trail rises over the wooded shoulder and passes just southeast of the summit of Cedar Swamp Mountain. A spur trail bears left to the summit. It drops to cross Little Harbor Brook at 1.2 mi. The trail then leaves the woods and rises sharply 0.4 mi. to a junction with the Sargent Pond Trail, which comes in from the right. The trail continues north over open granite ledges to the summit of Sargent, past junctions to the left with the Hadlock Brook Trail at 1.8 mi. and the Maple Spring Trail at 2.1 mi.

Distances from the Gate House

to Sargent Pond Trail: est. 0.7 mi., 30 min.
to Hadlock Brook Trail: est. 2.5 mi., 1 hr. 55 min.
to Maple Spring Trail: est. 2.8 mi., 2 hr. 5 min.
to Sargent summit: est. 3.1 mi. (5.0 km.), 2 hr. 15 min.

Giant Slide Trail

NPS rating: Ladder

This trail is the approach to the Sargent Mountain area from the northwest. The trail starts at St. James Church, a small stone chapel located on the east side of ME 198, about 0.3 mi. north of the intersection with ME 3 and 1.1 mi. south of the northern intersection with ME 233. The trail leads east 0.4 mi. to the Acadia National Park boundary and continues through woods up a gradual slope to a carriage road, at 0.7 mi. The trail turns sharply right (south) and, following Sargent Brook, rises steeply over the tumbled boulders of Giant Slide. At 1.8 mi., the Parkman Mountain Trail diverges right and the Sargent Mountain North Ridge Trail leaves left. The Giant Slide Trail continues through the notch between Parkman Mountain and Gilmore Peak at 2.4 mi. and descends to end at a junction with the Maple Spring Trail at 2.8 mi.

Distances from the St. James Church on ME 198

to carriage road crossing: 0.7 mi., 25 min.
to Parkman Mountain Trail and Sargent Mountain North
    Ridge Trail junction: 1.8 mi., 1 hr. 10 min.
to Maple Spring Trail junction: 2.8 mi. (4.5 km.), 1 hr. 45 min.

Sargent Mountain North Ridge Trail

NPS rating: Moderate

Leaving the Giant Slide Trail 1.8 mi. from ME 198, this trail ascends east and crosses a carriage road at 0.2 mi. Continuing essentially east, it rises over slanting pitches another 0.6 mi. to a sharp right (south) turn. The final 0.4 mi. to the summit of Sargent is over open ledges offering spectacular views.

Distance from Giant Slide Trail

to Sargent summit: 1.2 mi. (1.9 km.), 1 hr.

Hadlock Brook Trail and Maple Spring Trail

NPS rating: Strenuous

These are the principal routes to Sargent Mountain from the west. From the east side of ME 198 just north of Upper Hadlock Pond and opposite the Norumbega Mountain parking area, the Hadlock Brook Trail runs east 0.4 mi. to a junction, where the Maple Spring Trail leaves left and the Hadlock Brook Trail forks right. From here, there is little difference between the two trails. They are basically parallel, wooded, steep, and rugged, and terminate on the Sargent Mountain South Ridge Trail, south of the summit.

> to junction with the Bald Peak Trail: 0.3 mi., 10 min.
>
> to Sargent summit (via either route): 2 mi. (3.2 km.), 1 hr. 35 min.

Grandgent Trail

NPS rating: Strenuous

This trail runs between the summit of Sargent Mountain and the Giant Slide Trail. From the summit of Sargent, the trail leaves west and steeply descends into a saddle at the base of Gilmore Peak. After a short climb of 0.2 mi., the trail reaches Gilmore Peak. Then it gradually descends for 0.3 mi. to end at the Giant Slide Trail.

Distances from the summit of Sargent Mountain

> to saddle between Gilmore Peak and Sargent Mountain: 0.5 mi., 15 min.
>
> to Gilmore Peak: 0.7 mi., 25 min.
>
> to junction with the Giant Slide Trail: 1.0 mi. (1.6 km.), 35 min.

Parkman Mountain Trail

NPS rating: Moderate

The Parkman Mountain Trail starts out with the Hadlock Brook Trail but soon diverges north (left) to lead 1 mi. through woods and over a series of knobs to the summit of Parkman Mountain. The trail crosses a carriage road three times on the way to the summit. The Bald Peak Trail joins the trail from the right at 0.9 mi. At the summit, a trail that leaves right (east) connects with the Giant Slide Trail in the gap between Parkman Mountain and Gilmore Peak. The Parkman Mountain Trail continues north over open ledges, then through the woods, crossing a carriage road 0.5 mi. beyond the summit. The trail ends 0.2 mi. farther, at the junction of the Giant Slide Trail and the Sargent Mountain North Ridge Trail.

Distances from ME 198

> to Parkman summit: 1 mi., 50 min.
>
> to Giant Slide Trail-Sargent Mountain North Ridge Trail junction: 1.7 mi. (2.7 km.), 1 hr. 10 min.

Bald Peak Trail

NPS rating: Moderate

This trail connects the Hadlock Brook Trail to the Parkman Mountain Trail. The trail is reached by following the Hadlock Brook Trail for 0.3 mi. At this point, the Bald Peak Trail leaves left. Gradually climbing through the forest, the trail reaches the open Bald Peak at 0.8 mi. The trail reaches the Parkman Mountain Trail shortly beyond the summit of Bald Peak.

Distances from ME 198 (via the Hadlock Brook Trail)

to beginning of Bald Peak Trail: 0.3 mi., 10 min.
to summit of Bald Peak: 0.8 mi., 30 min.
to Parkman Mountain Trail: 0.9 mi. (1.5 km.), 35 min.

NORUMBEGA MOUNTAIN (852 ft./260 m.)

THIS SUMMIT is wooded, but the blueberries on the north slope make it attractive and appealing in season. The trail offers very good views of Somes Sound and the mountains west of the sound. Note: This area is honeycombed with abandoned and unoffical paths. Pay careful attention to trail markers and maps.

Norumbega Mountain Trail

NPS rating: Strenuous

This trail leaves the parking lot on the west side of ME 198 about 0.3 mi. north of Upper Hadlock Pond. It ascends quickly and steeply through woods to granite ledges, then swings south to the summit. The trail descends the south ridge through a particularly fine softwood forest to Lower Hadlock Pond. There, it turns north, following the shore of the pond and Hadlock Brook to Upper Hadlock Pond and ME 198.

Distance from ME 198 north of Upper Hadlock Pond

to ME 198 at Upper Hadlock Pond outlet: 2.5 mi. (4 km.), 1 hr. 35 min.

Western District
(West of Somes Sound)
ACADIA MOUNTAIN (681 ft./208 m.)

Acadia Mountain Trail

NPS rating: **Strenuous**

Parking is located at the Acadia Mountain parking area on the west side of
ME 102, 3 mi. south of Somesville and 3 mi. north of Southwest Harbor
(please do not block the fire road gates on the east side of ME 102). The
Acadia Mountain Trail begins on the east side of ME 102, across the road
from the parking area. Go left at the fork 0.1 mi. down the trail.

The trail ascends the west slope, soon leaving woods for open rocks
and frequent views. It passes over the highest summit and reaches the east
summit, with views of the sound, at about 1 mi. The trail then descends
southeast and south very steeply to cross Man o' War Brook. A junction
about 50 yd. beyond the stream marks the end of the Acadia Mountain
Trail. To return to ME 102 via the fire road, go west (right) at the junction
and proceed past trails to St. Sauveur and Valley Cove, which diverge left
about 100 yd. east of the stream. Go through a field for 200 yd. to the east
end of the Man o' War Brook fire road. Follow the fire road west over gradual grades about 1 mi. back to ME 102, 50 yd. north of the parking area
(you will cross the Acadia Mountain Trail shortly before ME 102; turn left
onto the trail to reach the parking lot directly).

Distances from ME 102

to Acadia Mountain, east summit: est. 1 mi. (45 min.)
to Man o' War Brook: est. 1.5 mi. (1 hr.)
to ME 102: est. 2.5 mi. (4 km.), 1 hr. 30 min.

ST. SAUVEUR MOUNTAIN (679 ft./207 m.)

THIS MOUNTAIN can be climbed from the north via the Man o' War Brook
fire road (NPS fire service road from ME 102), from ME 102 on the west,
and from the Fernald Cove Road on the south. There are good views of
Somes Sound from Eagle Cliff, just east of the summit.

St. Sauveur Trail

NPS rating: **Moderate**

This trail is an easy route to the summit of St. Sauveur Mountain from the north. Follow the Acadia Mountain Trail description to reach the parking lot and trailhead. Start 0.1 mi. down the Acadia Mountain Trail, and go right at the fork.

The path runs south through evergreens and over open slopes, rising constantly for 1 mi. to a junction with the Ledge Trail entering on the right. From there it is 0.3 mi. to the summit, where the St. Sauveur Trail joins the Valley Peak Trail.

Distances from ME 102

to Ledge Trail junction: 1 mi., 40 min.
to St. Sauveur summit: 1.3 mi. (2.1 km.), 55 min.

Ledge Trail

NPS rating: **Moderate**

This trail begins at St. Sauveur parking area on the east side of ME 102 about 0.2 mi. north of the entrance road to the NPS swimming facilities at the south end of Echo Lake. The parking area is also about 0.2 mi. south of the access road to the AMC Echo Lake Camp (contact the AMC for information:617-523-0636; 5 Joy St., Boston, MA 02108).

The path enters the woods and rises over ledges to its end. It meets the St. Sauveur Trail 0.5 mi. from the highway and about 0.3 mi. northwest of the summit.

Distances from ME 102

to St. Sauveur Trail junction: 0.5 mi., 25 min.
to St. Sauveur summit: 0.8 mi. (1.3 km.), 40 min.

Valley Peak Trail

NPS rating: **Strenuous**

This trail leaves the west side of the Valley Cove truck road a few yards north of the parking area at Fernald Cove. It rises steeply northwest through shady woods over Valley Peak (the south shoulder of St. Sauveur Mountain). The trail then skirts the top of Eagle Cliff, with outstanding views of Valley Cove below and the mountains to the east of Somes Sound. On the summit of St. Sauveur, at 0.8 mi., the St. Sauveur Trail merges from the left. The Valley Peak Trail continues fairly steeply down the northeast shoulder of St. Sauveur to end at a junction with the Acadia Mountain Trail near Man o' War Brook and the east terminus of the Man o' War Brook fire road.

Distances from the Valley Cove truck road

to St. Sauveur summit: 0.8 mi., 45 min.
to Acadia Mountain Trail junction: 1.6 mi. (2.6 km.), 1 hr. 10 min.

FLYING MOUNTAIN (284 ft./87 m.)

A FEW MINUTES climb to the open top gives a fine panorama of the sound, Southwest Harbor, Northeast Harbor, and the islands to the south: the Cranberries, Greening, Sutton, Baker, and Bear.

Flying Mountain Trail

NPS rating: Moderate

This scenic trail over tiny Flying Mountain leaves the east side of the parking area at the Fernald Cove end of the Valley Cove truck road and rises quickly and steeply through spruce woods. At the edge of Valley Cove, the trail follows the shore north over rock slides and under forbidding Eagle Cliff to end at a junction with the Acadia Mountain Trail at Man o' War Brook.

At Valley Cove, the north terminus of the truck road can be located up the bank about 75 yd. south from the water's edge. For an easy return to the Fernald Cove parking area, follow the road south for about 0.5 mi.

Distances from Fernald Cove parking area

to Flying Mountain summit: 0.3 mi., 15 min.
to Fernald Cove parking area (via truck road from Valley Cove): est. 1.2 mi. (1.9 km.), 45 min.
to Acadia Mountain Trail junction: 1.5 mi. (2.4 km.), 1 hr.

BEECH MOUNTAIN (839 ft./256 m.)

BEECH MOUNTAIN lies between Echo Lake and Long Pond (Great Pond on some maps). Its summit is easy to reach from either the Beech Cliff parking area (located at the end of Beech Hill Rd., in the notch between Beech Cliff and Beech Mountain) or the pumping station area at the foot of Long Pond. To reach the pumping station, follow Seal Cove Road west from Southwest Harbor. Take the first right (toward the landfill) and follow this road until it ends at the pumping station. Beech Mountain can also be climbed on its southwest flank, beginning at the south end of Long Pond. An added attraction near Beech Mountain is the Beech Cliff–Canada Cliff area just to the east of the Beech Cliff parking area. These rugged cliffs offer spectacular views of Echo Lake.

Canada Cliff Trail

NPS rating: Moderate (Beech Cliffs Trail: Ladder)

This trail offers access to the top of Beech Cliff via a ladder trail (not recommended for those uneasy about heights). It starts at the Beech Cliff parking area located at the end of Beech Hill Road. To reach this trailhead, follow ME 102 south through Somesville and take Pretty Marsh Rd., the first right after the fire station. Follow Pretty Marsh Rd. west for about 0.5 mi., where the Beech Hill Rd. intersects from the left. Follow Beech Hill Rd. south until it ends at the trailhead.

The trail leaves east and climbs quickly via switchbacks and ladders to a junction with the Canada Ridge Trail on the left. Follow the Canada Ridge Trail north to the Beech Cliff Trail and proceed out on the top of Beech Cliff for the views of Echo Lake, the ocean, and islands to the south. This route also provides access from the east to Beech Mountain and Long Pond.

Distance from Beech Cliff parking area

to Beech Cliff (via Canada Ridge and Beech Cliff trails): 0.5 mi. (0.8 km.), 30 min.

Beech Mountain Trail

NPS rating: Moderate

The trail leaves the northwest side of the Beech Cliff parking area and forks in 0.1 mi. The trail to the right (northwest) is 1 mi. long and provides a beautiful vista of Long Pond before climbing to the summit. The trail to the left (south) is 0.6 mi. long and climbs more steeply to the summit of Beech Mountain, with its firetower. The two trails can be combined to form a scenic loop hike.

From the summit, the Beech Mountain West Ridge and South Ridge Trails depart to the southwest and south, respectively.

Distances from Beech Cliff parking area

to Beech Mountain summit (via north fork): 1.1 mi., 45 min.
to Beech Cliff Parking area (via north fork, then south fork):
   1.8 mi. (2.9 km.), 1 hr. 15 min.

Valley Trail

NPS rating: Moderate

This graded path is a convenient link between the Long Pond area and the Beech Cliff parking area, which is located in the notch between Beech Cliff and Beech Mountain. It also permits a circuit or one-way trip over Beech Mountain, since it provides direct access to the South Ridge Trail.

The trail enters the woods on the east (right) side of the service road that skirts the east shore of the south end of Long Pond. The entrance is about 0.3 mi. north of the junction with the road to the pumping station. (Or, park at the pumping station. Take the trail east, go right at a fork in 40 or 50 yd. and cross the service road in about 0.3 mi.)

By easy grades over wooded slopes, the trail runs north briefly and then swings east (right) before entering a series of switchbacks on the south slopes of Beech Mountain. At about 0.3 mi., the South Ridge Trail to Beech Mountain leaves left. Continuing east the Valley Trail soon swings north to maintain altitude as it runs up the valley separating Beech Mountain and Canada Cliff. At about 1 mi., are the remains of the old road to Southwest Harbor and the Canada Ridge Trail comes in from the right. Continue directly ahead (north) 0.2 mi. to the Beech Cliff parking area.

Distances from service road at Long Pond

to Beech Mountain South Ridge Trail junction: 0.3 mi., 10
   min.
to Old Southwest Harbor Rd. and Canada Ridge Trail junction: 1 mi., 40 min.
to Beech Cliff parking area: 1.2 mi. (1.9 km.), 50 min.

Beech Mountain South Ridge Trail

NPS rating: Moderate

This well-marked trail diverges left from the Valley Trail about 0.3 mi. east of the service road and steadily ascends the south ridge to the summit along open ledges, offering views to the south.

Distances from service road at Long Pond

to start (via Valley Trail): 0.3 mi., 10 min.
to summit of Beech Mountain: 0.9 mi. (1.5 km.), 45 min.

Beech Mountain West Ridge Trail

NPS rating: Moderate

Leaving from the east side of the Long Pond pumping station, this trail skirts the edge of Long Pond for 0.3 mi. At this point the trail begins to climb from the shore. Rising steeply at times, there are ledges which offer good views of the pond and Mansell Mountain. It reaches the Beech Mountain Loop Trail at 0.9 mi.

Distances from pumping station

to junction with the Beech Mountain Loop Trail: 0.9 mi. (40 min.)
to summit of Beech Mountain (via the Loop Trail): 1.0 mi. (1.6 km.), 45 min.

Western Mountains

BERNARD MOUNTAIN (1,071 ft./326 m.)
MANSELL MOUNTAIN (949 ft./289 m.)

THIS AREA has two main summits: Bernard to the west and Mansell to the east. Both summits are wooded, and extensive views are rare. You can reach all of the southern approaches from the parking area at the foot of Long Pond near the pumping station. To reach the pumping station, follow Seal Cove Road west from Southwest Harbor. Take the first right (toward the landfill) and follow this road until it ends at the pumping station.

Western Trail

NPS rating: **Moderate**

This is the only trail providing access to the western mountains from the north. There are no open vistas. To reach the trailhead, go about 1 mi. east from the western loop of ME 102 on the Long Pond (Great Pond) fire road. Parking is available here. The fire road crosses ME 102 just north of Seal Cove Pond. The Western Trail starts on the southeast side of the road about 0.1 mi. beyond the Pine Hill turnaround and parking area.

The trail trends southeast and rises by easy grades to a junction with the Great Pond Trail (entering left) 1.9 mi. from the fire road. It ends in Great Notch at 2.3 mi. The Great Notch gives access to both western mountain peaks.

Distances from Great Pond fire road

to Great Pond Trail junction: 1.9 mi., 1 hr. 5 min.
to Great Notch: 2.3 mi. (3.7 km.), 1 hr. 25 min.

Long Pond (Great Pond) Trail

NPS rating: **Easy**

This excellent footpath starts at the pumping station at the foot of Long Pond. It follows the west shore of the pond for 1.5 mi., then bears west away from it. Turning south, the trail passes through a beautiful birch forest and follows Great Brook to a junction with the Western Trail. This route to the Western Trail leads to the complex of trails on Bernard and Mansell and completes a circuit back to the pumping station.

Distances from pumping station

to junction with Perpendicular Trail: 0.2 mi., 5 min.
to Western Trail junction: 2.9 mi. (4.7 km.), 1 hr. 40 min.

Perpendicular Trail

NPS rating: **Strenuous**

This trail, ascending Mansell peak, leaves left from the Long Pond Trail on the west shore of Long Pond, 0.2 mi. north of the pumping station. It follows a steep course up the east slope of Mansell, crossing a rock slide. The trail is very steep, much of it passing over stone steps. There are a few iron rungs and one iron ladder along the course of the trail. The upper portion has an excellent view southeast. At an open ledge near the top, watch for a sign marked Path, where an abrupt turn left leads down sharply into woods and marsh before the trail goes up to the actual summit. The summit is wooded.

Distances from pumping station

to start (via Long Pond Trail): 0.2 mi., 5 min.
to Mansell summit: 1.2 mi. (2.6 km.), 1 hr. 10 min.

Sluiceway Trail

NPS rating: Strenuous

This trail starts at Mill Field on the Western Mountain fire road. To reach Mill Field, follow Seal Cove Rd. west from ME 102 in Southwest Harbor. The pavement ends at the Acadia Park border. Take the first right off the dirt road, bear right at the first fork, and left at the second fork. The road ends at Mill Field. The trail runs north 0.6 mi. to a junction with the Great Notch Trail. At this junction, the Sluiceway Trail swings northwest and climbs rather steeply, to a junction with the South Face Trail 0.4 mi. farther. To reach Bernard Peak, follow the South Face Trail left (south) for 0.2 mi.

Distances from Western Mountain fire road

to Great Notch Trail junction: 0.6 mi., 25 min.
to South Face Trail junction: 1 mi., 50 min.
to Bernard summit (via South Face Trail): 1.1 mi. (1.8 km.), 1 hr.

Bernard Mountain South Face Trail

NPS rating: Strenuous

This trail also starts at Mill Field on the Western Mountain fire road. (For directions to Mill Field, see the Sluiceway Trail description.) As do many of the trails on the western mountains, it runs through a magnificent spruce-fir forest and affords fine views of western Mount Desert Island and Blue Hill Bay. It leads west 0.5 mi. and then rises north to Bernard peak at 1.7 mi. and ends in Little Notch at the junction with the Sluiceway Trail 0.2 mi. beyond.

Distances from Western Mountain fire road

to Bernard summit: 1.7 mi., 1 hr. 20 min.
to Little Notch: 1.9 mi. (3.1 km.), 1 hr. 25 min.

Razorback Trail

NPS rating: Strenuous

The Razorback Trail leaves from the Great Notch Trail, which in turn begins at Gilley Field. To reach Gilley Field, follow Seal Cove Rd. west from ME 102 in Southwest Harbor. The pavement ends at the Acadia Park border. Take the first right off the dirt road, bear right at the first fork, and right at the second fork. The road ends at Gilley Field. Follow the Great Notch Trail for 0.2 mi., where the Razorback Trail bears right.

This hike moderately climbs the western side of Mansell, offering views of the Great Notch and Bernard. The trail climbs over ledges and through softwood forest, to connect with the Mansell Peak Trail between the summit and Great Notch.

Distances from Gilley Field

to start of Razorback Trail (via Great Notch Trail): 0.2 mi., 5 min.
to junction with Mansell Peak Trail: 0.9 mi. (1.5 km.), 35 min.

Cold Brook Trail

NPS rating: Easy

This trail is an important link betweeen the Long Pond pumping station trailhead and the western mountains. Running between the Great Pond Trail and Gilley Field, this trail is an easy hike, following the lowlands around Mt. Mansell. It provides access to the Mansell Peak Trail. More importantly, it is a natural beginning or finish to a circuit hike over both Mansell and Bernard and is a lovely woodlands walk.

Distances from pumping station

to start of trail: 0.1 mi., 5 min.
to Gilley Field: 0.4 mi. (0.6 km.), 20 min.

Great Notch Trail

NPS rating: **Moderate**

This trail, leaving from Gilley Field, offers a pleasant walk through the notch separating Bernard and Mansell mountains. Gradually rising from the trailhead, the Great Notch Trail provides access to the Razorback Trail, Knight's Nubble, the Little Notch, and the summits of Bernard and Mansell.

Distances from Gilley Field

to Razorback Trail junction: 0.1 mi., 5 min.
to Great Notch: 1.1 mi. (1.8 km.), 45 min.

Mansell Mountain Trail

NPS Rating: **Moderate**

This trail leaves from Gilley Field and offers a beautiful hike up Mt. Mansell. Gradually climbing from the trailhead, this trail passes through softwood forest. It continues to climb onto ledges, giving views to the east and south of Southwest Harbor, Beech Mountain, Long Pond, and Northeast Harbor. It meets the Perpendicular Trail at the summit of Mansell.

Distances from Gilley Field

to outlook spur trail: 0.7 mi., 30 min.
to Mansell summit: 0.8 mi. (1.3 km.), 35 min.

West Ledge Trail

NPS rating: **Strenuous**

The West Ledge Trail connects the west end of Western Mountain Road to the system of trails on Bernard and Mansell Mountains. The views to the west of Blue Hill Bay, the Atlantic Ocean, and the islands south and west of Mt. Desert Island are spectacular. The trail begins from Western Mountain Rd., approximately 0.3 mile east of Seal Cove Pond. This road is closed to cars during the winter and early spring. The trail begins climbing moderately up the west face of Bernard Mountain, reaching open ledges very quickly. It briefly re-enters the woods twice before beginning a very steep climb over open granite ledges. From here, the views stretch from Bass Harbor to the Camden Hills, 30 miles to the west. After entering the woods, at 1.1 miles, the trail ends at its intersection with the Bernard Mountain South Face Trail.

Distances from Western Mountain Road:

to junction with Bernard Mountain South Face Trail 1.1 mi., 45 min.

to summit of Bernard Mountain via Bernard Mountain South Face Trail, 1.6 mi., 1 hr. 15 min.

Isle au Haut

A RANGE OF MOUNTAINS extends for 6 mi., the length of the island. Mount Champlain (543 ft.), near the north end, is its highest summit. Farther south along the ridge are Rocky Mountain (500 ft.), Sawyer Mountain (480 ft.), and Jerusalem Mountain (440 ft.). Near the southwest tip is Duck Harbor Mountain (314 ft.).

The island is reached by mail boat from Stonington (45 min.). The schedule should be checked locally.

About half of the island is within Acadia National Park. The NPS maintains a camping area at Duck Harbor, on the southwest side of the island and about 4 mi. from Isle au Haut Village. There are five lean-tos (no tent sites), which are available by reservation only. The NPS has established daily limits on the number of people allowed to visit Isle au Haut. For the latest information and reservations (available no earlier than April 1 for the following calendar year), call the park headquarters on Mount Desert Island (207-288-3338), or write to Acadia National Park, PO Box 177, Bar Harbor ME 04609.

The 12-mi. road around the island is partly paved. Some sections of the road, however, are very rough and not recommended for bike riding. The road passes the foot of Long Pond, where there is a place to swim.

Numerous trails offer opportunities to explore wild and rocky shoreline, heavily wooded uplands, marshes, and mountain summits. For current hiking information, write to Acadia National Park, stop at the park Visitor Center in Hulls Cove, or pick up a map from the mail-boat operators. From mid-May to mid-October, park rangers will meet the mail boat and provide you with detailed hiking information.

Goat Trail

NPS rating: Moderate

This trail runs from the southern portion of the main road to the Western Head Rd. It parallels the shoreline and offers spectacular views of Head Harbor, Merchant Cove, Barred Harbor, Squeaker Cove and Deep Cove.

The trail begins in a marshy lowland and gradually rises to the coastal ridge. Passing through an evergreen forest, at 0.6 mi. the trail emerges onto a rocky beach. Shortly thereafter, the trail climbs again and passes the southern terminus of the Median Ridge Trail (0.9 mi.). Once again, the trail passes intermittently through both beaches and highlands offering a variety of perspectives on the southern coast of Isle au Haut.

Distances from main road

to junction with Median Ridge Trail: 0.9 mi., 30 min.
to junction with Duck Harbor Mountain Trail: 1.8 mi., 1 hr.
to junction with Western Head Rd.: 2.2 mi. (3.5 km.), 1 hr. 15 min.

Cliff Trail

NPS rating: Moderate

This trail leaves from the Western Head Rd. It offers the shortest possible route to the Western Ear, which is a small island accessible only during low tide. It begins by climbing steeply (50 ft.) to reach the coastal ridge. Then, it follows the ridge, passing through an evergreen forest. At 0.6 mi. the trail passes through a rocky beach, offering views of Deep Cove and the coast.

Distances from Western Head Rd.

to junction with Western Head Trail: 0.7 mi., 40 min.
to Western Ear: 0.8 mi. (1.3 km.), 45 min.

Western Head Trail

NPS rating: Moderate

This trail follows the western shore of Western Head. It offers spectacular views of the ocean from oceanside cliffs. Included in these views are rock outcroppings in the Western Bay. Combined with the Cliff Trail, the Western Head Trail offers a very nice loop around Western Head. The trailheads are a short walk apart on the Western Head Road.

The trail begins in lowlands. At 0.2 mi., it begins to gradually climb to a shoreline ridge. Shortly thereafter, it crosses an active stream. While continuing to ascend through an evergreen forest upon a ledge, views of the coast are evident to the west. At 0.4 mi., the trail descends onto a rocky beach. The terrain continues to follow along the coast, ascending and descending between ridge and beach.

Distances from Western Head Rd.

to view of rock outcroppings in the Western Bay: 0.7 mi., 45 min.

to cliffs: 1.2 mi., 1 hr.

to junction with Cliff Trail: 1.6 mi. (2.6 km.), 1 hr. 15 min.

Duck Harbor Trail

NPS rating: Moderate

This trail begins at the park ranger station on the north end of the island. As a major connector, this trail offers hiking access to Duck Harbor, Moore's Harbor, Eli Creek, the Bowditch Trail, the Nat Merchant Trail, and the park campground.

Following the marshy lowlands, this trail passes through mature stands of softwoods. At 0.9 mi., a small pond will appear to the left. At 1.5 mi., the Bowditch Trail bears to the left. Shortly thereafter, another junction with the town road cuts off to the right. The trail crosses a sandy beach at 1.9 mi., offering views of the western coast. At 2.2 mi., a park service cabin will be visible. A small side trail which offers views of Deep Cove bears off to the right at 2.7 mi. After crossing the road, the trail offers outstanding views of the ocean and harbor.

Distances from park ranger station

to junction with Bowditch Trail: 1.5 mi., 45 min.

to junction with town road: 1.5 mi., 45 min.

to park service cabin: 2.3 mi., 1 hr. 10 min.

to junction with side trail to Deep Cove: 2.7 mi., 1 hr. 20 min.

to second junction with road: 3.0 mi., 1 hr. 30 min.

to views of harbor and ocean: 3.7 mi., 1 hr. 50 min.

to Duck Harbor and road: 3.9 mi. (6.2 km.), 2 hrs.

Duck Harbor Mountain Trail

NPS rating: Strenuous

This trail begins on the Western Head Rd. and is one of the most physically challenging trails on Isle au Haut. It climbs over Duck Harbor Mountain, offering terrific views of the harbor as well as the southern end of the island. The trail begins on rapidly ascending ledges. At 0.2 mi., the trail briefly crests. Then, at 0.3 mi., after a short descent, the trail again ascends steeply. It passes through a mixture of softwood forest and open ledge to the summit of Duck Harbor Mountain.

After the summit, this trail continues along the ridge. It goes over the Puddings, offering more views, and descends rapidly through softwood forest and ledges down to a junction with the Goat Trail.

Distances from Western Head Rd.

to summit of Duck Harbor Mountain: 0.4 mi., 35 min.
to junction with Goat Trail: 1.2 mi. (1.9 km.), 1 hr. 30 min.

Median Ridge Trail

NPS rating: Moderate

The trailhead is located on the main road in the southern part of the island. This trail has two spurs, north and south, from this point. The south spur connects quickly (0.3 mi.) with the Goat Trail by following low marshlands. The north spur quickly ascends to the ridge. At 0.3 mi., a blue blaze marks the park boundary. The trail follows the ridge into a Japanese garden, offering views to the east. At 0.7 mi., excellent views can be seen from a ledge area surrounded by small conifers. The trail then descends into a bog. At 1 mi., it crosses the Nat Merchant Trail. The trail continues through marsh, evergreens, and a cedar bog to a junction with the Long Pond Trail.

Distances from main road

to junction of south spur with the Goat Trail: 0.3 mi., 25 min.
to junction of north spur with the Nat Merchant Trail: 1 mi.,
    45 min.
to junction of north spur with the Long Pond Trail: 1.6 mi.
    (2.5 km.), 1 hr. 30 min.

Nat Merchant Trail

NPS rating: Moderate

The Nat Merchant Trail is located on the main road on the western shore of the island. This trail begins by entering low marshlands covered in cedar and pine. It crosses several intermittent streams until it meets with the Median Ridge Trail (0.8 mi.). After this junction, the trail begins to climb gradually. It passes over a boulder field and crests at the top of this field offering fine views. Once this ridge is crested, the trail passes through a softwood forest. The trail ends at the main road on the island's eastern side.

Distances from main road

to junction with Median Ridge Trail: 0.8 mi., 25 min.
to junction with road: 1.2 mi. (1.9 km.), 45 min.

Long Pond Trail

NPS rating: Strenuous

This trailhead is located on the main road on the western portion of the island. While this trail is relatively flat to begin, once on the loop the change of elevation is quite severe. Despite the difficult climb, this trail offers wonderful views of the largest pond on Isle au Haut, not to mention access to the summit of Bowditch Mountain, the Bowditch Trail, and the Median Ridge Trail. The trail forms a nice loop for a day hike.

Beginning at the road, the trail follows a low, wet area for 0.4 mi., where the trail meets the Median Ridge Trail (entering right) and splits into its two legs of the loop. The southern loop follows along an old stream bed for quite some time. At 1.1 mi., the trail passes over the old foundation of a building, follows along a stone wall, and then gradually climbs onto a ridge. At 1.7 mi., you will see Long Pond. The trail follows Long Pond north for a short time, bears west and climbs gradually through evergreens to the summit of Bowditch Mountain. At the summit, the Bowditch Trail enters from the right. The Long Pond Trail continues straight ahead and returns to the junction with the southern leg and the Median Ridge Trail.

Distances from main road

to junction with the Median Ridge Trail:0.4 mi., 15 min.
to foundation of old building:1.1 mi., 35 min.
to Long Pond (via south leg):1.7 mi., 55 min.

to summit and junction with Bowditch Trail (via south leg):2.4 mi., 1 hr. 30 min.

to complete the Long Pond Loop:3.2 mi. (4.6 km.), 2 hrs.

Bowditch Trail

NPS rating: **Moderate**

This trail runs between the Duck Harbor Trail and the Median Ridge Trail. If offers spectacular views from Bowditch Mountain.

Beginning from the Duck Harbor Trail, this trail follows low marshlands for its first 0.8 mi., where it crosses an active stream and turns onto an old firebreak. After following the firebreak, the trail begins to climb gradually, offering wonderful views of the ocean to the west. It continues to climb through a softwood forest over wet ledge for 1.1 mi., where it reaches the summit of Bowditch Mountain. At this point, it connects with the Median Ridge Trail.

Distances from junction with Duck Harbor Trail

to sign marking trail:1.1 mi., 40 min.

to ledges with views to the west:1.6 mi., 1 hr.

to summit and junction with Median Ridge Trail:2.0 mi. (3.2 km.), 1 hr., 30 min.

appendix b

recommended reading

Grierson, Ruth Gortner. *Wildlife Watcher's Guide: Acadia National Park*. North Word Press, 1995.

Hill, Ruth Ann. *Discovering Old Bar Harbor and Acadia National Park*. Down East Books, 1996.

Paigen, Jennifer Alisa. *The Sea Kayaker's Guide to Mount Desert Island*. Down East Books, 1997.

Roberts, Ann Rockefeller. *Mr. Rockefeller's Roads: The Untold Story of Acadia's Carriage Roads & Their Creator*. Down East Books, 1990.

St. Germain, Tom, and Jay Saunders. *Trails of History: The Story of Mount Desert Island's Paths from Norumbega to Acadia*. Parkman Publications, 1993.

Thayer, Robert A. *The Park Loop Road: A Guide to Acadia National Park's Scenic Byway*. Down Home Publications, 1999.

appendix c
lodging

LITERALLY HUNDREDS of choices for lodging exist in and around Acadia National Park. They range from basic campgrounds to very expensive, luxurious hotels and inns. Here are some resources to help you find the place that's right for your needs:

State of Maine Division of Tourism: 888-624-6345

Bar Harbor Chamber of Commerce: 800-288-5103

Mount Desert Chamber of Commerce: 207-276-5040

Southwest Harbor/Tremont Chamber of Commerce: 207-244-9264

Mount Desert Island Visitor Center at Thompson Island (seasonal): 207-288-3411

Acadia Information Center (seasonal): 800-358-8550

Down East Acadia/Bar Harbor Sunshine Guide: 207-594-8074

On the Internet

www.acadiaguide.com

www.downeastguide.com

www.maineguide.com

Campgrounds

NAME	PHONE	LOCATION	OPEN SEASON
Blackwoods	800-365--2267	Rt. 3, 5 min. from Bar Harbor	year-round
Seawall	207-288-3338	Seawall	seasonal
Echo Lake Camp	860-529-3666 (April 1–June 15) 207-244-3747 (after June 15)	Mt. Desert Island	seasonal
Bar Harbor Campground	207-288-5185	Rte. 3, Salisbury Cove	Seasonal
Barcadia Campground	207-288-3520	Jct. Rte. 3 & 102	Seasonal
Bass Harbor Campground	207-244-5857	Bass Harbor, ME	Seasonal
Hadley's Point Campground	207-288-4808	Bar Harbor, ME	Seasonal
Mount Desert Campground	207-244-3710	Somes Sound	Seasonal
Mount Desert Narrows Campground	207-288-4782	Bar Harbor, ME	Seasonal
Narrows Too	207-667-4300	Trenton, Rte. 3	Seasonal
Ocean Wood	207-963-7194	Birch Harbor, Schoodic Penn.	Seasonal
Quietside Camping	207-244-5992	West Tremont, Rte. 102	Seasonal
Somes Sound View Campground	207-244-3890	Hall Quarry Rd., Mount Desert	Seasonal
Spruce Valley Campground	207-288-5139	Bar Harbor, Rte. 102	Seasonal
Timberland Acres	207-667-3600	Rte. 3, Trenton	Seasonal
White Birches	207-244-3797	Seal Cove Rd. SW Harbor	Seasonal

SITES	RV/TENT	RESERV.	FLUSH TOILETS	SHOWERS	PETS	OTHER
300+	RV/tent	June-Sept.	Yes	Nearby	Leashed	National park campground, wooded sites, short walk to ocean
200+	RV/tent	No	Yes	Nearby	Leashed	National park campground, wooded sites, short walk to ocean
N/A	Use their permanent tents	Yes, weekly only	Yes	Yes	No	Tents with floor boards beds, mattresses, & pillows provided; family-style meals included
300	RV/tent	No	Yes	Yes	Yes	Views of Frenchman Bay swim pool, laundromat, arcade, games TV room
200	RV/tent	Yes	Yes	Yes	Leashed Limit 2	Ocean front, laundry, store game room, games, private beach, trailer rentals
130	RV/tent	Yes	Yes	Yes	No	Heated pool, cable TV, laundry, camp store, playground
180	RV/tent	Yes	Yes	Yes	Yes	Heated pool, laundry, store, playground, walk to beach
150	RV/tent	Yes	Yes	Yes	Yes	Tenting along the shore of the sound, canoe & kayak rentals; dock
200	RV/tent	Yes	Yes	Yes	Yes	Entertainment, heated pool, playground, canoe rental, game room, ocean front, store
120	RV/tent	Yes	Yes	Yes	Yes	Ocean front, laundry, game room, store, cabins, heated pool, playground
70	RV/tent	Yes	Yes	Yes	Leashed in certain sites	For nature lovers only! Heavy restrictions on noise; on coast; .25-acre sites
37	RV/tent/ cabins	Yes	Yes	Yes	Yes	Camp store, games, hiker oriented
60	Tent/few RVs	Yes	Yes	Yes	Leashed w/shots	Simple camping on Somes Sound; boat launch for kayaks and canoes
100	RV/tent	Yes	Yes	Yes	Leashed Limit 1	Store, laundry, heated pool, games, rec room, free cable
211	RV/tent	Yes	Yes	Yes	Yes	Rec room, laundry, pool, playground, horseshoes
60	Tent/few RVs	Yes	Yes	Yes	Yes	Small camp store; hiker oriented

appendix d
outfitters

NAME	ADDRESS	PHONE	OPEN SEASON
Acadia Bike	48 Cottage St., Bar Harbor	207-288-9605	All Year
Acadia Outfitters	106 Cottage St., Bar Harbor	207-288-8118	May–Oct.
Bar Harbor Bicycle	193 Main St., Ellsworth	207-667-6886	March–Dec.
Bar Harbor Bicycle	141 Cottage St., Bar Harbor	207-288-3886	March–Dec.
Coastal Kayaking Tours	48 Cottage St., Bar Harbor	207-288-8118	All Year
Island Adventure	137 Cottage St., Bar Harbor	207-288-3886	Mem. Day–October
Loon Bay Kayak	Trenton & Seawall	888-786-0676	May–Oct.
National Park Canoe and Kayak	Pond's End (Long Pond), Somesville	207-244-5854	May–Oct.
National Park Rental Center	Routes 102/198, Town Hill, Bar Harbor	207-288-1151	May–Oct.
National Park Sea Kayaking Tours	39 Cottage St., Bar Harbor	207-288-0342 or 800-347-0940	May–Oct.
Southwest Cycle	Main St., Southwest Harbor	207-244-5856	All Year

RENT BIKES	FIX BIKES	SELL BIKES	RENT KAYAKS	SELL KAYAKS	KAYAK TOURS	RENT CANOES	OTHER
Yes	Yes	Yes	No	No	No	No	Bike accessories, group rentals & tours
Yes	Yes	Yes	Yes	Yes	Yes	Yes	Kayak tours. Max. 10 people per trip
Yes	Yes	Yes	No	Yes	No	No	Snowboards/ skateboards
Yes	Yes	Yes	No	Yes	No	No	Baby joggers/ Accessories
No	No	No	Yes	Yes	Yes	Yes	Wide variety of tours 2 guides/trip; max. 16 people/trip
No	No	No	Yes, to experienced	Yes	Yes	No	
No	No	No	Yes	No	Yes	Yes	Guide was a chef for 25 yrs. Cooks seafood lunch on half- and all-day tours
No	No	No	Yes	Yes	No	Yes	
Yes	No	Yes	Yes	Yes	Yes (freshwater)	Yes	Cartop racks/supplies
No	No	No	No	No	Yes	No	
Yes	Yes	Yes	No	No	No	No	Accessories

appendix e
boat trips

COMPANY	PHONE	BOAT NAME
Bar Harbor Whale Watch	800-942-5374 www.whalesrus.com	Friendship V
		Friendship V
Beal & Bunker Mailboat Ferry	207-244-3575	Sea Queen
Cranberry Cove Boating Co.	207-244-5882	Southwest Harbor Ferry
Down East Windjammer	207-288-4585 207-546-2927 (winter)	Margaret Todd
		Seal
		Bar Harbor Ferry Co.
Isle Au Haut Co.	207-367-5193	Miss Lizzy & Mink
Isleford Ferry Co.	207-276-3717	Isleford Ferry
		Isleford Ferry
		Isleford Ferry
Island Cruises	207-244-5785	RL Gott & Christina
		RL Gott & Christina
Sea Bird Watcher	800-247-3794	Acadian Whale Watcher
		Acadian Whale Watcher

TRIP/ DESTINATION	LEAVES FROM	NOTES
Morning whale and puffin cruise	Bar Harbor Regency Holiday Inn 39 Cottage St. for tickets	High-speed catamaran Cash-back guaranteee
Afternoon whale watch	Bar Harbor Regency Holiday Inn 39 Cottage St. for tickets	High-speed catamaran Cash-back guaranteee
Ferry to Cranberry Islands charter trips available	NE Harbor	Runs all year
Ferry to Isleford/ Cranberry Islands	SW Harbor	
2-hour windjammer cruise	Bar Harbor Inn pier	150-ft. 4-masted schooner
4-hour fishing trips	Bar Harbor Inn pier	
Ferry from Bar Harbor to Little Cranberry & SW Harbor	Bar Harbor Inn pier	
Ferry to Isle au Haut. Either Town Landing or Duck Harbor	Stonington	Runs Mon.–Sat. all year to village. Only goes to Duck Harbor 6/14–9/1. No rides on holidays.
Little Cranberry	NE Harbor	2-3/4 hour trip
Baker Island with a park-ranger-led hike around the island	NE Harbor	4-1/2 hour trip
Sunset cruise	NE Harbor	2-hour trip with no stops
Lunch cruise to Frenchboro	Bass Harbor	Stops on Long Island for lunch and a walk around Frenchboro
Afternoon nature cruise	Bass Harbor	
Morning whale and puffin cruise	Golden Anchor Inn pier, Bar Harbor	Guarantee if you don't see whale, standby ticket for another trip or gift certificate to whale museum
Afternoon lighthouses and seals	Golden Anchor Inn pier, Bar Harbor	

COMPANY	PHONE	BOAT NAME
Sea Princess Cruises	207-276-5352	Sea Princess
		Sea Princess
		Sea Princess
Sea Venture Custom Boat Tours	207-288-3931 or 207-288-3355	Reflection
Swans Island Ferry	207-244-3254	Captain Henry Lee
Whale Watcher Inc.	207-288-3322	Atlantis
		Acadian
		Acadian
		Acadian
		Acadian
		Katherine

TRIP/ DESTINATION	LEAVES FROM	NOTES
Little Cranberry, Somes Sound, lighthouse narr. by a Park Service Naturalist	NE Harbor	2-3/4 hour trip
Somes Sound	NE Harbor	1-1/2 hours
Little Cranberry Island, dinner trip	NE Harbor	Dinner on Little Cranberry Island
Customized boat tours, will show you whatever you want to see!	Atlantic Oaks pier, Bar Harbor	Bald Eagle researcher will let you design your own trip. Spec. birds & wildlife, nature & lighthouses
Swans Island	Bass Harbor	Runs all year
Whale watch with a wildlife naturalist on board	One West St., Harbor Place, downtown Bar Harbor	Whale-watching newest vessel—300 pass. Cashback guarantee
Nature cruise & sightseeing with park naturalist	One West St., Harbor Place, downtown Bar Harbor	180 passengers
Afternoon trip specializes in homes and history	One West St., Harbor Place, downtown Bar Harbor	180 passengers
Evening nature cruise	One West St., Harbor Place, downtown Bar Harbor	180 passengers
Lighthouse cruise	One West St., Harbor Place, downtown Bar Harbor	180 passengers
Lobster fishing & seal watch on a working lobster boat	One West St., Harbor Place, downtown Bar Harbor	40 passengers for this 1-1/2 hour trip

appendix f

environmental organizations

American Oceans Campaign: 800-8OCEAN-0; www.americanoceans.org

Friends of Acadia: 207-288-3340; www.foacadia.org

Island Institute: 207-594-9209; www.islandinstitute.org

Leave No Trace: 303-442-8222; www.lnt.org

Maine Audubon Society: 207-781-2330; www.maineaudubon.org

The Nature Conservancy: 207-729-5181; www.tnc.org

Natural Resources Council of Maine: 207-289-1110; www.nrcm.org

Maine Island Trail Association: 207-594-9209; www.mita.org

about the authors

JERRY AND MARCY MONKMAN specialize in ecophotography, creating images that depict nature and man's interaction with nature. Their home base is in Portsmouth, New Hampshire, but they spend as much time as possible hiking, biking, and paddling around New England, capturing it all on film. Their photos of the Northeast are published regularly by the Appalachian Mountain Club, the Northern Forest Alliance, and the Appalachian Trail Conference. Since 1994 they have worked as photography editors for APPALACHIA, the 120-year-old literary journal of the Appalachian Mountain Club. Their work has also appeared in *Backpacker, Outdoor Photographer, Canoe and Kayak, Conservation Sciences, Yankee, Country Journal,* and *Natural History* magazine, as well as in National Audubon Society and National Geographic field guides. They maintain a website full of pictures and travel essays at www.ecophotography.com. *Discover Acadia* is their first book.

about the amc

SINCE 1876, the Appalachian Mountain Club has helped people experience the majesty and solitude of the Northeast outdoors. We offer outdoor skills workshops, guided trips, and lodging options for all levels of outdoor adventuring. Our conservation programs include trail maintenance, air and water quality research, and advocacy work to preserve the special outdoor places we love and enjoy for future generations.

Join the Adventure!

Take a hike, ride a bike, paddle a canoe. We believe that people who enjoy breathing fresh air, climbing mountains, splashing in streams, and walking on trails have more fun and take better care of the outdoors. Join the fun today. Call 617-523-0636 for membership information.

Outdoor Adventures

From beginner backpacking to advanced backcountry skiing, we teach outdoor skills workshops to suit your interest and experience. If you prefer the company of others and skilled leaders, we also offer guided hiking and paddling trips. Our five outdoor education centers guarantee year -round adventures.

Huts, Lodges, and Visitor Centers

With accommodations throughout the Northeast, you don't have to travel to the ends of the earth to see nature's beauty and experience unique wilderness lodging. Accessible by car or on foot, our lodges and huts are perfect for families, couples, groups, and individuals.

Books and Maps

We can lead you to the best hiking, biking, skiing, and paddling destinations from Maine to North Carolina. With more than 50 books and maps published, we're your definitive resource for discovering wonderful outdoor places. For ordering information call 1-800-262-4455.

Check us out online at www.outdoors.org, where there's lots going on.

Appalachian Mountain Club
5 Joy Street
Boston, MA 02108-1490
617-523-0636